T0320050

# The Social Challenge of Job Creation

# The Social Challenge of Job Creation

## Combating Unemployment in Europe

*Edited by*

**Jordi Gual**

*Economic Adviser, Economic and Financial Affairs, European Commission and Professor, IESE, University of Navarra, Barcelona, Spain.*

**Edward Elgar**
Cheltenham, UK. Brookfield, US

© Jordi Gual 1996

All rights reserved. No part of this publication may be reproduced, stored in a retrieval system or transmitted in any form or by any means, electronic, mechanical, photocopying, recording or otherwise without the prior permission of the publisher,

Published by
Edward Elgar Publishing Limited
8 Lansdown Place
Cheltenham
Glos GL50 2HU
UK

Edward Elgar Publishing Company
Old Post Road
Brookfield
Vermont 05036
US

**British Library Cataloguing in Publication Data**
The social challenge of job creation: combating
    unemployment in Europe
    1. Job creation – Europe 2. Manpower policy – Europe
    I. Gual, Jordi
    331.1'25'094

**Library of Congress Cataloguing in Publication Data**
The social challenge of job creation: combating unemployment in
    Europe / edited by Jordi Gual.
        Includes bibliographical references and index
        1. Job creation—European Union countries—Congresses. 2. Full
    employment policies—European Union countries—Congresses. 3. Job
    creation—Spain—Congresses. 4. Full employment policies—Spain–
    –Congress. I. Gual, Jordi
    HD5764.A6S63  1996                                          96–15145
    331.12'042'0942—dc20                                        CIP

1 85898 459 9

Printed and bound in Great Britain by
Biddles Limited, Guildford and King's Lynn

# Contents

Contributors                                                                vii

Prologue                                                                     ix
*Carlos Cavallé*

**INTRODUCTION**

1. Four Myths about Employment                                               3
   *Jordi Gual*

**PART I**
**POLICIES AND INSTITUTIONS FOR JOB CREATION**

2. Employment in Europe                                                      29
   *Jacques H. Drèze*

3. Preventing Long-Term Unemployment: An Economic Analysis    55
   *Richard Layard*

4. Does it Fit? Drawing Lessons From Differing Labour Practices   70
   *Richard B. Freeman*

**PART II**
**SPAIN: LESSONS FROM A FAILURE IN JOB CREATION**

5. Job Creation in Spain: A Macroeconomic View                   91
   *José Viñals*

6. Creating Employment in Spain: Labour Market Imperfections   119
   *Carlos Sebastián*

**PART III**
**CULTURAL VALUES AND LABOUR MARKET INSTITUTIONS**

7. The Institutional Structuring of Firms' Strategies          157
   *Richard Whitley*

8. Knowledge and Ideas for Job Creation          190
   *José Luis Alvarez*

   Index          215

# Contributors

Professor **José Luis Alvarez**
IESE (Universidad de Navarra)

Professor **Carlos Cavallé**
Dean of IESE (Universidad de Navarra)

Professor **Jacques H. Drèze**
CORE (Université Catholique de Louvain)

Professor **Richard B. Freeman**
Harvard University, NBER, and Center for Economic Performance (LSE)

Professor **Jordi Gual**
IESE (Universidad de Navarra), European Commission and CEPR

Professor **Richard Layard**
Center for Economic Performance (London School of Economics)

Professor **Carlos Sebastián**
Universidad Complutense de Madrid

Dr **José Viñals**
Banco de España and CEPR

Professor **Richard Whitley**
Manchester Business School

# Prologue

Like many other European citizens, I am concerned about the acknowledged inability of the European Union (EU) to create jobs - in either sufficient quantity or quality, or in keeping with Europe's natural, technical and in particular human resources. Some may argue that the job-creation problem is worldwide, occurring especially in less developed countries and in almost all industrialised countries. But in my judgment this reasoning is neither reassuring nor convincing.

Europe is the birthplace of Western culture and civilisation, of technical and economic development, and of social progress. It ought to be better than other economic blocs at resolving one of the most critical problems that humanity stands to face in the next decade - fulfilling people's right to a decently paid, dignified job. Only then will the individual be able to fully develop his or her God-given abilities, and to put these abilities at the service of others, to bring up and educate a family, and to play an active role in the economic and social development of Europe and the world.

I am making neither a political claim nor a public statement about human ecology. A decently paid, dignified job is a reality to which all human beings legitimately aspire as the unquestionable right for themselves, for their families and friends - and it should be something that they desire for other human beings as well. Evidence of Europe's inability to create work is made manifest with every publication of unemployment figures. No week passes without the international press highlighting the blight of unemployment. And with similar frequency, numerous publications analyse its causes, point out its consequences and offer solutions.

The unemployment issue is seen from different angles within the EU, whether by member countries or by various political spheres. At present, of increasing concern is the repercussion on whether the hopes of the different state pension systems can be fulfilled. And with good reason. The dependency coefficient - the percentage of people of retirement age in relation to those of working age - is discussed with increasing frequency. In the EU, the coefficient was 21% in 1990. And it is due to reach 43% in 2040. In other words, for every retired person there will be just over one person of working age. This forecast is rendered bleaker if the active person lacks sufficient work and sufficiently well-paid work. This is the case in Europe today.

To explain the problem further, allow me to recall some simple, orientational figures regarding unemployment in the EU. After five years of an improving employment situation, coinciding with the economic expansion of 1985-90, unemployment rose alarmingly to reach almost 12% of the active population. A high percentage of these unemployed are 15- to 24-year-olds; about 40% in Spain, 30% in Italy, 20% in France and 15% in the UK. Only Germany, with its dual training plan, has low youth unemployment, at about 5%, says the Organisation for Economic Cooperation and Development (OECD).

Different studies have already stressed the consequences of youth unemployment: a waste of young people's energies and talents, and the creation of frustration at the beginning of a professional life, which can have serious ramifications for society as well as for the unemployed youths in question. I will not expand on this point, but I want to bring it up in the hope of making the reader more aware of the need to solve as soon as possible this human and social problem, for which all of us, to a greater or lesser extent, are responsible.

The EU has also a disquietingly high number of long-term unemployed, those looking for a stable job for a year or more. According to the OECD, the rate is 58% in Italy, 50% in Spain, 34% in France and 33% in Germany. Numerous studies analyse this harsh reality. I use the word "harsh" because, in many cases, long-term unemployment leads to a growing inability to remain in the labour market, with an increasing probability of falling out completely and having to accept definitive unemployment benefits, early retirement or some other undesirable solution.

The magnitude of the problem is set out in the EU White Paper. Europe needs to create 15 million net jobs between now and the end of the century, assuming that people's aspirations to a dignified and reasonably paid job do not change substantially. This compares with the 6 million net jobs created in the 20 years between 1972 and 1992: that is to say, less than half the jobs that need to be created by the year 2000, in a quarter of the time. Mission impossible? Perhaps not.

To offer hope regarding the EU's difficult and uncertain future in job creation, my suggestion is to look at what happened in the US during the same 20-year period. The US created 22 million net jobs between 1972 and 1992, enabling the country to maintain its unemployment rate at between 5 and 6%, and at only 12% among the long-term unemployed. My question is: if the US can, why cannot Europe? This is not a trivial question, but a useful and illuminating one. It would lead us to compare the US's economic development with that of Europe. We Europeans must be thankful that US specialists, including Professor Richard Freeman, have rigorously done this already. Some of their interesting contributions are gathered together in this book.

To add another factor of particular interest, Europe's Gross Domestic Product experienced a growth parallel to that of the US's between 1970 and 1994. Both reached the mark of 180, taking 1970 as a base of 100, according to the International Monetary Fund. The growth of capital stock was also similar, rising to 220 in 1994. The difference, though, resides in how the available capital was used to buoy growth. In Europe, the ratio of capital invested per worker grew quickly, to a mark of 210 in 1994, while in the US this growth was slower, reaching only 140. Hence, Europe showed a stronger tendency than the US to substitute labour for capital, which explains in part why the two areas have differing abilities to create net jobs.

If we compare the growth of real salaries in the US and in Europe, nominal salaries in the US grew at the same rate as inflation, whereas in Europe they grew at an annual average of more than 1.5 percentage points above inflation. In this way, real salaries grew by 3.9% in the US between 1975 and 1993, compared with 24.6% in Europe. One may conclude that whereas the US has chosen to expand its economy through stable salaries and employment, Europe has opted for increased labour productivity and salaries.

It is not my intention to enlarge on this intriguing comparison of the two main Western economic blocs. The reader will find more and better references to it in several chapters of the book. But I would like to underline the importance for Europe of continuing to study in depth the job-creation differences between itself and the US, an area in which the US is ahead of Europe. In other words, the EU would benefit from having a good "benchmarking" with the US. From IESE, the International Graduate School of Management of the University of Navarre, we will continue to stimulate this discussion, and we will try to be up to date in obtaining the results and to divulge them accordingly.

Given the cultural, social and political differences between Europe and the US, benchmarking should in my judgment be considered a way of reflection rather than a solution. I am convinced that what the European Union needs most at present is to reflect deeply about its present instability and its uncertain future. I hope that the EU's Inter-Governmental Conference of 1996 will be an opportunity to do this.

One area for reflection is the unfortunate European tendency to enlarge the public sector. The firm is the main protagonist in economic and social development, especially in the private sector: it is the major contributor to the issue of job creation. When politicians promise to create a certain number of jobs, usually at the beginning of their mandate, they are robbing the private company of its role. It is the private company that can create the necessary employment, so long as the prevailing economic and labour conditions allow it to do so. In this respect, Europe must look to the US, where the public sector has a larger subsidiary role, including in job creation.

The educational system is civil society's other important protagonist. In the case of the university, its mission is to advance in the fields of knowledge related to understanding society better and to helping resolve not only society's technical problems, but especially its human and social ones.

Therefore, I believe that the university must become a habitual forum for debating the causes and consequences of Europe's incapacity to create decent jobs for its citizens, and to examine viable lines of action.

IESE, aware of its responsibility, decided two years ago to take a step forward in its contribution to the important task of job creation in Europe and the rest of the world. It set out to attempt to join the forces of international experts: academics who could provide the necessary interdisciplinary dimension in areas such as economics, management, sociology and psychology, as well as insightful and thoughtful business executives who could add the practical dimension. We are hoping to contribute to civil society's two main protagonists, the firm and the university, being able to reconcile the various aspects that affect job creation within dimensions that are relevant, interdisciplinary and international.

IESE recognised the breadth and complexity of the task, so we have decided to plan a series of International Conferences on Job Creation, to be held annually over the next ten years. By the time these pages appear, God willing, we will have held the second conference. I hope that this next congress will be at least as successful as the first, since it will take as its basis everything that we have learnt from the excellent contributions made from participants in that first conference. I trust that our readers will acknowledge this to be the case, and that they will join me in my unreserved thanks to the authors.

Professor Carlos Cavallé
Dean of IESE, University of Navarre

# INTRODUCTION

# 1.    Four Myths about Employment

## Jordi Gual*

The creation of jobs is the main goal of the social and economic policies of most industrial countries today. This is particularly true of Europe. The poor employment performance of most European countries over the last 20 years has brought employment policies to the forefront of political and social debate.

Employment is the key economic policy objective of the countries of the European Union (EU) as established at the Essen European Council of December 1994. Building on the strategy outlined in the December 1993 White Paper on Growth, Competitiveness and Employment prepared by the European Commission, the countries of the EU have agreed on an action plan which covers measures on vocational training, the employment intensity of growth, the reduction of non-wage labour costs, the impact of labour market policies on incentives, and aid to groups which are especially hard hit by unemployment.

The renewed policy interest in the employment problem has sparked a major research effort by the academic community. It has become increasingly clear that the underlying forces which hinder the generation of employment are multidimensional and very complex. They lie partially in the traditional domain of economics (for instance, the incentives of economic agents, the functioning of markets), but cannot be fully apprehended without the insights and tools of other disciplines such as sociology. The role of the culture of society (for example, values and attitudes toward work) and its institutions (firm, family, state) is drawn coherently into the analysis by a sociological approach, which ought to complement economics in any comprehensive discussion of employment creation.

This multidisciplinary research effort is not easy because of the traditional communication difficulties across academic disciplines. Nevertheless, the need for such a broad view has led to the decision to hold the international conference on employment creation which is at the root of this book. Both the conference and the book are the result of the commitment of the International Graduate School of Management (IESE) to a long-term research effort in this field. It is only natural that

3

the multidisciplinary approach of IESE to business education was reflected in the conference.

This gathering took place in Barcelona in the autumn of 1994 and brought together economists, philosophers, sociologists and business leaders from several countries to discuss policy proposals that could aid in the generation of employment, particularly in Europe. Some of the papers presented at the conference are collected in this volume.

This introductory chapter will discuss four common fallacies about the difficulties of generating employment in industrialised countries. It does not pretend to constitute a survey of all that is known about employment creation.[1] Rather, it looks at a few common misunderstandings about the factors that contribute to job creation, as a motivation for presenting the papers included in this volume.

Three of the myths to be examined are directly or indirectly discussed in detail in the chapters that follow. We will thus place the contributions of this book in a broader context. The fourth myth, which refers to the relationship between employment and trade, is not covered in this volume, and will therefore be the subject of a more complete discussion. This last section can be seen as a selective survey of a topic which is currently the subject of hot debate.

## 1.1.    EMPLOYMENT AND TECHNOLOGICAL CHANGE

There has always been a misunderstanding of the impact of technological change on employment. This erroneous perception was already present during the industrial revolution and has been recurrent in periods of rapid technological progress. Our first myth can be stated as follows:

*Myth 1. Given the current trends in technological change, there are not going to be enough jobs for the whole population. The citizens of industrial societies will have to accept "technological" unemployment and adapt to an increase in leisure time.*

The fears of technological unemployment are widespread, particularly among European citizens, as they witness that each new economic expansion over the last 20 years has been unable to bring unemployment back down to the level attained in the previous cyclical peak.

It is certainly true that Western societies will have to adapt to a reduction in work time. However, this is nothing but the continuation of a long-established trend and a reflection of the augmented well-being of society. This betterment stems precisely from the total factor productivity increases which technological change has brought about. This growth in real income has in turn led to an increase in the value that citizens attach to leisure.

But despite these arguments, the main problem with this first fallacy is that it constitutes a well-known but still common misconception. It is based upon the idea that the total amount of jobs is fixed, determined by what is required in order to produce the goods and services demanded in the marketplace. If technological change allows the satisfaction of this demand with a diminished use of workers, the story goes, then these are jobs that are lost.

Of course, this argument is wrong. As Professor Layard points out in his contribution to this volume, aggregate demand is not the main constraint on job availability. If necessary, monetary and fiscal authorities can always transitorily generate more demand. Moreover, technological change - with the subsequent increase in total factor productivity - generates real returns, either in the form of lower final prices for goods or in increased wages and profits. These are increases in real income which in the end result in higher demand. Although technological change may be the direct cause of job losses in a particular sector, the increase in income heightens the demand for labour elsewhere in the economy.

Indeed, jobs cannot be created simply by artificially increasing the aggregate demand of the economy. The true constraint for employment creation is the inflation constraint. The inflation target determines the level of aggregate demand, but the number of jobs compatible with that inflation level is determined entirely by the supply side of the economy: what Professor Layard calls the "employability" of the labour force.

A worker's employability depends on her willingness to accept a job and on her adequacy to the job market's requirements. A more "employable" labour force will make a higher level of employment compatible with a given inflation target. The explanation is simple. When aggregate demand peaks up, the employable workers limit the reappearance of inflation since they are able to compete for the new jobs. Non-employable workers cannot bid for the new jobs, and the expansion of aggregate demand may lead to wage inflation. In his paper, Professor Layard exploits the notion of employability to design a plan to reduce long-term unemployment. This kind of unemployment is the natural target for measures that attempt to reduce the number of unemployed without increasing the rate of inflation, since long-term unemployed workers exert no downward pressure on labour markets.

The notion of employability is intimately linked to the implications of technological change for labour markets. Rapid technological change displaces workers with outdated abilities and creates demand for workers with a different expertise. Technological change does not create aggregate unemployment; it triggers profound changes in the structure of labour demand. The difficulties for employment arise due to the inability of the labour supply to adjust quickly to the new demands of the labour market so that enough employable workers are available. The decline in employability means that only a reduced number of jobs will be compatible with the inflation target.

One further issue is the potential impact of what is usually known as labour-saving technological change: technical progress which is biased against the use of labour. This progress, however, does not fundamentally change our argument. Technological change will be biased to the extent that firms have an incentive to invest in this type of technology. This will be basically determined by the current and expected evolution of the relative price of productive factors per unit of output.

If the unit labour cost of low-skill labour tends to grow faster than that of skilled labour, this will lead to an investment in technologies that save on low-skill labour. With an unchanged labour supply - that is, without changes in employability - the adjustment takes place through wages or through decreased employment.

In his contribution to this volume, Professor Jacques Drèze points out the importance of preserving an undistorted relative price of labour. As he notes, taxes on labour use cause an inefficient allocation of resources in the economy. This is particularly important for low-skill labour. For this type of labour, in most European countries the private cost of employing an additional worker is substantially higher than its corresponding social cost. This inefficient pricing leads to an under-utilisation of this type of worker.

The evidence on the importance of technological change over the last 20 years is mixed. Overall technical progress has, if anything, slowed down in comparison to the changes observed in the previous two decades, as reflected by the decline in the rate of growth of total factor productivity detected in most studies on this subject. However, there is some suggestive, albeit limited, evidence on the importance of biased technological change as a factor behind the changing pattern of labour demand. For example, Berman et al. (1994) find a strong correlation between the use of non-production workers and investment in R&D, and Drèze and Sneessens (1994) report on two studies for the UK and France which estimate production functions and find evidence of technical change which is significantly biased in favour of skilled workers.

In sum, then, technological progress does not lead to the destruction of jobs. Rather, it modifies the distribution of jobs in the economy. The overall number of jobs is determined fundamentally by the employability of the labour force. Excessive real wage increases (relative to productivity improvements) and/or the structure of taxation and other benefits may contribute to biased technical change, and therefore both to labour-capital substitution and to the substitution between skilled and unskilled labour. The source of the problem, however, is the distorted relative price, not technological change. Moreover, if high taxes reduce the demand for low-skill workers, changes in their employability can limit the impact in terms of unemployment.

## 1.2.    EMPLOYMENT AND AGGREGATE DEMAND

The pervasive influence of the new classical economics in the formation of economic policy has led to the development of a second employment fallacy which I believe merits discussion. This myth excludes aggregate demand from the employment debate.

*Myth 2. Unemployment due to insufficient aggregate demand is nothing to be concerned about. Either there is no such thing as insufficient demand or, if there is, it leads only to temporary unemployment, which should not be a matter of policy concern, since fine-tuning the economy to eliminate these cyclical fluctuations would be counterproductive.*

This myth is of a different nature than the first. For one thing, the presumption that there cannot be insufficient demand can be contested. Moreover, there are also reasons to be concerned about purely cyclical drops in demand.

Professor Jacques Drèze provides the main arguments behind what is sometimes known as the neo-Keynesian response. The basic message is that the incompleteness of contingent markets and the lack of coordination in the markets for goods may explain why the markets can achieve an equilibrium with low demand. The possibility of insufficient demand is reinforced by the process of increased interdependence among industrialised economies. Since expansionary aggregate demand policies entail risks in terms of budgetary balances and inflation, countries have an incentive to free-ride on the expansionary policies of their partners, and an overall low demand equilibrium becomes a distinct possibility.

In any case, the existence of economic cycles and the appearance of cyclical unemployment is a fact well-accepted by mainstream economists and policy makers. It is true, as we have argued before, that the number of jobs is determined by the supply side of the economy and not by aggregate demand. Nonetheless, temporary drops in demand should be a matter of concern for at least two reasons.

First, with the rapid changes in technology, and the existing training and welfare systems, there is a clear risk that spells of unemployment due to temporary drops in demand may result in a decrease in the degree of employability of the labour force.

Second, some of the features of the labour market (to which we will return in the next section) lead to the existence of persistence mechanisms, whereby cyclical drops in demand can have long-lasting effects on employment. Bean (1994a) provides a summary of the features of the labour market which lead to this "hysteresis" effect. As an example, he argues that in light of the high cost of hiring and firing, firms may take on additional workers only if they expect a sustained recovery in demand.

This will lead to a slow employment reaction in recoveries and to an excessive persistence of high unemployment levels. Other persistence mechanisms are the result of the dual structure of the labour market, with insiders and outsiders exhibiting different behaviour in terms of wage negotiations and attitudes toward work.

Recent claims that demand policies should be used in the fight against unemployment (see for example Blanchard et al., 1994 and Alogouskoufis et al., 1995) can therefore be justified on several counts from a theoretical perspective. This, however, is still not a predominant view among practitioners, particularly in terms of the policy prescriptions of most international organisations. Their recommendations grant clear priority to fiscal consolidation and the fight against inflation. While recognising that it is dangerous to advise policy makers to engage in fine-tuning and that there can be no long-term trade-off between inflation and unemployment, the proponents of active demand management emphasise the high costs in terms of employment and output which may result from the combination of sharp drops in aggregate demand and the hysteresis effects pervasive in employment markets.

## 1.3.   EMPLOYMENT AND THE STRUCTURE OF LABOUR MARKETS

A consensus appears to be taking shape among the major international organisations with regard to the need to liberalise labour markets in order to improve the employment situation in industrialised countries.[2]

This view has been greatly influenced by the relative employment performances of the US and the EU over the last 20 years. As Dr Viñals points out in his essay, both areas grew at an average annual rate of 2-2.2% over the period, but the US was able to increase employment yearly at a rate of 1.6%, whereas Europe managed only 0.5%. If the Spanish case is worth examining at all, it is because not only did Spain fail to create employment, it actually destroyed it, at a rate of -0.4% per year.

General political trends, as well as the development of new thinking in economics, have contributed to the increasing popularity of the deregulation of markets, and in particular of the labour market. Although it is true that prices set freely by private economic actors tend to clear markets (as does, in principle, the wage), I believe that the present state of opinion has led to the development of a third myth, which can be stated as follows:

*Myth 3. The deregulation of labour markets, in terms of both wage-setting procedures and contractual conditions, will facilitate the creation of employment and thus contribute to an overall improvement in living standards.*

The fundamental problem with the deregulation of labour markets is not that it might fail to generate employment. It would probably succeed. The key issue is whether such deregulation would lead to employment creation's ultimate goal: namely, the improvement of living standards for a broad majority of the population.

There are at least two reasons to doubt that a thorough deregulation of labour markets constitutes the right strategy if one seeks to create jobs that will lead to a widespread improvement in the standard of living.

The first argument is based upon the observation of employment trends and real earnings in the United States. Professor Richard Freeman sets it out clearly when he observes that fully employed American workers with low wages have living standards below those of similar workers in Europe, despite the fact that the US enjoys a higher overall standard of living. The strong US performance in employment creation has been accompanied by an increase in wage inequality among workers with different skills, and by an actual decline in real wages for the low-skilled. Concomitantly, US society has shown disquieting indicators of the growth of a permanent underclass, with sharp increases in poverty rates and in crime (this point is also put forward by Professor Drèze in his paper). As Professor Freeman writes, "Countries that maintained the earnings of the less skilled seemingly 'paid' in terms of high unemployment; while the US 'paid' for its growth of employment through falling real earnings."

The second reason to question full deregulation has to do with the imperfect nature of labour markets. Although it is probably true that most labour markets in Europe are overregulated, it does not follow that the appropriate policy is to dismantle all regulations. There are some sound reasons to regulate certain features of the labour market. Reforms should scrap unnecessary rigidities and restrictions but preserve those regulations that attempt to correct the imperfections of the market.

Professor Drèze argues that full labour market flexibility would subject workers to excessive income uncertainty. On the one hand, this could lead to inefficient levels of volatility in aggregate demand. On the other, more fundamentally, workers invest in human capital which cannot be diversified away as easily as other forms of wealth. This may justify a reduction of income volatility through some degree of rigidity in real wages.

There are other possible justifications for some degree of regulation in labour markets. Prominent among these are the existence of an asymmetrical distribution of information in that market and the problem of time inconsistency in the contractual relationship.[3]

Asymmetrical information can be significant to the extent that workers may have difficulties in assessing the characteristics of the jobs being offered (e.g., in terms of health and safety), whereas employers are likely to be much better informed.

The problem of time inconsistency refers to the acquisition of firm-specific knowledge by workers. Once this know-how has been acquired, there is no incentive on the part of the firm to provide the workers with an appropriate reward and the worker, anticipating this, might be reluctant to invest in socially profitable firm-specific training.

A clear assessment of the cases in which some regulation of the market is justified in terms of efficiency is a helpful exercise, because it provides a benchmark for labour market reform. Although full deregulation should not be the objective, the previous account of the main reasons behind regulation makes it clear that some markets are in need of substantial changes to approximate an optimal level of state intervention. This is, of course, the case of the Spanish market.

The papers by Dr Viñals and Professor Sebastián included in this volume provide a complete analysis of the large number of distortions prevalent in the Spanish labour market. Discussion of these suggests that few of the regulations improve market efficiency. Quite the contrary: they have lain at the root of its extremely poor performance over the last two decades.

It is useful to classify the distortions of the Spanish labour market under two headings. First, we have restrictions on the nature of contracts in terms of their duration and the costs and flexibility of starting and finalising the contractual relationship (for example, temporary versus indefinite contracts, severance pay, part-time contracts). Second, there are restrictions on the nature of the working conditions that may be established in contracts (for example, mobility across production centres and professional categories, flexibility in pay structure, flexibility of working time).

In principle, these limitations constitute restrictions on a firm's choice of the optimal use of its labour. Of course, they exert an indirect effect on price. More specifically, they lead to real wage inflexibility. This is particularly true of restrictions on types of contracts. Such limitations have generated an insider/outsider structure in the Spanish labour market which, apart from considerations of fairness, leads to profoundly negative macroeconomic effects through the reinforcement of real wage inflexibility. Adjustments to changes in the economic cycle take place via quantities rather than wages.

These consequences in terms of the imperfect adjustment of the labour market are, of course, very important, since they imply a higher rate of unemployment compatible with non-accelerating inflation. Viñals argues that rigidities in markets other than labour worsen the situation,[4] so that the non-accelerating inflation rate of unemployment (NAIRU) in Spain is as high as 19.5%.

Other market distortions affect the process of wage formation. These include: 1) the presence of a significant tax wedge which adversely affects the relative price of labour, in particular low-skill labour; 2) the availability of unemployment benefits, which negatively affect the willingness to engage in a job search; 3) the minimum wage level; and 4) the rules that govern collective bargaining.

The fact that the Spanish labour market is full of government interventions does not mean that all of these should be eliminated. As we have argued before, labour markets are far from perfect markets, and some degree of regulation might indeed be desirable, if it adequately corrects the imperfections.

Although most of the interventions in the Spanish labour market might in theory respond to or correct some sort of market failure, the discussion by Viñals and Sebastián shows that the extent of intervention is leading to extremely counterproductive effects in terms of employment. Viñals and Sebastián consider that the most harmful features of the Spanish labour market are the differentiation between temporary and indefinite contracts, the extreme rigidity of contract conditions, the collective bargaining system, the high tax wedge and the favourable conditions of unemployment benefits.

Clearly this calls for a very ambitious agenda for action. Other recent contributions on this subject (see Blanchard et al., 1994) have narrowed down the list of urgent reforms, arguing that most of the employment-destruction features of the Spanish labour market can be attributed to a few of the distortions (the report by Blanchard and his colleagues focuses on the insider/outsider problem and on collective bargaining). Focusing on certain aspects of reform is undoubtedly necessary when one is attempting to achieve political and social acceptance. Nonetheless, selecting the components of the institutional system which need to be adjusted is no easy task. Some of the essays in this volume point out the need to look carefully at the "fit" of the new labour regulations with other labour market institutions and even with other aspects of a society's institutions and culture.

A related issue is the extent to which, in seeking to reform the Spanish (or European) labour market, one may draw upon the experiences of other labour systems which have been more successful at the creation of employment. In this regard, the contributions to this volume by Professors Freeman, Alvarez and Whitley sound a note of caution with respect to the transferability of labour market institutions across national boundaries.

Richard Freeman offers a starting point for the development of a conceptual framework. His contribution goes beyond the basic idea that by importing the US labour market and social institutions into Europe one could only be exchanging less unemployment for more inequality and poverty. According to Freeman, labour markets and the whole labour relations system are complex, dynamic systems with many independent yet interrelated actors. The effectiveness of alternative institutions is not independent of the whole set of existing labour relations.

Freeman provides an interesting example of the complexity of the interactions between labour market institutions. A few years ago, both Spain and Germany introduced contracts of limited duration, but with quite different results for their respective labour markets. Germany's well-developed apprenticeship system meant its firms continued to show an interest in permanent contracts to a much greater extent than their Spanish counterparts.

These ideas are articulated by the notions of an institution's fitness and supermodularity advanced by Freeman. These are concepts which focus the attention of policy makers on the need to carefully evaluate the interrelationship between institutions before borrowing models applied elsewhere. The questions to be asked are the following: how great will the benefits of the new institution be, given the specific set of other institutions already in place? Will these benefits outweigh the costs of introduction? And, most fundamentally, is there a need for "importing" more than one institution, in order to reap the full benefits of change or reform?

The discussion of labour market reform in Spain provides an interesting case study of the potential use of this conceptual framework. As argued earlier, the changes in the range of possible labour contracts and their applicability has to be appraised in a comprehensive manner. As Professor Sebastián makes clear in his contribution to this volume, the recent reform (1994) has rightly eliminated the contract of limited duration, except where justified by the nature of the economic activity (seasonality) and has appropriately developed part-time contracts and apprenticeship contracts. This is a model in which indefinite contracts are the standard contractual form, since they provide the appropriate incentives to both parties of the agreement with regard to investment in job-specific skills. However, indefinite contracts should not mean jobs for life. In practice, the high cost of dismissal for indefinite contracts means that firms are tempted to use part-time and apprenticeship contracts where indefinite contracts would be appropriate. One could, therefore, argue that the reform should have been complemented by a substantial decline in firing costs.

Freeman also distinguishes two interesting institutional dimensions which should be taken into account when assessing the transferability of specific institutions to different social and labour systems: malleability and catalytic power. Malleable institutions are robust ones, in the sense that they work well under different social/labour systems, even if not fully implemented. Catalytic institutions are those which have the potential to spur change in other parts of the system.

When assessing the recommendations for labour market reforms in the EU and in particular in an overregulated market like Spain's, it is interesting to evaluate the proposed changes in light of these dimensions.

The 1994 reform of the Spanish labour market allows significant freedom on the part of social agents to determine many aspects of labour relations within the setting of collective agreements. However, actual change in labour relations and new regulations of working conditions will in reality hinge on substantial changes in the attitudes of the key social actors (see Sebastián), which itself may require a change in the way these institutions (unions, employers' federations) operate. One can therefore conclude that this particular change envisaged by the reform is fundamental. It could be the catalyst for deep reforms in the Spanish labour market, changing the nature of the interaction between social actors and possibly leading to new actions and collaboration by these actors in other very important domains, such as professional training.

It is more difficult to find examples of malleable institutions that could easily be adapted to the Spanish labour market. Arguably, one could include in this category changes in social security contributions, or a reform of the unemployment subsidy system. Changes in these areas could be carried out without requiring complementary changes in other types of labour market institutions.

The contributions of Professors Alvarez and Whitley in this book go even further than that of Professor Freeman by arguing that changes in the labour market should be compatible with (or else may trigger changes in) other aspects of the business system. Their arguments touch upon cultural, political and financial facets of society.

Alvarez uses the case of the international diffusion of entrepreneurship ideas to argue that a society's prevalent values and ideas on economic issues are very important for the acceptance and effectiveness of policy changes. According to Alvarez, the promotion of job creation requires that the ideas on the role of entrepreneurship in the generation of employment become a shared belief among the members of society. This can be achieved only if some domestic social groups adopt a leadership role in spreading these values and in importing and adapting to local circumstances business practices from abroad.

According to Whitley, employment relations - whether in developing countries or in Western societies - develop in the context of systems of norms and rules which govern the exchange relationships between economic actors (the cultural system); the role of the state (the political system); the distribution and pricing of capital (the financial system); and the development, certification and exchange of skills (the labour market system). Whitley stresses that the complex interactions of these systems affect the deployment of business strategies and the development of employment relations and labour management practises. Whitley's essay makes clear that long-term employment patterns and the impact of efforts to change them are highly constrained by the nature of dominant institutions in each economy.

Although these ideas are less formalised than those presented by Freeman, it is not difficult to illustrate their relevance in the case of wide-ranging labour market reforms, like the one recently implemented in the Spanish labour market. Sebastián points out in his paper that the reform implemented thus far leaves a substantial degree of discretion to the judiciary in the termination of contracts. As a consequence, the effectiveness of the reform is contingent upon the interpretation of the spirit of the law by the judges. Early indications are not encouraging, since they do not reflect a market-oriented view of contract termination (see Ortega, 1995). If the reform fails in this respect, it may be the consequence of the lack of simultaneous reforms in other areas of Spanish society: in particular, the political system and the widespread popular perception of the paternalistic role of the state.

Yet another example of the interaction between labour institutions and other, broader aspects of society is supplied by the already-mentioned increased importance of collective agreements for the determination of working conditions. The effectiveness of the reform could be seriously undermined by the fact that the institutions which represent workers and employers in labour markets are weak, and rely on political actions to obtain their goals, much as indicated by Professor Whitley for the case of France. The new role of collective bargaining is therefore a risky bet. It could act as a catalyst if it leads to change in the organisations that represent labour and employers. But it might lead to a failed reform if these institutions do not respond to the challenge.

## 1.4.   EMPLOYMENT AND TRADE

Several recent developments in the international economy have led to the re-emergence of another well-known fallacy: that trade destroys employment in some of the trading partners to the benefit of others. This myth can be stated bluntly: .

*Myth 4. Trade with an increasingly competitive Third World is tearing apart the developed world's social fabric: destroying jobs in Europe and increasing wage disparities in the US, thus condemning low-skill workers to increasing levels of poverty.*

The argument, of course, is that Third World countries compete with very low wages[5] and thus displace labour-intensive sectors of the developed world. That displacement occurs in the domestic and export markets and, in some versions of the story, can also result from foreign direct investment (FDI) or the delocalisation of domestic plants. The debate is further cluttered by arguments over the extent to which the competitiveness advantage is due to wage differentials or to differences in total labour costs, including social charges and working conditions.

In Europe, concern over the employment effect of trade with the Third World is the result of the coincidence of an increased integration of the world economy (Third World countries are adopting increasingly export-led strategies and are growing much more receptive to direct foreign investment) with the surge of unemployment in the 1980s. As to FDI, there is a heated debate over outward FDI: what is known as the delocalisation problem.[6] In the US, the issue has come to the forefront of the economic and social debate in relation to the observed widening of the wage gap within the US labour force, and also as a result of the policy of commercial integration with developing countries, such as Mexico.

The assessment of the employment effects of trade poses difficult theoretical and empirical problems; it is therefore not surprising that it should be the subject of such substantial controversy. Three broad categories of studies have been conducted. We will briefly review their approaches and main results.

(a)   The employment content of imports
The classic methodology that has been used to assess the employment impact of trade is the analysis of the so-called factor content of trade.[7] Essentially, this method attempts to measure the employment displaced by trade by looking at the labour content of net trade flows, taking into account the effects on intermediate production. It is assumed that in the absence of trade the jobs involved in the production of exports would not be available and, at the same time, that the domestic production of imports would increase domestic employment. The precise amount of domestic labour that would be employed by the substitution of imports is computed under the assumption that domestic and foreign productivity are the same.

Needless to say, this is a very crude approximation of the employment impact of trade, and is plagued by theoretical pitfalls. Some of these problems have long been recognised. For example,[8] if imports were produced domestically, their price would be higher and the quantity produced lower, so that the effect on total spending in previously imported goods would be uncertain. Moreover, it is also unclear to what extent imports can be substituted by domestic production using the same quantity of labour per unit of output. In principle it seems reasonable to assume that, since the product would otherwise be imported, domestic production is less efficient and involves a higher labour cost per unit of output. Most probably, domestic production would entail the use of less labour-intensive techniques. Moreover, it is even possible that some products could not be produced domestically, in which case imports would not be substituting for any domestic employment (unless, of course, one assumes that spending would be redirected to goods which could be produced domestically)[9]. Finally - and this is probably the main criticism of this methodology - the approach disregards general equilibrium effects. In particular, reduced exports would lead to changes in factor demands which, in turn, would affect labour market conditions.

Nonetheless, the employment content method is a simple and readily understandable methodology. Some authors have recently arrived at sizable estimates of the employment impact of trade. For example, Sachs and Shatz (1994) argue that trade in the US - mostly with the developing world - resulted in a drop of almost 6% in manufacturing employment between 1978 and 1990. The calculations of these authors show that the decline in employment was concentrated in low-skill jobs.

(b)     Changes in international relative prices and their impact on relative factor prices (for example, the wages of skilled versus unskilled workers)

The unsatisfactory theoretical basis of employment content studies has led to the application of the conventional general equilibrium trade framework: the Heckscher-Ohlin model. The advantage of this approach is that under the precise assumptions of the model (that is, imposing perfect competition, constant returns to scale and incomplete specialisation) the theory provides a clear link between trade and factor markets through one of the famous results of international trade: the Stolper-Samuelson theorem. In the case of two goods and two factors, this theorem establishes the existence of a positive partial correlation between relative international prices and relative factor prices. If the price of the good which is relatively intensive in one factor goes up, so does the relative price of that factor.

Two important remarks should be made with regard to this theorem. First, it does not establish a link between international prices and the evolution of unemployment. Nonetheless, the evolution of relative factor prices is a key determinant of the evolution of employment and wages for the different categories of labour. As pointed out by Sachs and Shatz (op. cit., p. 15), the theorem is developed under the conditions of full employment and wage flexibility. With fixed factor supplies, this means that any increase in the demand for skilled workers due to the shift of production toward skill-intensive sectors will be exactly compensated for by the shift within sectors from skilled to unskilled employment. Sachs and Shatz argue that low-wage competition will do more than reallocate labour between and within sectors due to the presence of labour market imperfections.

A second point is that the theorem is useful empirically provided that one can control for the evolution of factor supplies and technology, since these are the other determinants of relative factor prices. Lawrence and Slaughter have used this framework to analyse the evolution of the relative wages of skilled and unskilled[10] labour in the US. These authors show that during the

1980s the international relative price of the goods that require intensive use of production workers (as compared to non-production workers) actually increased slightly, and that only after controlling for the evolution of total factor productivity (TFP) in the two kinds of industries (that is, using what is sometimes known as "effective" prices), one finds a relative decline of the price of goods intensive in production workers.[11]

This evolution is consistent with an increase in the relative wage of non-production versus production workers. This is what was actually observed in the US during the 1980s, and the fact that the relative supply of non-production workers also increased during the same period means that the demand shift compatible with the evolution of relative effective prices was indeed substantial.

Lawrence and Slaughter conclude, however, that trade (through the change in relative effective prices) was not the main force driving the evolution of relative factor prices over that period. If that had been the case, one would have observed a decline in the use of non-production versus production workers in all industries - but precisely the opposite was detected. Lawrence and Slaughter argue that biased technical change which favours the demand for non-production workers is the only explanation for the observed shifts in relative wages, prices and employment by skill categories in the 1980s.[12]

The use of the Stolper-Samuelson theorem offers guidance in empirical analysis, but one must recall that it yields a theoretical result the validity of which is unclear in the context of imperfectly competitive markets. In such a situation (see, for example, Helpman and Krugman, 1985, Chapter 9) it may well happen that trade benefits all factors if the changes in relative factor prices are not too great and if they are outweighed by the gains from exhausting scale economies. Oliveira Martins (1994) and Neven and Wyplosz (1994) have recently addressed the issue of the effects of trade on employment in a way that takes into account the imperfect competition perspective. Oliveira Martins uses regression analysis with a sample of 25 industries corresponding to 12 OECD countries and finds that import competition reduces wages and employment only in those industries characterised by product homogeneity and very fragmented market structures. Moreover, he finds that the trade variable contributes positively to wages in other types of industries where product differentiation and investment in intangibles are important. In those cases, trade benefits all factors of production involved in the exporting country. These are suggestive results. However - and this is in contrast with the econometric results of Revenga (1992), which we review later - there is a problem with the interpretation of the parameters, given the partial linkage of the specification with the underlying theory.

Neven and Wyplosz examine the evolution of relative prices, real output and the use of labour in two sets of European industries: labour-intensive and technology-intensive. By selecting these types of industries they attempt to disentangle technology from trade shocks. Although they do not control for changes in TFP, they argue that the price of both technology-intensive and labour-intensive goods falls over time relative to the overall price level. Output increases in high-tech industries (relative to total output) and falls in labour-intensive industries. This might indicate that labour-intensive industries were subject to a negative trade shock, whereas in the case of high-tech industries the data would be consistent with a positive technology shock. Employment data corroborate this interpretation. Relative employment falls in the labour-intensive industries but does so in high-tech industries as well, albeit to a lesser extent. This could be the result of the higher labour productivity of these sectors, but it is also consistent with labour-saving technical progress.

(c)     The labour market approach: import competition and the adjustment of labour markets
The previous discussion makes clear that the general equilibrium method, though theoretically sound, is difficult to implement in practise. Labour economists have taken quite a different approach. They have focused on the estimation of labour supply-and-demand equations where import prices appear as a significant explanatory variable.

Revenga (op. cit.) estimates such a system of equations for a sample of 38 US industries and uses quarterly data corresponding to the period 1977-87. She finds that the major decline in import prices brought about by the strong appreciation of the dollar had significant effects on wages and employment. Her estimates suggest that, ceteris paribus, a 10% reduction in import prices leads to an average employment reduction ranging from 2.5% to 4%, and to a wage decline of 0.5-1%. These results seem to indicate that labour markets in specific industries are particularly sensitive to import competition, but that adjustment takes place through the reallocation of labour across industries rather than through a decline in industry-specific wages.[13]

(d)     What can we conclude?
The studies based on the factor content method have led to an unwarranted alarm about the effects of trade on employment and wages. Despite its intuitive appeal, this methodology is

insufficiently reliable; the conclusions reached by this strand of research cannot be the basis of policy formulation.

A more insightful analysis has been obtained by the research into the evolution of relative prices. The trade theory tradition has contributed by pointing out that the evolution of international relative prices, factor supplies and factor prices is not consistent with a dominant role of trade as a factor explaining high unemployment (or low wages) for unskilled workers. Some of the work by labour economists has tackled the issue by looking directly at the effect of import prices on employment markets across industries. The results, at least for the US, are not inconsistent with the aggregate picture. Trade effects at the level of specific industries are significant, but there is a substantial adjustment of employment across industries, which need not affect aggregate (manufacturing) employment. A similar inter-sectoral mobility effect could take place between manufacturing and services, although there is no formal evidence of this so far.

Unfortunately, the evidence available for the European labour market is still very scarce, and the results which are valid for the US need not apply to Europe, where labour market rigidities may limit or hinder inter-sectoral employment flows.

In sum: the belief that trade liberalisation contributes to the destruction of employment is unfounded. An expansion of trade results in lower prices, which should lead to an increase in consumer surplus and end up in an overall increase in demand. Of course, such a beneficial demand increase is unlikely to spread evenly over all sectors of the economy, and demand will increase more in some sectors than in others. In fact, as real income increases, demand is likely to rise proportionally more in services than in manufacturing, which tends to have a lower income elasticity. The uneven distribution of demand growth across sectors leads to an uneven demand for different types of labour. Like technological change, trade also brings an overall increase in welfare, but its full benefits require a swift adaptation of labour supply. Also like technological change, trade[14] exerts pressure for change in the labour market structures of the developed world. It is not the culprit to be blamed for unemployment: rather, it is a catalyst for change in the labour market. Unemployment is created by the lagging pace at which our institutions and markets develop and alter workers' skills to adapt them to the changing needs of firms, consumers and society at large.

## 1.5.    CONCLUSIONS

This volume has brought together experts from several areas in sociology and economics, such as organisational sociology, labour economics and macroeconomics. The main purpose of the papers is to contribute to the debate on the definition of policy alternatives for the creation of employment. This explains why (by and large) they are not unduly technical and remain accessible to a wide audience.

Policy proposals in the field of employment should be based on a multidisciplinary analysis which recognises the multiple facets of modern societies. To this end, this book assembles contributions from two of the most relevant fields. The acknowledgement of the social and cultural dimensions of the employment problem should enrich the policy analysis and may facilitate the social acceptance (and political viability) of policy reform if that acknowledgement is worked into its design.

This introductory chapter has presented the main themes of the volume in a somewhat unorthodox fashion. As a non-specialist in this topic, I have tried to show how the contributions to this book shed light on some popular misconceptions regarding the question of employment. Moreover, as an economist interested in the impact of economic integration, I have deemed it worthwhile to include a discussion of the relationship between trade and employment, a controversial issue not covered by the essays collected here.

As a concluding note to this chapter, I would like to highlight some of the main ideas included in this book which I believe should be present in the employment debate.

First, there is the emphasis on the key role of the employability of the labour force. It is a challenge to both the private and the public sector in industrialised countries to augment the abilities of their population, and in particular of the less skilled, in order to confront the changing requirements of labour demand which are primarily due to technological progress, but also, to a lesser extent, to economic integration.

Technological progress, even if unbiased, changes the structure of labour demand and, in the absence of appropriate action in education and training, may reduce the employability of the labour force, and thus the number of jobs. If technological change is biased against low-skill labour, it will be particularly important to ensure that the relative price of this labour is not made excessively high by taxes and other regulations. The preservation of the living standards of the low-skilled should be achieved by income support mechanisms which encourage firms to employ workers from this sector of the population; such mechanisms should not limit the incentives to join the labour force and actively seek work. The difficulty of providing education and training to large numbers of unemployed people, together with the fact that employability is enhanced by actual employment, means that there is a special need to eliminate the distortions that penalise the low-skilled. General education and training designed to adapt the labour force to a changing labour demand should be specially targeted to youth, in order to avoid their entry into the pool of the long-term unemployed.

Economic integration, in the form of lower trade barriers and increased international trade and investment flows, has contributed only moderately to the changing nature of jobs in industrialised countries. Reports ascribing a significant employment effect to trade are grossly exaggerated due to faulty methodologies. Trade appears to exert a significant effect on employment only at the sectoral level, within the tradables industries. The effects however, disappear at the aggregate level if the economy shows sufficient inter-sectoral mobility. Like technological progress, trade is a source of gains in welfare which translate into jobs - provided that the supply of employable people responds appropriately.

A second central idea focuses on labour market institutions. The contributions to this book clearly indicate that an appropriate reform of labour markets need not involve, in general, their full deregulation, since there are sound reasons to regulate certain aspects of the relationship between workers and their employers. Nonetheless, in cases such as that of the Spanish market, these essays demonstrate that profound changes are necessary in order to liberalise an overwhelmingly rigid system.

The acknowledgement that some degree of regulation of labour markets and institutions is needed points to one of the book's key themes: the question of labour market reform and the potential adaptation of labour market institutions borrowed from abroad. The essays emphasise the interaction between labour market institutions and shows that any plan of labour market reform should take into account broad packages of institutions as well as their relation to other aspects of a society and its business culture.

This means that policy changes may have unintended consequences or remain ineffectual unless accompanied by broad reforms in several institutions of society. Incremental reforms - such as those advocated by Alogouskoufis et al. (1995) - will be effective only if they focus on the few labour market institutions whose performance is independent of the rest of the system. Otherwise, the avenue of wide-ranging reforms is more promising. However, even then - as Freeman points out in this book - a high degree of uncertainty about the (distributional) outcome of reforms remains, and this explains the resistance to change in industrial societies despite the gravity of the employment problem.

The third main message concerns the demand side of the economy. Although the solution to the employment problem is on the supply side, lying as it does in the reform of labour market institutions, demand management aspects cannot be disregarded. Demand may be insufficient because of several market imperfections. But even if the shortfall of demand is purely cyclical, its (negative) effects on employment can be lasting, and may justify a counteracting intervention. True, the persistence mechanisms operating in the labour market are largely the result of labour market regulations and institutions. But, as we have already indicated, the nature of the labour market is such that these regulations (and their costs in terms of the persistence of negative demand shocks) cannot be simply swept away.

## NOTES

*   The views expressed in this article are personal and do not reflect the opinion of the European Commission. I want to thank Professor José Luis Alvarez for his help during the preparation of this volume. The paper has also benefited from the comments by Professor Antonio Argandoña and Professor André Sapir. Finally, I would like to thank Professor Carlos Cavallé and Professor Jordi Canals for their continuous encouragement and support during the preparation of this volume and the conference on which it is based.

1   Among the main contributions on this subject in recent years see, for example, Drèze and Bean (1990), Layard et al. (1991) and Bean (1994b).

2   See, for example, OECD Jobs Study (OECD Paris, 1994). The recent International Labour Office Employment Report (ILO, 1995) is, however, an exception to this trend.

3   See, for example, Begg et al. (1993; pp.106-108).

4   Imperfections in other markets allow firms to pass on to consumers a substantial part of the wage increases. Although Viñals does not explicitly formalise his argument, this feature shows up neatly in the simple model used by R. Layard. A recent report by MacKinsey Global Institute (1994) has stressed the significance of product market restrictions as a factor underlying poor employment performance.

5   The argument should refer to low wages per unit of output, with the underlying idea that it is not hard for developing countries to obtain the physical capital and the technology that will allow them to obtain high levels of productivity.

6   Robert Lawrence (1995) reports on the pattern of wages and employment of US multinationals in the US and abroad. According to his data, the ratio of production to non-production workers has dropped both in the US and abroad. Similarly, relative wages of production workers have fallen worldwide. These trends are not consistent with a substantial effect of outward FDI on US wage inequality.

7   Another popular methodology is the input-output accounting decomposition of employment changes, taking into consideration the evolution of (apparent) labour productivity and the composition of final demand (see, for example, OECD, 1992). Such a decomposition is subject to even more criticism than the factor content approach (see, for example, Baldwin, 1995).

8   Some of these points are discussed by Wood (1994).

9    Wood (op. cit.) has attempted to correct for some of these problems. He computes the factor content of exports from the South to the North assuming that the input combination used in the South is the result of cost minimisation at the prevailing factor prices. Data on factor use and some extraneous information on the elasticities of substitution allow the calibration of the technology parameters, which are then used to infer the "counterfactual" factor use in the North at the North factor prices. Wood obtains very high estimates for the effect of North-South trade on employment, but his methodology is controversial (see, for example, Krugman, 1994). In related work, Deardoff and Staiger (1988) show that the factor content method can be used to assess directly the effects of trade on factor rewards only under very restrictive assumptions on preferences and technology. Under more general specifications, the results are substantially weaker.

10   Lawrence and Slaughter do not actually work with skill categories; rather, they distinguish between production and non-production workers, a classification which - they argue - is closely correlated with skill categories. Despite some sharp criticisms of the use of this proxy (see Leamer, 1994), data presented by Berman et al. (1994) confirm the usefulness of the variable.

11   When total factor productivity (TFP) grows quickly, observed prices may be misleading as indicators of price changes. The percentage change in effective prices is computed as the difference between the percentage change in observed prices minus the percentage change in TFP. Lawrence and Slaughter find that TFP grows faster in industries which use skilled workers, and this more than compensates for the evolution of observed prices. Sachs and Shatz (1994) rightly point out that the Stolper-Samuelson theorem requires the use of effective prices, since it assumes that the countries have the same technology. These authors criticise the data set used by Lawrence and Slaughter, argue that the price of computers should be removed from the sample, and use a different statistical technique (simple regression with a computer dummy). Their results indicate that the relative price of unskilled-intensive goods falls, but that this drop is softened by the effect of the evolution of total factor productivity. This implies that TFP grows faster precisely in the industries which are intensive in unskilled workers: the exact opposite of what is found in the Lawrence and Slaughter data. However, the results obtained by Sachs and Shatz are not statistically significant for the case of effective prices, and therefore do not invalidate the evidence presented by Lawrence and Slaughter. Moreover, the latter results have been extended to Germany and Japan (Lawrence, 1995).

12   Leamer (1994) has also been critical of the results obtained by Lawrence and Slaughter. Although his results are very preliminary, his contribution points out the need to estimate fully specified models where the link between relative factor prices, technological change and changes in relative prices is well established. He uses 1976-86 data for 450 manufacturing industries to assess the relationship between initial input use and payroll savings. In a simple Heckscher-Ohlin model with constant international relative prices, the parameters of such a regression provide an approximation of the changes in relative wages due to changes in input requirements. His surprising results indicate that technological change has tended to favour an increase in the relative wage of unskilled labour.

13   In the US, this is consistent with the finding that most of the widening gap be-
      tween the wages of the skilled and the unskilled takes place within industries.
14   Although this section has argued that trade does not significantly affect aggregate
      wages and employment, this should not prevent the discussion of a potential
      indirect effect of trade pressure. Import competition could have an indirect effect
      on wages and employment if it created or accelerated labour-saving technical
      change. Not many systematic studies have addressed this issue. Neven and
      Wyplosz (1994) have looked at how German labour-intensive industries have
      changed technology, presumably as a response to increased competitive pressure
      from low-wage countries. Their work is still in the exploratory stages. They
      measure technology changes by statistically significant changes in some proxies
      of input composition, and find that only a few of these industries have responded
      to foreign competition by increasing the human capital content of production (thus
      demanding fewer unskilled workers). Their results lend support to the view that
      the trade effects on employment - even if they occur through the indirect effect on
      technology - are very much industry-specific.

# REFERENCES

Alogouskoufis, G. et al. (1995), *Unemployment: Choices for Europe*, CEPR, 5th
   Report on Monitoring European Integration.
Bhagwati, J. and M. Kosters (eds.) (1994), *Trade and Wages*, Washington, D.C.:
   American Enterprise Institute.
Baldwin, Robert E. (1995), 'The Effects of Trade and Foreign Direct Investment on
   Employment and Relative Wages', *The OECD Jobs Study Working Papers* n°4.
Bean, C. (1994a), 'The Role of Demand Management Policies in Reducing
   Unemployment', paper presented at the symposium Reducing Unemployment:
   Current Issues and Policy Options of the Federal Reserve Bank of Kansas City at
   Jackson Hole, 25-27 Aug.
Bean, C. (1994b), 'European Unemployment: A Survey', *Journal of Economic
   Literature*, vol. XXXII, 2, June. pp.573-619.
Begg, D. et al. (1993), *Making Sense of Subsidiarity. How much Centralisation for
   Europe?* CEPR, 4th Report on Monitoring European Integration.
Berman, Eli, John Bound and Zvi Griliches (1994),'*Changes in the Demand for Skilled
   Labor Within U.S. Manufacturing Industries'*, Quarterly Journal of Economics,
   109(2): 367-397.
Blanchard, O. et al., (1994), *El paro en España: ¿Tiene solución?* Report prepared by
   CEPR (Consejo Superior de Cámaras de Comercio, Industria y Navegación),
   December.
Deardoff, A.V. and R.W. Staiger (1988), 'An Interpretation of the Factor Content of
   Trade', *Journal of International Economics,* 24 1/2: 93-107.
Drèze, J. and C. Bean (1990), *Europe's Unemployment Problem,* Cambridge, Mass.:
   MIT Press.

Drèze, J. and H. Sneessens (1994), 'Technical Development, Competition from Low-Wage Economies and Low-Skilled Unemployment' in *Swedish Economic Policy Review*, vol. 1, n°1-2, Autumn.

Freeman, R. (ed.) (1994), W*orking Under Different Rules*, Russell Sage.

Helpman, E. and P. Krugman (1985), *Market Structure and Foreign Trade. Increasing Returns, Imperfect Competition and the International Economy*, Cambridge, Mass.: MIT Press.

International Labour Office (1995), *World Employment 1995*, Geneva.

Krugman, P. (1994), 'Past and Prospective Causes of High Unemployment', paper presented at the symposium Reducing Unemployment: Current Issues and Policy Options of the Federal Reserve Bank of Kansas City at Jackson Hole, 25-27 Aug.

Krugman, P. and R. Lawrence (1994), 'Trade, Jobs and Wages', *Scientific American*, April.

Lawrence, Robert Z. (1995), 'U.S. Wage Trends in the 1980's: The Role of International Factors' in *Federal Reserve Bank of New York Economic Policy Review* vol. 1, n°1, January.

Lawrence, Robert Z. and Matthew Slaughter (1993), 'Trade and U.S. Wages: Giant Sucking Sound or Small Hiccup?' *Brookings Papers on Economic Activity Microeconomics,* vol. 2, pp. 161-226.

Layard, R.G., S.J. Nickell and R.A. Jackman (1991), *Unemployment: Macroeconomic Performance and the Labour Market*, Oxford: Oxford University Press.

Leamer, E. (1994), *'Trade, Wages and Revolving Door Ideas',* NBER Working Paper n°4716, April.

McKinsey Global Institute (1994), *Employment Performance*, Washington, D.C., November.

Neven, D. and C. Wyplosz (1994), 'Trade and European Labor Markets', Mimeo, September.

OECD (1992), *Structural Change and Industrial Performance: A Seven Country Growth Decomposition Study*, Paris.

OECD ( 1994), *Jobs Study, Evidence and Explanations,* Paris.

Oliveira Martins, J. (1994), 'Market Structure, Trade and Industry Wages' in *OECD Economic Studies,* n°22, Spring.

Ortega, R. (1995), 'La contrarreforma laboral' in *La Vanguardia*, 12 February.

Revenga, A. (1992), 'Exporting Jobs: The Impact of Import Competition on Employment and Wages in US Manufacturing', *Quarterly Journal of Economics* 92, 225-286, February.

Sachs, J. and H.J. Shatz (1994),'Trade and Jobs in U.S. Manufacturing' in *Brookings Papers on Economic Activity*, vol. 1, pp.1-84.

Wood, A. (1994), *North-South Trade, Employment and Inequality: Changing Fortunes in a Skill Driven World*, Oxford: Clarendon Press.

# PART I

# POLICIES AND INSTITUTIONS
# FOR JOB CREATION

# 2.    Employment in Europe

## Jacques H. Drèze*

---

## 2.1.    UNEMPLOYMENT, EUROPE'S NUMBER ONE PROBLEM

Unemployment is unmistakably Europe's number one problem. With more than 18 million unemployed (Eurostat definition) in the European Union today, the record rate of 11.6% of the labour force prevails. This also means that unemployment rates for the young, the less skilled or the less prosperous regions exceed 20%, and even more where there is a combination of these unfavourable features. The persistence of that situation raises doubts about the prospects for a return to full employment. Many refer to a structural break, not a temporary recession. Social exclusion and despair, but also confused prospects, breed excessive or even extreme reactions, which threaten our economic and democratic institutions.

And yet: between 1987 and 1990, nine million jobs were created in the European Union, on a net basis (net increase in employment); in terms of full-time equivalents, the increase still exceeds eight million. That result has been achieved through a revival of growth, reaching an average (over four years) 3.5% per year for the GNP of the EU 12, and 1.4% for employment. A slight increase of the population of working age, a somewhat faster increase of the labour force kept the rate of decline in employment to 0.7% per year, or 2.8% over the four years. Europe's unemployment thus fell only to 8% - but nine million jobs had been created, and youth unemployment was receding markedly.

Had growth continued at the same pace between 1990 and 1994, today's unemployment rate in Europe would be below 5.5%, less than half of what we observe. Our outlook on economic conditions, on the performance of our economies, and on the prospects for European integration, would be markedly different. It sounds like a dream - but it is not science fiction. It could have happened, and should be our goal for tomorrow.

I wish to stress at the outset my firm belief that progress in our societies calls for reducing unemployment, hence for creating jobs; that jobs come from growth; and that growth is possible, in economic as well as

29

ecological terms. The concern for employment is fully consistent with the concern for the environment. But balanced growth is always fragile; it requires consistent economic developments, social cohesiveness, and protection from external shocks. It requires today concerted action mobilising economic, social and political forces at the European level. The prospects for such concerted action are unfortunately slim.

Eliminating our excessive unemployment will require a full decade of sustained growth. We know by now that growth of output must be at least 2% for non-declining employment and 3% for declining unemployment. Thus, we must grow for ten years at a rate regarded by some as close to our potential. (I am personally more optimistic about our ability to invest and grow.) There is no miraculous short-term solution. The objective can only be reached after following a narrow path for ten years. We cannot neglect medium-term policies, with effects spreading over time. The problem will not be solved before these effects materialise. Medium term, unfortunately, is also the horizon over which economic analysis is least informative.

## 2.2.   THE WEAKENED POSITION OF UNSKILLED LABOUR

One cannot discuss European unemployment today without stressing that it is largely concentrated among low-skilled workers.[1] We had sensed it for a while, we know it today: the market position of less-skilled workers has deteriorated, in the US and Europe alike, over the past ten years.[2]

The main reasons are:

(i)     First and foremost, skill-biased technological change, largely linked to computers. The implications for employment gain momentum as the new technologies invade services, which account today for two jobs out of three.
(ii)    Competiton from low-wage economies, whose quantitative impact is still modest, but growing inexorably. In Western Europe, the pressure from the East, where wage costs are lower by a factor of 1 to 6 or sometimes even 10, is mounting and bound to become quantitatively significant.
(iii)   Decline of blue-collar employment in manufacturing, previously a source of well-paid but largely accessible jobs, now less abundant due to high productivity and international specialisation.

In the US, the deterioration shows up mostly in wages. Wage inequality has increased markedly during the eighties, the number of low-paid workers is growing, poverty is spreading. In 1990, over 30% of US workers earned less than two-thirds of the median wage - as opposed to

10% in Europe (5% in Belgium). Europe has not followed the American model which in this respect is entirely unappealing. Minimum wages and social protection prevent wages from falling to the low US levels, but a price has to be paid in the form of high unemployment rates. Still the root cause is the same, and the phenomenon will expand. Corrective action is much needed.

## 2.3. THE TWO PILLARS OF GROWTH

Balanced growth rests fundamentally on two complementary pillars: demand growth and realistic wage developments. When these two conditions prevail, the benefits of growth pervade the economy. In particular, public deficits can be controlled and objectives of budgetary restraint, as listed in the Maastricht treaty, become realistic.[3] On the contrary, insufficient demand and excessive wage pressure are the proximate causes of unemployment.

I will develop these two themes (demand and wages), which are the key to sustained and sustainable growth. I will relate them to the persistence of unemployment, then to medium-term macroeconomic policies.

### 2.3.1 Aggregate demand

Volatility of aggregate demand is a recurrent weakness of decentralised market economies.The main body of evidence to that effect comes from econometric work.[4] More transparent illustrations are easy to give.

Often, acceleration or reversal of growth can be traced directly to demand movements. Illustrations include the 1984 boom in the US following the Reagan tax reform; the 1986 investment boom in Europe induced by the single market prospects; or the 1990 turning point both in Europe, and then in US where economists impute it to an unexplained slowdown in private consumption (most naturally understood as a change in expectations, perhaps due in part to the Gulf War).[5] The role of investment, notoriously volatile, was stressed forcefully by Keynes; it is illustrated in Figures 2.1.a and 2.1.b for Europe.

Other accidents originate elsewhere, but get transmitted to output and employment through the demand channel. Thus, the first oil shock, by nature a supply shock, did affect aggregate demand through the temporary sterilisation of oil revenues which were not immediately turned into real spending, and through the postponement of investments, pending clarification of the size and persistence of the oil price hike. The second oil shock similarly affected demand through investment and through the restrictive monetary policies aimed at forestalling a (partly unavoidable) surge of inflation. These demand contractions in turn depressed output and employment.

These observations are not new - even if the importance of aggregate demand is curiously neglected by "new classical" macroeconomists, or by "natural unemployment" theorists, of which there are many. Whereas "new Keynesian" macroeconomists are mostly concerned with alternative explanations of the frictions which slow down adjustment towards equilibrium, I pay special attention to the persistence of demand effects.

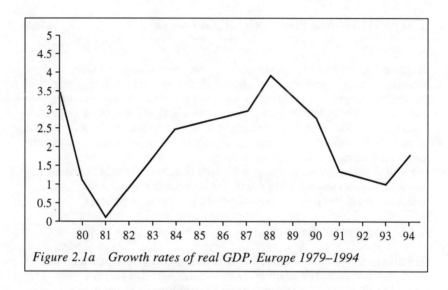

*Figure 2.1a    Growth rates of real GDP, Europe 1979–1994*

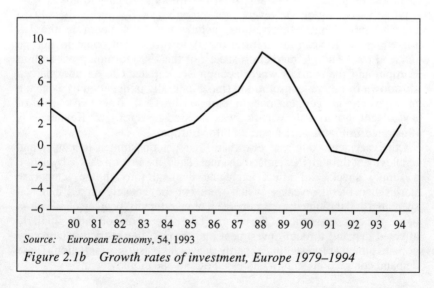

*Source:   European Economy,* 54, 1993

*Figure 2.1b    Growth rates of investment, Europe 1979–1994*

The persistence is due, in my opinion,[6] to two limitations inherent in the functioning of a decentralised market economy: first, the absence of simultaneity in the clearing of markets for a myriad of goods and services; and second, the absence of markets for forward or contingent transactions on these goods and services.[7] These two limitations entail coordination failures, which cannot be overcome by existing markets or by initiatives of individual agents. There results a multiplicity of equilibria (with no self-correcting tendencies) and persistent inefficiencies.[8]

I will explain, starting with the absence of simultaneity. In decentralised market economics, most prices (not all, a majority) are set by firms, who then meet demand within the limits of their profitable capacities. Price-making is decentralised - in contrast to what happens on a stock exchange, where equilibrium prices for a range of assets are determined simultaneously.

At the prevailing prices, excess supply can prevail simultaneously on many markets - markets for goods, where excess capacities prevail, and markets for labour services, where unemployment prevails. This has indeed been the typical situation in Europe over the past 20 years, as revealed by Figure 2.2. Excess supply persists, because it corresponds to a non-cooperative, or Nash, equilibrium. Firms do not hire due to lack of demand; the unemployed do not buy, due to lack of income. And yet, there exist other equilibria, with more output and employment, at the same prices and wages. These equilibria could only be reached through coordinated increases in quantities - sales and hirings. But the basis of the required coordination is wide. It is wider than one firm, one region or even one country - all of which are too open for domestic demand to reconstruct the wage bill (for Say's Law to operate).

That superior equilibria exist, at the same wages and salaries, is true as a close approximation. I do not mean at exactly the same price for each specific good or the same wage for each specific labour qualification. I mean rather at the same overall level of prices and wages. There are enough firms operating under decreasing average costs and non-increasing marginal costs to offset the opposite cases.[9] This is also the main reason why unused capacities do not lead firms to lower prices, as hoped by Pigou and after him a generation of macroeconomists. (Why wages do not fall is taken up below.)

The absence of markets for forward or contingent transactions reinforces the persistence of equilibria with excess capacities and unemployment. An analogy is instructive. It comes from the theory of peak-load pricing, i.e. pricing of periodic demand. Electricity is the standard example. Efficiency calls for prices equal to marginal, i.e. variable, cost at times of excess capacity (low demand). All the costs due to capacity investment, or fixed costs, are covered thanks to the higher prices charged on peak demand (when capacity is fully used). The same logic applied to macroeconomic fluctuations calls for recouping investment costs through a high mark-up

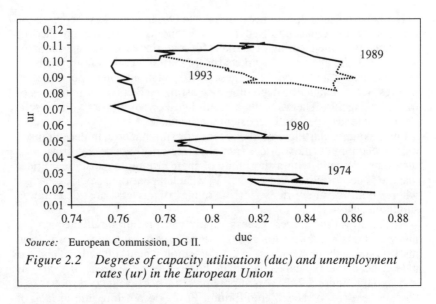

*Source:*   European Commission, DG II.

*Figure 2.2    Degrees of capacity utilisation (duc) and unemployment
             rates (ur) in the European Union*

in the case of full use of capacity, while covering variable costs alone in
the case of excess capacity.

Because we are now considering mutually exclusive uncertain paths, the
solvency of firms in recessions would require financial contracts,
transferring a share of the excess margins in states of full activity to the
states of under-activity. Equity financing can do that - but it applies to a
small share of investment flows.[10] Retained earnings and fixed debentures
instead lead firms to maintain solvency by collectively charging prices in
excess of variable costs even in recession, which limits downward price
flexibility and accounts for the persistence of under-activity with excess
capacities.[11] Of course, excess capacities are eventually removed by non-
replacement, in contrast to excess labour supply, which explains the
pattern of Figure 2.2: successive returns to high rates of capacity utilisation
have been associated with successively higher rates of unemployment.

One might hope that business firms be relieved, at least partly, of their
financial burdens, during recessions. The social cost of additional output
is then lower than at future times when excess capacities will have
disappeared, so that real interest rates should be negative. But nominal
interest rates cannot become negative. Hence, negative real rates call for
anticipated inflation exceeding nominal rates. But monetary authorities
react to inflation forecasts by raising nominal rates, and thus bar the road
to financial relief.

I conclude that demand stabilisation policies are needed, in
decentralised market economies. Such policies are met with justified
scepticism, when they aim at fine tuning: our tools for measurement and

control are not fine! But I am not advocating fine tuning. I am advocating support of growth over a decade to reduce mass unemployment by 7 or 8%. Demand stabilisation policies, however, must be pursued at a European-wide level. Europe is sufficiently closed to make such policies effective, since foreign trade accounts for only 9% of EU 12 GDP (a percentage that will decrease further with the entry of new members). Demand stabilisation on a narrower basis is illusory, as was revealed for instance by the German "locomotive experiment" after 1978 or by the French isolated expansion after 1981.

### 2.3.2    Wage moderation

I turn now to wage developments. The level of real wages matters on three counts:

(i)     The first count is capital-labour substitution - the engine of long-term growth, but a form of waste under unemployment. In gross terms, i.e. ignoring the labour content of capital equipment, this substitution reduces employment in Europe (but not in the US) at the rate of roughly 1% per year. It is likely - though not documented econometrically, to my knowledge - that this process boils down in large part to substitution of skilled labour for unskilled labour. (In small countries, it also amounts to substituting imported capital goods for domestic labour.)

(ii)    The second count is international competitiveness. High wages curtail exports and encourage imports. That aspect is very important for small open economies like Belgium, much less so for relatively closed areas like Europe.

(iii)   The third count is profitability, without which investment stalls and reorganisations with negative employment consequences are carried out.

These three effects would seem to overpower the positive contribution of wages to consumer demand stabilisation.

Next to the level of real wages, their evolution matters: any sign of wage inflation triggers - rightly or wrongly, meaning sometimes rightly and sometimes wrongly - restrictive monetary policies; these discourage investment, curtail profitability and induce pessimistic expectations, with further negative effects on consumption and investment.

The contrast between wage and employment developments in Europe and in the US is striking, as illustrated by Table 2.1 or Figures 2.3.a-2.3.b.

Table 2.1    Comparisons Europe 12 – United States

| Growth rates 1960–1990 | % | |
| --- | --- | --- |
| | Europe | United States |
| Real GDP | 3.3 | 3 |
| Employment | 0.3 | 2 |
| Real wages | 3.0 | 1 |

Source:   European Economy, 54.

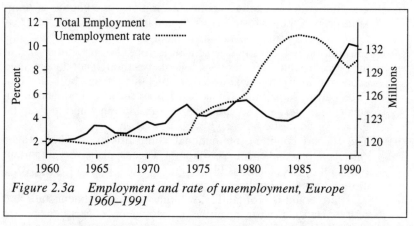

Figure 2.3a    Employment and rate of unemployment, Europe
               1960–1991

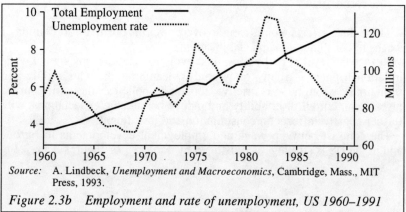

Source:   A. Lindbeck, Unemployment and Macroeconomics, Cambridge, Mass., MIT
          Press, 1993.

Figure 2.3b    Employment and rate of unemployment, US 1960–1991

Wage formation in Europe has witnessed some errors - like the rise of real wages in 1974-76 (over 10% for EU 12, 14% for France, 16% for Belgium), at a time of collective impoverishment through terms of trade deterioration. There is also a statistical error. Wages in Europe (but not in the US) incorporate rapidly and almost fully gains in gross average productivity (value added per worker), without regard for the fact that these productivity gains: (i) reflect in part capital-labour substitution induced by the wage increases - which creates a spiral: wages-productivity-wages-prices-wages;[12] (ii) reflect in some cases scrapping of older idle equipment and not technological or managerial advances.

How do we explain the resistance of real wages in the face of persistent unemployment? We need to look separately at different labour markets. At the low end of the skills ladder, where unemployment is most severe, the wage floor comes from unemployment benefits and minimum wages (either legal or negotiated). This floor has no counterpart in the US, where benefit payments last at most six months while minimum wages are either non-existent (in some states) or ineffective. In Europe, the wage floor seems to reflect a broad social consensus, a collective desire to guarantee to every worker a minimal income, still not generous for families with no other source of income.[13] In most European countries, the wage floor has prevented the rise of poverty witnessed in the US. We must maintain that kind of income protection for low-skilled workers, while continually trying to find more efficient schemes.

At the upper end of the skill ladder, on the other hand, wages and salaries are geared to equilibrium of supply and demand. True, markets remain imperfect; salary differentials between firms exceed plausible compensating differentials; but there is no evidence of either upward or downward bias, except for narrowly defined jobs where wages come closer to a contest outcome than to a competitive outcome.

Between these two extremes, there is a broad range of intermediate qualifications, where long-term unemployment is rare, but work below qualification is frequent, especially among young workers. In that range, where wages are to some extent lifted from above and propped from below, negotiations between employers and trade unions play the major role.

The recurrent plea for flexibility is presumably addressed primarily to that middle range. It should however be stressed that full wage flexibility is inefficient, when aggregate demand is volatile and long-run labour contracts are limited in scope. If the wages did adjust continuously to clear all labour markets, the resulting income volatility and uncertainty would be a hardship to workers, who cannot diversify risks on their human capital to the extent made possible for non-human wealth by investment funds and related assets. That income uncertainty must be curtailed, all the more so as it would exacerbate demand volatility. Constraining real net wages, both upward and downward, is more efficient.[14] It also follows that some resistance of real wages in the face of persistent unemployment is justified on efficiency grounds.

From a positive viewpoint, the dominant opinion among macroeconomists is that wage inflation is negatively related to unemployment: the Phillips curve.[15] Under that relationship, a fall in unemployment automatically triggers some wage inflation, unless the process of wage formation is tampered with. That viewpoint, which underpins the plea for structural flexibility, seems hardly convincing at unemployment rates approaching 12%. Yet I have heard serious macroeconomists advertise - *horresco referens!* - an equilibrium rate of unemployment of some 10% in Europe today. A more reasonable, and widely accepted, viewpoint suggests leaving out of these calculations the long-term unemployed and low-skilled workers. This provides yet another reason to concentrate on creating low-skill jobs.

To conclude: persistent unemployment is accompanied by a major distortion of the price system. The wage costs of firms do not reflect correctly the scarcity of low-skilled labour. The wedge between private and social costs includes all labour taxes[16] (social insurance contributions and income taxes), plus some unemployment benefits. Two-thirds of the labour costs saved by a firm that does not replace a retiring worker are borne by public budgets. Our economies operate with a fundamental price, the low-skilled wage, which is grossly biased relative to the underlying reality. That blatant distortion must be corrected, knowing that a return to full employment is ten years distant, at best.

## 2.4.    POLICIES FOR GROWTH

How can we bring about a decade of employment-generating growth? By bringing about sustained growth of aggregate demand and reasonable wage developments. Is that possible? Does that correspond to the current orientation of macroeconomic policies in Europe? Let us take a look.

### 2.4.1    The recommendations

In the current publications of international institutions, for instance the OECD jobs study or the annual report of the European Commission, three lines of action are stressed:

(i)    Budgetary restraint and inflation control, as per the guidelines of the Maastricht treaty, should pave the way for lower interest rates, and for realisation of the European Monetary Union. Lower interest rates will then stimulate investment demand.

(ii)   Labour market flexibility should spur employment. A long list of proposals covers flexible wages and hours, part-time work, elimination or flexibility of minimum wages, lower social insurance contributions, especially on low wages, firm-level rather than higher level wage bargaining and so on.

(iii) Education, training and active labour market policies should increase the employment prospects of low-skilled or long-term unemployed workers.

These recommendations are generally well-founded (with some exceptions, like elimination of minimum wages). But they fall short of target. I am of course in favour of lower interest rates, but I do not think that monetary policy alone can stimulate and stabilise aggregate demand (due in particular to the non-negativity constraint on nominal rates). Flexibility stimulates hirings in a growing economy, but it stimulates firings during recessions, as was confirmed recently. The link between labour market flexibility and wage moderation remains indirect and perhaps tenuous. Flexibility is not the universal remedy which is sometimes advertised. Training and active labour market policies bring their beneficiaries closer to the head of the queue of job-seekers, but they do not reduce the overall length of the queue - not until full employment is in sight, as might hopefully be the case in 7 or 8 years.

The White Paper on *Growth, Competitiveness and Employment* of the European Commission is more ambitious. It does not diverge from the above recommendations. But it introduces some specific targets - like a lowering of social insurance contributions on low wages amounting to 1 or 2% of GDP by year 2000, with substitute funding coming from a European-level tax on energy ($CO_2$) or a uniform withholding tax on interest income. The White Paper also contains some investment proposals, extending the Edinburgh growth initiative. These concern in the first place transeuropean networks for transportation, energy and information. They concern new investments related to environmental protection, to reconcile growth and ecology. They also concern - in less specific terms, unfortunately - investment in urban renewal, low-cost housing, urban transportation, and so on. These programmes are not motivated by a demand stimulation goal, but rather as contributions to the growth potential or to social welfare.[17]

Needless to say, my quotations from these documents are a biased selection. I read them in the wake of the attempt by a group of a dozen economists, convened by Edmond Malinvaud and myself,[18] to define the scope of a European growth and employment initiative. That attempt has led to a consistent set of policy proposals,[19] ranging through lower interest rates, budget restructuring and wage moderation, with special emphasis on two essential medium-term policies: lower wage costs for unskilled labour, through elimination of employers, social insurance contributions on minimum wages (with substitute funding from a tax on energy or interest income, or from VAT); and demand stimulation through investment programmes in urban renewal, low cost housing, urban transportation and transeuropean networks, with employment subsidies (relief from labour taxes) on the labour content of the investments. We are back to the two pillars of sustained growth: wages and aggregate demand.

### 2.4.2   Investment

Regarding investment, I do naturally deplore the lack of concern for demand stabilisation in the OECD study and in the White Paper. The current state of macroeconomic thinking is reflected there. And I regret the vagueness and lack of instruments in the presentation of the White Paper - except perhaps for transeuropean networks and environmental protection. In these two areas, the list of projects is impressive. It adds up to 574 billion ECUs over the period 1994-99,[20] or some 1.5% of GDP over the six years. This would undoubtedly make a significant contribution to aggregate demand. The order of magnitude is similar to that advanced by our group before seeing the figures in the White Paper. Our proposal puts more emphasis on projects using extensively low-skilled labour, while meeting unfilled needs - namely urban renewal and low-cost housing.

I realise that our proposal to subsidise the labour content of investments calls for preparations, hence delay. But it provides the needed correction to the two price distortions noted above, namely wages and real interest rates. This is in the spirit of second-best theory. It may be hoped - subject to verification - that employment subsidies with neutral budgetary implications would suffice to bring forward in time, and make financially viable, investments with adequate social returns.

The growth rates for the coming years are highly uncertain. We need a portfolio of investments from which to draw in order to stabilise aggregate demand, if it falls short of what is needed to reduce unemployment. Preparing the portfolio is an urgent task, to be undertaken at once. That is the agenda on the demand side.

### 2.4.3   Wages

Regarding wage costs, we were gratified by the attention paid by the Community services to our proposal. The Directorate for Economic and Financial Affairs (DG II) speedily produced econometric simulations of the impact of cutting labour taxes on low wages with substitute funding from the energy tax already under consideration by the Commission.[21] The simulations suggest gains in employment, after 4 or 5 years, exceeding 2% of the labour force - but also 6% of the low-skilled labour force, which is the order of magnitude of supplementary unemployment for that group. The result is achieved with a slight budgetary improvement. The merits of that proposal are thus substantial.[22] I am pleased to find the proposal reflected - though less ambitiously - in the White Paper and also to some extent in the OECD study. A first step toward implementation has been taken in Belgium. Elsewhere, the virtues of targeting on low wages are not yet fully appreciated.

Over the past year, I have looked more carefully at the deterioration of the market position of low-skilled workers.[23] I have come to fear that labour tax exemptions - a once for all measure - may prove insufficient to reconcile decent incomes for all with full employment. Minimum wages and unemployment benefits will remain a major policy instrument in Europe. Perhaps we shall need some day to proceed further, through an "earned income tax credit" or subsidies for low-skilled employment. It is urgent that we look more deeply into the logic and consistency of suitable policies.

More generally, it should be realised that policy proposals, including our own, are more explicit about the objective of wage moderation than about ways of attaining it. We propose the objective of negotiating constant real wages[24] - expecting a wage drift of some 1% per year, well within the margin of productivity growth. Is that objective realistic? Most - not all - members of our group think that the objective would be fostered by a more equitable tax treatment of property versus labour incomes. This would also restore the effective labour share. But the contribution to wage moderation is highly indirect. The question raised here is difficult. To what extent could unemployment abatement favour wage moderation - contrary to the theory of equilibrium unemployment (Phillips curve) mentioned above? The main difficulty is to link wage moderation to job creation in terms credible to labour unions, which are little inclined to sign blank cheques. The notion of a "pact", reflecting a broad social consensus to favour employment over wages, remains abstract. Wage moderation is a challenge that we might be unable to meet.[25]

## 2.5.   EUROPE AND EMPLOYMENT

At the end of this broad presentation, centred on macroeconomics, I wish to come back to my opening statement: "Unemployment is unmistakably Europe's number one problem". I have attempted to sketch some paths along which the problem could be met. Will Europe follow these paths?

The question is broader than just economics. It concerns the political consensus needed to tackle macroeconomic stabilisation at the European level, and the social consensus needed to favour employment over wages. The twin consensus should emerge simultaneously in the European Union and in member states.

I see two stumbling blocks at the European level. First, Europe's responsibilities towards a growth and employment initiative remain ambiguous. Second, that middle-term objective must be fitted into the long-term integration programme, of which the next step on the agenda is Monetary Union.

That Europe is not prepared to accept operational responsibilities toward growth and employment is clearly illustrated by the White Paper, which culminates in a "Call for Action", where we read:

"As for Community action proper, it is proposed to impart a new impetus or give a new form, but only in accordance with five priorities:

-       Making the most of the single market;
-       Supporting the development and adaptation of small and medium-sized enterprises;
-       Pursuing the social dialogue that has, to date, made for fruitful cooperation and joint decision-making by the two sides of industry, thereby assisting the work of the Community;
-       Creating the major European infrastructure networks;
-       Preparing forthwith and laying the foundations for the information society."

There is no consensus on the energy tax or the uniform withholding of interest income - which still require a unanimity decision and are blocked by those opposing any new tax instrument. The very idea of "cooperative expansion", which prevailed in the mid-eighties, has fallen into oblivion. The problems of "growth, competitiveness and employment" are perceived, but the agenda is different. The current priority goes to Monetary Union, at the price of deflationary fiscal guidelines and of measures inspired by extreme inflation-aversion.[26]

Clearly, Monetary Union promises major benefits: it is the only definitive way to forestall competitive devaluations which export but do not reduce unemployment, to free national policies from the consequences of exchange rate overshooting, or to stabilise relative prices across regions of Europe.

Under present circumstances, however, these benefits should be weighed against job creation, the number one priority, relative to which Monetary Union comes second. Unfortunately, such arbitrage is not a realistic prospect, under the political constraints surrounding the construction of Europe. It would appear counterproductive to attempt improving the terms of a treaty which in itself was a laborious accomplishment, requiring unanimity from 12 partners with asymmetrical objectives (regarding unemployment and inflation, for instance), asymmetrical views about economic mechanisms, and asymmetrical strategies regarding European integration - not to mention asymmetrical real circumstances.

It would be tempting - but unproductive - to conclude that economic and monetary integration comes after, not before political integration. Political integration is required to overcome the unanimity rule, to permit expression of socio-political forces at the European level, and to place at that single level the call for political consensus and for social consensus. But there is little scope for reversing a historical trend - one can only hope that relations with Eastern Europe may speed up the process of political integration. In the meantime, it seems more fruitful to call on research and imagination toward reconciling the middle-term growth priority with the agenda of Monetary Union. We now have an explicit proposal of two-speed Monetary Union, with France and Germany in the hard core. It will be the responsibility of France to indicate whether or not it wishes to go that way.[27] The stakes are high. Does a fully credible alternative exist? In order to clarify their reaction to a potential two-speed development, other major countries, like Italy and Spain, should study carefully the risks linked to an audacious reaction; namely, tie their own currency formally, under the "currency board" regime,[28] to the ECU (or possibly to the new European currency) which would acquire the status of domestic legal tender. This would de facto speed up the Monetary Union, at no risk for the hard core countries. The risks, born by the "currency board" countries, would concern ability to control inflation and to raise the overall efficiency of the public sector - two real problems worth attacking in any case. Research on this avenue is needed, urgently so, because it is important to eliminate as soon as possible the institutional uncertainties about monetary Europe.

This last suggestion is highly speculative. I take the liberty of concluding in such terms, because recent experience has confirmed my belief that the tempo and orientation of economic research do matter. Over the past few months, the idea of partially correcting the distorted price of unskilled labour has progressed substantially. Seven years ago,[29] that idea was not considered seriously. In the meantime, it has been further specified and documented. I like to think that the more positive response today is linked to the strength of the arguments. At the same time, the idea of macroeconomic demand stabilisation has regressed into near oblivion. It is kept alive by a minority, though a qualitatively outstanding minority, in the US as well as in Europe. That idea also needs to be specified and documented anew, so as to persuade. Patience as well as research energy are needed. The time has come to broaden our frame of thoughts on Monetary Union. A research effort is called for in that direction as well.

## Appendix 1

### Unemployment Rates by Level of Educational Attainment

| Country | Pre-Primary and Primary | Lower Secondary | Upper Secondary | Higher Education Non-University | Higher Education University | Total |
|---|---|---|---|---|---|---|
| United States | 8.5 | 9.1 | 4.6 | 3.3 | 2.2 | 4.4 |
| Japan | – | 7.0 | 6.5 | 7.7 | 2.3 | 4.4 |
| Germany | – | 13.8 | 6.8 | 3.7 | 4.5 | 7.3 |
| France | 11.8 | 10.5 | 6.6 | 3.4 | 3.0 | 8.1 |
| Italy | 5.9 | 6.8 | 7.7 | – | 4.8 | 6.6 |
| United Kingdom | – | 10.0 | 5.6 | 2.7 | 2.4 | 6.4 |
| Canada | 10.3 | 9.8 | 6.8 | 5.0 | 3.6 | 6.7 |
| Australia | 8.1 | 7.0 | 4.2 | 4.6 | 3.7 | 5.4 |
| Austria | – | 3.6 | 2.4 | – | 1.1 | 2.7 |
| Belgium | 14.0 | 9.2 | 4.7 | 2.7 | 2.0 | 7.5 |
| Denmark | – | 12.1 | 7.1 | 4.0 | 3.4 | 8.3 |
| Finland | – | 4.1 | 3.1 | 1.6 | 1.7 | 3.0 |
| Ireland | 25.8 | 15.1 | 6.6 | 3.9 | 2.6 | 13.9 |
| Netherlands | 13.6 | 7.6 | 4.8 | 4.6 | 5.0 | 6.5 |
| New Zealand | 9.3 | 4.7 | 4.9 | 5.1 | 2.9 | 6.0 |
| Portugal | 6.0 | 5.8 | 6.4 | 6.0 | 6.1 | 6.0 |
| Spain | 12.7 | 15.6 | 13.1 | – | 10.7 | 12.9 |
| Sweden | – | 1.4 | 0.9 | 0.9 | 1.0 | 1.0 |
| Switzerland | – | 1.4 | 0.6 | 0.3 | 0.8 | 0.8 |
| Simple average | 10.9 | 8.4 | 5.7 | 3.9 | 3.4 | 6.3 |

\* Adult population aged 25–64 in 1989, except Japan (1987), Denmark (1988), New Zealand (1990) and the Netherlands (1990).

**Source**: CERC (1991), 'Les bas salaires dans les pays de la CEE', *La Documentation Française*, 101, 3–86.

# Appendix 2

## Minimum Wages in Western Europe

| Country | Year | System | Level (ECU's per month) | Ratio to median wage (%) | Exceptions |
|---|---|---|---|---|---|
| Belgium | 1988 | economy-wide at age 21 | 783 | 66 | −7.5% per year of age below 21 |
| Germany | | negotiated at sectoral regional level | | | |
| Spain | 1991 | economy-wide at age 18 | 399 | 54 | −39% at age 17 −61% below age 17 |
| France | 1987 | economy-wide at age 18 | 556 | 61 | not applicable below age 18 |
| Greece | 1988 | economy-wide private sector public sector | 332 418 | 67 | depends upon marital status and seniority |
| Ireland | | no minimum wage | | | |
| Italy | | negotiated at sectoral level | | | |
| Netherlands | 1988 | economy-wide at age 23 | 898 | 72 | −10% per year of age below 23 |
| Portugal | 1985 | economy-wide at age 18 | 148 | 73 | −25% below age 18 −17% for domestic services |
| UK | | no minimum wage | | | |

**Source:**   CERC (1991), op. cit.

## Appendix 3

### Social Insurance Contributions (SIC) and Income Tax at Average Earnings (blue collar workers), 1991

|                  | SIC Rates | | Average Income Tax Rate | Wedge as % of Private Cost |
|------------------|-----------|----------|--------|--------|
|                  | Employer  | Employee |        |        |
| Belgium          | 41.9      | 12.1     | 11.6   | 46.2   |
| Denmark          | 0.0       | 2.5      | 36.0   | 38.5   |
| France           | 43.8      | 17.1     | 1.0    | 43.1   |
| Germany          | 18.2      | 18.2     | 8.7    | 38.1   |
| Ireland          | 12.2      | 7.8      | 16.4   | 32.4   |
| Italy            | 50.1      | 9.0      | 14.2   | 48.9   |
| Netherlands      | 10.8      | 10.7     | 32.5   | 48.8   |
| Portugal         | 24.5      | 11.0     | 0.9    | 29.2   |
| UK               | 10.4      | 7.6      | 15.5   | 30.3   |
| Unweighted mean  | 23.5      | 10.7     | 15.2   | 39.5   |
| US               | 7.7       | 7.7      | 11.3   | 24.8   |
| Japan            | 7.6       | 7.0      | 2.4    | 15.8   |

**Source**:     OECD, *Economic Perspectives*, January 1993.

## Appendix 4

### Sources of new jobs

The scope of job creation depends largely on the existing structures and services in each country, lifestyles, and tax rules.

However, several estimates agree that some 3 million new jobs could be created in the Community, covering local services, improvements in the quality of life and environmental protection.

### Examples

## Local services

- Home help for the elderly and handicapped, health care, meal preparation and housework
- Minding pre-school-age children and schoolchildren before and after school, including taking them to and from school
- Assistance to young people facing difficulties, comprising help with schoolwork, provision of leisure facilities, especially sports, and support for the most disadvantaged
- Security in blocks of flats
- Local shops kept in business in rural areas, and also in outlying suburban areas

## Audiovisual

## Provision of leisure and cultural facilities

## Improvements in the quality of life

- Renovation of rundown areas and old housing with a view to increasing comfort (installation of bathrooms and noise insulation) and safety
- Development of local public transport service, which should be made more comfortable, more frequent, accesible (to the handicapped) and safe, and the provision of new services such as shared taxis in rural areas

## Environmental protection

- Maintenance of natural areas and public areas (local waste recycling)
- Water purification and the cleaning-up of polluted areas
- Monitoring of quality standards
- Energy-saving equipment, particularly in housing

**Source**: Commission of the European Communities, *Growth, Competitiveness, Employment*, White Paper, p. 17, 1993.

## Appendix 5

### Budgetary and Institutional Implications of Proposed Measures

| Section | Measure | Budgetary implications | Level of responsibility |
|---|---|---|---|
| 3 | Lower short-term interest rates | Lower cost of servicing public debt, with country specific quantitative impact | Central banks |
| 4.3 | ESIC exemption on minimum wages | Uniform exemption would cost about 3% of GDP, degressive exemption about 1.2% with substantial country differences | National governments, typically in concertation with labour unions and employers' organisations |
| 4.4 | $CO_2$ tax | As currently considered, would bring 1% of GDP or more | Under consideration at EC level |
| 5.5 | Targeted investment programmes | Might deserve wage subsidies up to 1% of GDP | Programmes to be defined by national governments (housing, urban renewal or transportation) or possibly by EC instances; wages subsidies to be decided by national governments; funding involves specialised intermediaries |
| 7 | Welfare programmes | In some but not all countries aim should be to reduce expenditures by 1 or 2% of GDP | National governments, typically in concertation with labour unions and employers' organisation |
| 8 | Withholding tax on interest income | Could bring in 1% of GDP or more | EC decision subject to unanimity rule |
| 8 | Wage moderation | Neutral for public budgets except through inflation and interest rates | Wage bargaining institutions, country specific |

**Source**:    J. H. Drèze and E. Malinvaud, 'Growth and Employment: The Scope of a European Initiative', *European Economic Review*, 1994, 38, 489–504.

## Appendix 6

## Investing in the Competitiveness of Europe*

The Commission's analysis of the trans-European networks and large environmental projects and their financing requirements can be summarized as follows:

## 1. Transport and energy - ECU 250 billion by the year 2000 (ECU 95 billion priority projects)

These networks of transport infrastructures will enable our citizens to travel more quickly, more safely, and more cheaply, thus improving competitiveness. They will also form links to Eastern Europe and to North Africa. In total some ECU 400 billion of investments in the transport and energy trans-European networks will be required in the next 15 years, of which some ECU 250 billion by 1999.

Article 129b of the Treaty makes clear how to proceed. The Community[1] establishes a set of guidelines that identify projects of common interest. It then supports the financial efforts of the Member States (feasibility studies, loan guarantees, interest rate subsidies). It can also contribute to the coordination of the Member States' policies and cooperate with third countries.

The principal guidelines of the networks (master plans) have been proposed by the Commission or adopted by the Council and the Parliament. The Commission has identified a series of priority projects for the next five years - 26 transport projects (ECU 82 billion) and energy projects (ECU 13 billion).

## 2. Telecommunications - ECU 150 billiion by the year 2000 (ECU 67 billion priority projects)

A system of information highways for the Community will provide the best means to create, manage, access and transfer information. It involves:

- the creation of infrastructures (cable and land or satellite based radio communication), including integrated digital networks,
- the development of services (electronic images, data bases, electronic mail),
- promoting applications (teleworking, teletraining, linked administrations).

The amount of investments that could be put into effect by the end of the century has been estimated at ECU 150 billion. A series of priority projects to the value of ECU 67 billion has been identified by the Commission for the period 1994-99.

## 3. Environment - ECU 174 billion on large environmental projects by the year 2000.

The environment is an integral part of the trans-European networks, for example concerning combined transport networks designed to get traffic off the roads onto rail.

The Commission also has environmental programmes of sufficient size to merit eligibility for financial support from the Community. By way of an indication, these projects concern water control, urban waste water treatment, renovation of water supply distribution systems, and Mediterranean and Baltic Sea clean-ups at an estimated cost of ECU 314 billion in total over 12 years or ECU 174 billion by the end of the century. The Community could help finance some ECU 25 billion in this area of environmental concern over the period 1994-99.

## 4. Financing the trans-European networks and large environmental projects

The major portion of finance for these investments will be raised at the level of Member State, either through private investors (especially in the telecoms sector) or via public enterprises. The Community can, however, play a role, as foreseen in the Treaty, by supporting the financial efforts of the Member States and mobilizing private capital.[2] This requires a panoply of financial instruments, as set out in the Table below, some of which exist already and two of which are new ("Union Bonds", "Convertibles"). The new instruments are needed for projects specifically included in the Master Plans and complement the lending of the European Investment Bank, which is more general. The budgetary elements remain within the Edinburgh ceilings. National budgets would not be required to support additional financing. In the case of the new instruments, the capital and interest would be repaid by the promoters of the projects, with the Community budget available to back the repayment of the Union Bonds and the capital of the European Investment Fund available in the case of the Convertibles. There would be no risk of destabilizing the capital markets given that the amounts concerned represent less than 1% of the Eurobond and bank credit markets.

**Community financing of the trans-European networks**

**(average financing per year 1994-99)**

| Source: | Amount in ecus |
|---|---|
| **Community budget:** of which | **5.3 billion** |
| Trans-European networks (TENs): | 0.50 billion |
| Structural Funds    (TENs): | 1.35 billion |
| (environment): | 0.60 billion |
| Cohesion Fund    (TENs): | 1.15 billion |
| (environment): | 1.15 billion |
| Research and development  (telecoms): | 0.50 billion |
| (transport): | 0.05 billion |
| **European Investment Bank** (loans): | **6.7 billion** |
| **Union Bonds[3]** (esp. transport and energy): | **7.0 billion** |
| **Convertibles[4] guaranteed by EIF** (esp. telecoms): | **1.0 billion** |
| **Total** | **20.0 billion** |

## New facilities

### "Union Bonds"

"Union Bonds" for growth would be issued on tap by the Union for long maturities to promote major infrastructure projects of strategic interest covering the trans-European networks plus cross-border projects with EFTA, Central and Eastern Europe and North Africa. The beneficiaries would be project promoters (public sector agencies, private companies) directly involved in TENs. The EIB would be invited to appraise and advise the Commission on the overall structure of the financial arrangements and act as agent for individual loan contracts.

### "Convertibles" guaranteed by European Investment Fund

Bonds issued for long maturities by the private or public company promoting the project, guaranteed by the European Investment Fund. These would be either:
- convertible wholly or partly into shares or investment certificates; or
- be accompanied by subscription warrants giving the holder the right to buy shares at a certain price; or
- performance-related through a share in the profits of the company or venture concerned.

The maturities of the bonds and of the exchange terms would be coherent between the expected returns of the project and the exercise period of the option. The EIF would create a special window for this type of guarantee, especially for major projects linked to telecommunications networks.

---

\* **Source:** Commission of the European Communities, *Growth, Competitiveness, Employment*, White Paper, p. 17, 1993.
1 The Council decides by qualified majority in co-decision with the European Parliament (Article 189b); guidelines and projects of common interest which relate to the territory of a Member State require the approval of the Member State concerned.
2 In addition the EIF can guarantee up to a total of ECU 6 billion of private loans for large infrastructure projects, averaging 1 billion per year to 1999.
3 See below.
4 See below.

# NOTES

\*    I am grateful to Michel Mouchart for his helpful comments.
1    Appendix 1 illustrates that point for the (relatively favourable) year 1989.
2    Cf. J.H. Drèze and H. Sneessens, "Technological Development, Competition from Low-Wage Economies and Low-Skilled Unemployment", *Swedish Economic Policy Review*, 1, 185-214, 1994.
3    The budgetary cost of today's unemployment is evaluated by the European Commission at 4% of EU 12 GDP, whereas budget deficits exceed by 2.5% the Maastricht guidelines.
4    Including J.H. Drèze and C. Bean, "Europe's Unemployment Problem: Introduction and Synthesis", in *Europe's Unemployment Problem,* J.H. Drèze, C. Bean, J.P. Lambert, F. Mehta and H. Sneessens, (eds), MIT Press, Cambridge, Mass., 1990.
5    Cf. O.J. Blanchard, "Consumption and the Recession of 1990-91", R.E. Hall, "Macro Theory and the Recession of 1990-91", *American Economic Review*, 270-74 and 275-79, 1993.
6    The argument to follow is partly original, with the informal presentation here anticipating the necessary formalisation. But most elements are well-known. A related formulation (still distinct in several important respects) can be found in J. Tobin, "Price Flexibility and Output Stability", *Journal of Economic Perspectives*, 7, 1, 45-65, 1993.
7    Contingent transactions make delivery conditional on future events, hence contingent; contracts for contingent deliveries are more similar to insurance contracts than to options.
8    Multiple equilibria pose a genuine challenge to empirical (econometric) research.
9    The indeterminateness of equilibrium, at competitive prices and wages, is established explicitly for the case of constant returns to scale by J. Roberts, 'Equilibrium without Market Clearing', Chap. 6, pp. 145-158 in *Contributions to Operations Research and Economics*, B. Cornet and H. Tulkens, (eds), MIT Press, Cambridge, Mass.,1989. Constant returns to scale in the long run (with an adjusted capital stock) imply in the short run fixed costs, that is a cost structure similar to that characteristic of increasing returns. An equilibrium concept covering these situations is proposed in J.H. Drèze and P. Dehez, "Competitive Equilibria with Quantity-Taking Producers and Increasing Returns to Scale", *Journal of Mathematical Economics*, 1988, 209-30. Using that equilibrium concept, one can extend the analysis of Roberts (where a zero profits condition plays a central role) to the case of increasing returns, which is the more typical in my opinion. A further extension of the argument is needed to encompass diminishing returns as well. The analysis of Roberts demonstrates unambiguouly the multiplicity of allocations decentralised by competitive prices and wages, and provides a convincing argument for the stability of output prices. The downward rigidity of wages requires an additional argument, of which several versions exist.
10   Cf. J. Corbett and T. Jenkinson, "The Financing of Industry, 1970-89: An International Comparison", CEPR Discussion Paper 948, 1994.

11    The impact of interest payments on business profitability, stressed by I. Fisher in his book *Booms and Depressions* (Adelphi, New York, 1932), has recently received renewed attention, for instance in the Presidential Address by M. King, "Debt Deflation: Theory and Evidence", *European Economic Review*, 1994, 419-45. But the implications of financial fixed costs for the pricing policies of firms have not been spelled out, because theorists are reluctant to entertain equilibria under increasing returns.

12    Cf. J.H. Drèze and C. Bean, op. cit.

13    Appendix 2 contains some information about minimum wages in Europe.

14    This point is unambigouously established in J.H. Drèze and C. Gollier, "Risk Sharing on the Labour Market and Second-Best Wage Rigidities", *European Economic Review*, 37, 1457-82, North-Holland, 1993, and in the references given there.

15    Empirical work in which I have been involved - cf. J.H. Drèze and C. Bean, op. cit. - suggests instead a long-term relationship between unemployment and the share of wages in value added, rather than wage inflation. Recent microeconometric work links conclusively individual wage levels to local unemployment rates; see Blanchflower and A. Oswald, *The Wage Curve*, MIT Press, 1995.

16    Appendix 3 reveals their magnitude, but also substantial differences between countries.

17    The White Paper also contains a specific recommendation - formulated more precisely in the summary chapter than in the supporting chapter; namely, the promotion of "proximity services", seen as an answer to unfilled needs, but also as a source of potential jobs. (See Appendix 4 for details.) The specific suggestions even include "service-vouchers", a French innovation meant to spur demand for proximity services through price rebates; and subsidies to non-profit organisations apt to organise the supply.

18    Cf. J.H. Drèze and E. Malinvaud with Paul De Grauwe, Louis Gevers, Alexander Italianer, Olivier Lefebvre, Maurice Marchand, Henri Sneessens, Alfred Steinherr and Paul Champsaur, Jean-Michel Charpin, Jean-Paul Fitoussi, Guy Laroque, "Growth and Employment: The Scope for a European Initiative", *European Economy (Reports and Studies)*, 1, 75-106, 1994; "Croissance et emploi: l'ambition d'une initiative européenne", *Revue de l'OFCE*, 49, 247-88, 1994.

19    They are summarised in Appendix 5.

20    The overview in the White Paper is reproduced as Appendix 6.

21    The Commission evaluates the cost externality of private transportation (pollution, accidents, congestion) at 3 or 4% of GDP. There lies a main justification of the energy tax.

22    These merits are also spelled out in the book *Pour L'Emploi et la Cohésion Sociale,* written by A.B. Atkinson, O.J. Blanchard, J.P. Fitoussi, J.S. Flemming, E. Malinvaud, E.S. Phelps, R.M. Solow, Fondation Nationale des Sciences Politiques, Paris, 1994.

23    Cf. Drèze-Sneessens, op. cit.

24    The Belgian government has in the meantime imposed constant real wages for the years 1995 and 1996.

25  An innovative suggestion has been voiced recently by Belgium's Finance Minister Maystadt. The goal is to transfer into jobs some of the gains accruing to prosperous firms thanks to the 1995-96 wage freeze. Exceptions to the freeze would be authorised if they took the form of "service-vouchers", usable by households to purchase proximity services (see footnote 18 above). The face value of the vouchers would be treated on par with wages for assessment of labour taxes and income taxes. The vouchers would be tradable. The idea is to generate a demand for proximity services high enough to induce a corresponding supply by non-profit organisations.

26  My views on the fiscal guidelines are given in "1 Market + 1 (tight) Money = 2 Rules of Fiscal Discipline: Europe's Fiscal Stance Deserves Another Look", in *European Economic Integration: A Challenge in a Changing World*, M. Dewatripont and V. Ginsburgh, (eds), North-Holland, Amsterdam, 1994. I touch on some aspects of monetary policy in *Money and Uncertainty: Inflation, Interest, Indexation*, Banca d'Italia, Lezioni Paolo Baffi di Moneta E Finanza, Edizioni Dell' Elefante, Roma.

27  Perhaps against the advice of an impressive group of MIT economists?

28  Under that regime, domestic money creation is subject to 100% reserves in the reference currency.

29  Cf. "Priorité à l'Emploi", a manifesto by 72 French-speaking Belgian economists in January 1987.

# 3. Preventing Long-Term Unenployment: An Economic Analysis

## Richard Layard*

## 3.1. INTRODUCTION AND SUMMARY

The European Union has set the target of halving unemployment by the year 2,000 (EU, 1994). How can it be done without increasing inflation? The strategy must be to reduce those kinds of unemployment which do little to restrain inflation. The most obvious such category is long-term unemployment.

### 3.1.1 Effects of long-term unemployment

Let us examine the evidence. In wage equations long-term unemployment is usually found to have a very small (or zero) effect in reducing wage pressure.[1] The reasons for this are obvious: long-term unemployed people are not good fillers of vacancies. This can be seen from data on exit rates from unemployment: exit rates decline sharply as duration increases. Equally, aggregate time-series show that, for a given level of unemployment, vacancies increase the higher the proportion of unemployed who are long-term unemployed.

If long-term unemployment is an optional extra, depending on social institutions, it is not surprising that there are striking differences in its prevalence across countries. As Table 3.1 shows, in the 1980s the majority of countries had between 3 and 6 per cent of the labour force in short-term unemployment (of under a year). But there were huge differences in long-term unemployment. It was under 1 per cent in the US, Japan, Canada and Sweden and over 8 per cent in Spain, Belgium and Ireland.

Clearly some short-term unemployment is necessary in any economy, to avoid the inflationary pressure which would develop in an over-tight labour market. But long-term unemployment is not needed for this purpose.

### 3.1.2 Causes of long-term unemployment

So how can it be prevented? To consider this we need to know under what conditions it occurs. Figure 3.1 provides a striking clue. It shows on the vertical axis the maximum duration of benefit in each country and on the horizontal axis the percentage of unemployed people in long-term unemployment (over a year). In countries like the US, Japan, Canada and Sweden benefits run out within a year and so unemployment lasting more than a year is rare. By contrast in the main EU countries benefits have typically been available indefinitely or for a long period, and long-term unemployment is high.

The relationship shown in Figure 3.1 is of course a partial correlation. But if one allows for multiple causation, the effect of benefit duration upon the aggregate unemployment rate remains strong and clear.[2]

The effect of unemployment benefit availability upon unemployment is not surprising. Unemployment benefits are a subsidy to idleness, and it should not be surprising if they lead to an increase in idleness. In principle of course the benefits are meant to protect individuals against an exogenous misfortune and there is meant to be a test of willingness to work. But in practice it is impossible to operate a "work test" without offering actual work. So after a period of disheartening job search, unemployed individuals often adjust to unemployment as a different life-style.

### 3.1.3 Preventing long-term unemployment

What should we do about the situation? One possibility would be to reduce the duration of benefits to say one year and put nothing else in its place. This would be the American-style solution. But we know this only works because people thrown onto the labour market accept an ever-widening inequality of wages.

A much better approach would be to help people to become more employable so that they would justify a better wage. This leads to our central proposal.

After 12 months the state should stop paying people for doing nothing. But at the same time it should accept a responsibility to find them temporary work for at least 6 months.[3]

In return the individual would recognise that if he wishes to receive income, he must accept one of a few reasonable offers. These offers would be guaranteed through the state paying to any employer for 6 months the benefit to which the unemployed individual would otherwise have been entitled.

This would have huge advantages:

(i)     After the 12th month, it would relieve the public finances of any responsibility for people who are already in work.[4] It is very difficult to prevent fraud without being able to offer full-time work.

(ii)     Between months 12 and 18, people would be producing something rather than nothing.

(iii)    But the biggest effect would come after the 18th month. Provided the temporary work had been real work with regular employers, unemployed people would have re-acquired work habits plus the ability to prove their working capacity. They would have a regular employer who could provide a reference - or (even better) retain the individual on a permanent basis. The main justification for the proposal is not that it employs people on a subsidised basis but that, by doing so, it restores them to the universe of employable people. This is an investment in human capital.

That is the central objective of the exercise. Job creation schemes in the past have often failed because the jobs have been marginal and have failed to make the individual more employable thereafter. The job subsidy should therefore be available to any employer (private or public). There should also be the least possible restrictions on the kind of work that could be done. Clearly no employer should be allowed to employ subsidised workers if he was at the same time dismissing regular workers. But there should be no condition (as there was in the UK's former Community Programme) that the work done should be work that would not otherwise be done for the next two years. Such a requirement is a formula for ineffectiveness.

The reason why job creation schemes have so often had these disastrous limiting conditions is the fear of substitution and displacement. This fear is understandable but misplaced.

### 3.1.4    Substitution and displacement

Most opposition to active labour market measures is based on fears of displacement and substitution. In their extreme form these derive from the "lump-of-labour fallacy": there are only so many jobs, so, if we enable Mr. X to get one of them, some other person goes without work. This is a complete fallacy.

However it is easy to see how it arises. In the most immediate sense, the proposition is true. If an employer has a vacancy and, due to a job subsidy, Mr. X gets it rather than Mr. Y, Mr. Y remains temporarily unemployed. But by definition Mr. Y is inherently employable. If he does not get this job, he will offer himself for others. Employers will find there are more employable people in the market and that they can more easily fill their vacancies. This increases downward pressure on wages, making possible a higher level of employment at the same level of inflationary pressure.

On average over the cycle the level of unemployment is determined at the level needed to hold inflation stable. Active labour market policy increases the number of employable workers, and thus reduces the unemployment needed to control inflation. Equally, in the short-run a government that has a given inflation target (or exchange rate target) will allow more economic expansion if it finds that inflationary pressures are less than would otherwise be expected.

Many people find it difficult to believe that (inflationary pressure equal) jobs automatically expand in relation to the employable labour force. So we devote the whole of Section 3.2 of the paper to that issue.

### 3.1.5   Benefits and costs

We can now proceed to sum up the effects of the scheme and its impact on human welfare. In a formal sense it would abolish long-term unemployment. However this is to overclaim since someone who reverts to unemployment after 18 months (after his temporary job) is not really short-term unemployed, even though this would be his classification in the statistics. So let us consider the impacts on the flow of a cohort entering unemployment.

During the first 12 months, some people may, it is true, delay taking a job because their potential employer has an incentive to wait for the subsidy. But more people will take a job who would not otherwise have done so because they would not like to end up on the programme. The hope is that a completely new climate would develop in which neither individuals nor the Employment Service accept the idea that someone should reach the humiliating position of being confronted with temporary work as the only possible source of income. In Sweden in the 1980s typically about 3 per cent of the workforce reached the 14th month of unemployment (when benefit ran out): in Britain the figure was about five times larger.

Going on, between the 12th and 18th months all the cohort is now employed. After the 18th month the proportion employed should be very much higher than it would have been, due to the employability of those concerned.

Thus it is reasonable to suppose that unemployment would fall by roughly the same size as the stock of long-term unemployed, leading to a substantial increase in production. Suppose average European unemployment fell to 5 per cent compared with a counterfactual rate of say 9 per cent. Output would be at a minimum 2 per cent higher.

This is the social gain (not to mention an additional non-income related gain in psychic well-being among those affected). What is the social cost? Very little. The employment service would need more administrative staff, but this is a tiny cost compared with the gain.[5] (The typical EC country spends only 0.1% of GNP on its employment service.)

The balance is also favourable if we focus exclusively on the benefits and costs to the public finances:

(i)     After the 12th month the taxpayers stop supporting those who are already fraudulently in work.
(ii)    Between the 12th and 18th month, the taxpayers keep paying benefit but now it goes to employers not workers. However an employer who would anyway have hired somebody unemployed between 12 and 18 months will of course claim the subsidy, so that there would on this account be some deadweight - i.e. extra expenditure.
(iii)   After the 18th month, there will be major savings on benefits and extra taxes received. On any reasonable estimate the total of all these will be a positive saving to the government, and a saving higher than the extra cost of the Employment Service.

### 3.1.6   Carrot and stick

Why does this analysis seem so much more cost-effective than most existing active labour market policy? Because it is much more drastic. Job subsidies without compulsion to accept an offer can easily be ineffective.

Consider for example the proposal put forward by Snower (1994) which has inspired a recent British government initiative. The idea here is to make possible the conversion of a person's unemployment benefit into an employment subsidy, but not to make it mandatory. While the social net benefits should be positive, they may well be small. Major falls in unemployment are unlikely down this route. What is needed is a shift of regime.[6]

No one would now design a system like the existing one. But it requires courage and commitment to change it. One thing however is sure. Unless it is changed, we shall be almost as far from the EU's target early next century as we are now.

In the rest of the paper, we first discuss the issue of substitution and displacement (Section 2). We then in Section 3.3 review the effects of existing work-based policies in Sweden and the US, as a basis for evaluation of our own proposal.

## 3.2.   SUBSTITUTION AND DISPLACEMENT

Programmes to help unemployed people have always been subject to two types of criticism. First, they may help people to do things they would have done anyway. Such expenditure is called "deadweight" since it has no effect but involves a public outlay. The social cost of this public outlay is the excess burden of the tax that financed the outlay. While this can be an important issue, it is not the main criticism.

The second and more serious objection is that, if unemployed workers get jobs they would not otherwise have got, this may not increase total employment but simply deprive other workers of jobs. This can happen either if each firm employs the same number of people as before but just substitutes one lot of workers for another, or if some firms expand employment and output but displace employment in other firms.

### 3.2.1    No job fund

Such arguments taken to the limit are based on the idea that the total number of jobs is somehow fixed, presumably by the level of aggregate demand. But there is no reason to suppose that demand is ever the main constraint in an economy. The monetary and fiscal authorities can always generate more demand. The constraint is the inflation constraint.

This is illustrated by the Phillips curve $A_0A_0$ in Figure 3.2. When the employment rate is above $(1-u_0^*)$ inflation tends to rise, and vice versa. Most governments and electorates seem to have some kind of inflation objective. Given this objective, the level of employment depends on $u^*$. Only policies which alter $u_0^*$ will change the actual level of unemployment. But, conversely, if a policy reduces $u_0^*$, it will reduce u. This is illustrated by the new inflation constraint $A_1A_1$.

There is no fixed number of jobs to be done. Given the inflation target, the number of jobs is fixed entirely on the supply side of the economy.

### 3.2.2    Employability

The main thing that determines the number of jobs is the number of "employable" people in the economy. Economists generally take for granted the idea that ceteris paribus the number of jobs rises in proportion to the labour force, so we will for the moment take that as read. The more difficult issue is the notion of "employability". People clearly differ along a wide spectrum of employability. Near one end is Mr. A: a skilled worker who is willing to take any job and searches every day. Near the other is Mr. B: unskilled worker with an excessive reservation wage who only samples the job market once a month. If there are vacancies, Mr. A will probably be hired soon and Mr. B after a longer spell of unemployment.

More specifically, we can denote the "employability" of an individual $c_i$ and the average employability of all unemployed people c. Then the total number of unemployed people hired in a given period (H) will depend on the number of vacancies (V) and on the number of unemployed people (U) weighted by their average employability(c).[7] Hence

$$H = f(V, cU)    f_1, f_2 > 0    \text{(1)}$$

Thus our concept of employability refers to the capacity to fill vacancies.

How then does the employability of the unemployed affect the number of jobs - for a given inflation path? The path of inflation is given by the wage-price spiral, which we shall depict in the simplest possible form. Prices (p) are a mark-up on expected wages ($w^e$) so that, using small letters for logarithms:

$$p - w^e = b_0 \qquad (2)$$

Wages (w) are a mark-up on expected prices ($p^e$), and this mark-up is affected by "inflationary pressure", denoted by ø and defined below. Thus

$$w - p^e = y_0 + \emptyset \qquad (3)$$

Substituting expected prices from (2) we have

$$w - w^e = \beta_0 + y_0 + \emptyset$$

If price inflation is perceived as a random walk, then when $w=w^e$ inflation is stable; when $w>w^e$ inflation rises; and when $w<w^e$ inflation falls.

Thus the key determinant of the inflation path is ø. Evidence suggests strongly that inflationary pressure increases with the chances of finding work for an unemployed person of given employability i.e. (H/cU).[8] Thus

$$w - w^e = \beta_0 + y_0 + y_1 (H / cU)$$

If unemployment is constant, hires equal separations i.e. employment (N) times the separation rate (s). So

$$w - w^e = \beta_0 + y_0 + y_1 s / (cU / N)$$

Hence for a given inflation path, unemployment is inversely proportional to average employability (c).[9]

The basic concept of this paper is that cU is a constant. More generally, if $U_i$ is the number of unemployed of type i, $\Sigma c_i U_i$=constant. Going on, we could for simplicity assume that there are only two types of unemployment, short-term and long-term, and that long-term unemployment causes people to be less employable ($c_L<c_S$).[10] It follows that

$$c_S U_S + c_L U_L = constant$$

From this position we can immediately understand the effect of measures to increase the employability of the long-term unemployed (i.e. to raise $c_L$). It will be clearest if we simply compare the equilibrium positions before and after $c_L$ is reduced.[11] After $c_L$ has fallen, this is what we observe:

(i)     The inflow into unemployment (sN) is unchanged (and so therefore is the outflow H).[12]

(ii)    The exit rate from unemployment for a person with given employability is unchanged, since:

$$H_i \, / \, c_i \, U_i = H \, / \, cU$$

Therefore the exit rate from short-term unemployment is unchanged.

(iii)   Since (i) the entry to short-term unemployment is unchanged and (ii) the exit rate is unchanged, the stock of short-term unemployment is unchanged. Therefore $c_s U_s$ is unchanged.

(iv)    It follows that $U_L$ is lower by the same proportion that $c_L$ is higher. Since the outflow from long-term unemployment is given by

$$H_L \, / \, c_L \, U_L = H \, / \, cU$$

it follows that the long-term unemployed are filling exactly the same number of vacancies per period as before. They do not prevent a single extra short-term unemployed person from being hired. What happens is that there are fewer long-term employed but they are being hired at a faster rate. The position is illustrated in Figure 3.3.

Thus there is no substitution or displacement whatever in aggregate terms. Because long-term unemployed are more employable, their numbers fall. Total hirings of long-term unemployed have not increased.

In the transition from one equilibrium to another the hirings of long-term unemployed people do of course increase. But so of course do total hirings, which is the method by which employment increases and unemployment falls.

### 3.2.3   The proposed scheme

The preceding analysis does not of course reflect in detail our proposed scheme. In Figure 3.3 we assume that all who complete short-term unemployment (STU) enter long-term unemployment (LTU) but that people are helped to leave LTU at double the previous rate. We can now depict our own scheme more exactly in Figure 3.4. In between STU and LTU there is a 6 month period of temporary work. This leads to two extra flows. Some people who complete STU do not take temporary jobs (J). And some who take temporary jobs never reenter unemployment at the 18th month. Total unemployment falls by the fall in $U_L$.

### 3.2.4 People cause jobs

Finally we revert to the question of whether in given institutional conditions the labour force determines the number of jobs (taking the cycle as a whole). Economists take this for granted but rarely bother to document it. This is done in Figure 3.5. As the graph shows, there is nothing special about the US or Japan as creators of jobs, as is constantly alleged. They just happen to be good creators of people.[13]

To ram home the point, Figure 3.6 shows that the same applies to "jobs for men" and "jobs for women". These do not go their own merry way. They respond with remarkable precision to the ratios of men and women in the labour force. In almost every country the proportion of men aged 16-64 wanting to work has fallen and the proportion of women wanting to work has risen. This is the overwhelming source of the fall in the male/female ratio in employment, which has tended to occur within nearly all industries.

## 3.3.   RELEVANT EXPERIENCE

What empirical evidence is there that could throw light on the feasibility of our proposal or its effects. We are aware of only two main types of evidence that really help.

First there is cross-sectional evidence of decadal unemployment rates across countries having different ways of treating unemployed people. In Layard et al. (1994) we estimated such a regression which showed that unemployment increases with the duration of unemployment benefit and falls with expenditure on active labour market policy (per unemployed person). Only with these variables is it possible to explain the extraordinarily low rate of unemployment in Sweden throughout the 1970s and 1980s (around 2% on average). Sweden operated and still operates essentially the system we have been advocating.

Second, there are the randomised experiments with "conditionality" for recipients of AFDC in the US (Gueron, 1990). These show that AFDC recipients who were exposed to work requirements subsequently became more likely to be in work, and had higher earnings and lower AFDC receipts - adding up to higher total incomes.

Our proposal is, we believe, immune to the criticisms of many training programmes offered to unemployed people. These often show a poor rate of return, especially when those retrained had little previous skill or where the quality of training was poor. For most people whose previous work experience was semi or unskilled the best way to become employable is to work. We believe that only a regime change which makes this the normal course of affairs can make major inroads on European unemployment.

*Table 3.1   Short- and Long-Term Unemployment as Percentage of Labour Force (1980s Average)*

|             | Long-Term | Short-Term | Total |
|-------------|-----------|------------|-------|
| Australia   | 1.9       | 5.5        | 7.4   |
| Belgium     | 8.0       | 3.0        | 11.1  |
| Canada      | 0.8       | 8.4        | 9.2   |
| Denmark     | 2.4       | 5.6        | 8.0   |
| Finland     | 0.7       | 4.1        | 4.8   |
| France      | 3.9       | 5.0        | 9.0   |
| Germany     | 3.0       | 3.6        | 6.7   |
| Greece      | 2.9       | 3.6        | 6.6   |
| Ireland     | 8.1       | 6.1        | 14.2  |
| Italy       | 6.4       | 3.4        | 9.9   |
| Japan       | 0.4       | 2.0        | 2.4   |
| Netherlands | 4.7       | 5.0        | 9.7   |
| New Zealand | 0.4       | 4.1        | 4.5   |
| Norway      | 0.2       | 2.5        | 2.7   |
| Portugal    | 2.5       | 4.7        | 7.3   |
| Spain       | 10.1      | 7.4        | 17.5  |
| Sweden      | 0.2       | 2.2        | 2.4   |
| UK          | 4.2       | 5.2        | 9.5   |
| US          | 0.6       | 6.5        | 7.1   |

*Sources*:   OECD, *Employment Outlook* and OECD, *Labour Force Survey*

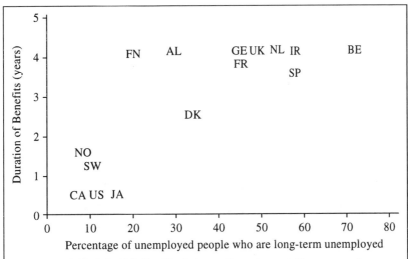

*Source:*  R. Layard, S. Nickell and R. Jackman, *Unemployment: Macroeconomic
Performance and the Labour Market*, Oxford, Oxford University Press, 1991.

*Figure 3.1*   *Percentage of unemployed people out of work over 12
months by maximum duration of benefits (1984)*

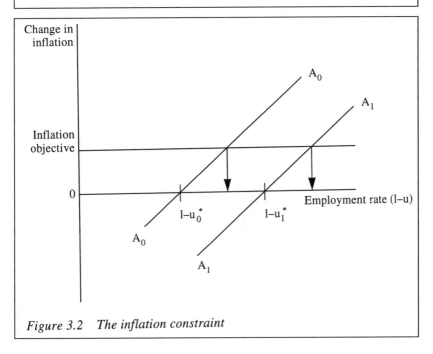

*Figure 3.2*   *The inflation constraint*

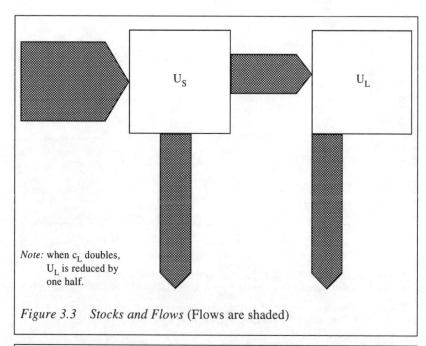

*Note:* when $c_L$ doubles, $U_L$ is reduced by one half.

*Figure 3.3    Stocks and Flows* (Flows are shaded)

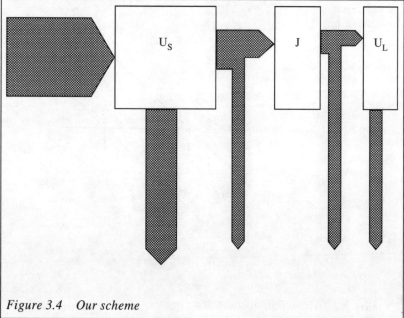

*Figure 3.4    Our scheme*

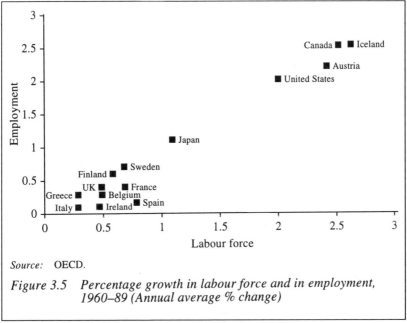

*Source:* OECD.

*Figure 3.5 Percentage growth in labour force and in employment, 1960–89 (Annual average % change)*

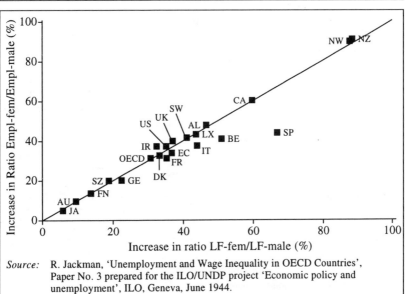

*Source:* R. Jackman, 'Unemployment and Wage Inequality in OECD Countries', Paper No. 3 prepared for the ILO/UNDP project 'Economic policy and unemployment', ILO, Geneva, June 1944.

*Figure 3.6 Change in relative labour force, and change in relative employment: by sex, 1970–90*

## NOTES

\*    I am most grateful to Richard Jackman for his generous help and ideas.

1    All remarks in this paragraph are based on Layard et al. (1991), Chapter 4. They apply only to countries which encourage long-term unemployment. The situation is different in the US where there are no unemployment insurance benefits for the long-term unemployed.

2    Layard et al., 1994, p.82. The other causal variables in the equation relate to the replacement ratio, active labour market policy, collective bargaining and the change in inflation.

3    As in Sweden, anyone who failed to find regular work within that period would be entitled to go back onto benefits after 6 months; but re-entry onto benefits would be conditional on having worked at least 15 out of the last 52 weeks.

4    In Sweden 2/3 of those entitled to temporary jobs because their benefits have come to an end do not exercise their right to subsidised work.

5    We personally strongly favour more retraining of skilled workers with obsolete skills but in this paper we focus on a virtually costless proposal.

6    In passing, note that we have not suggested doing anything extra for the existing long-term unemployed. This is deliberate. Helping people who are already LTU is very difficult and can easily fail. Therefore prevent long-term unemployment, and let the existing LTU find their own solutions within the existing programmes, as eventually they will.

7    It is easy to allow for job competition from other employed people but this makes no difference of substance.

8    It may also increase with the duration of vacancies

$$(V/H)$$

But from equation (1) these two variables are positively related. Since (1) must exhibit constant returns to scale (in a large enough market),

and
$$(H/cU) = f(V/cU, 1)$$
$$1 = f(V/H, cU/H)$$

9    In a more fully dynamic context we need to allow for changes in U. Since $\Delta U = sN - H$, $H/cU = (s - (\Delta U)/N)/cU/N$.

10   There are also of course selectivity reasons why LTU have lower exit rates than STU. But Layard et al. (1991) provide powerful evidence that LTU also causes lower employability.

11   During the transition the possibility of substitution and displacement is even less since $H > sN$ while unemployment falls.

12   If s is constant there is a second-order rise in sN and H, due to the rise in N.

13   If the population of working age is used on the horizontal axis, the diagram still works well.

## REFERENCES

European Commission, *Growth, Competitiveness, Employment. The Challenges and Ways Forward into the 21st Century*, Brussels, European Commission, 1994.

Gueron, J.M., "Work and Welfare: Lessons on Employment Programs", *Journal of Economic Perspectives*, Vol.4, No.1, p. 79-98, 1990.

Layard, R., Nickell, S., Jackman, R., *Unemployment: Macroeconomic Performance and the Labour Market*, Oxford, Oxford University Press, 1991.

Layard, R., Nickell, S., Jackman, R., *The Unemployment Crisis*, Oxford, Oxford University Press, 1994.

Snower, D., "Converting Unemployment Benefits into Employment Subsidies", London, Centre for Economic Policy Research, Discussion Paper No.930, 1994.

# 4. Does it Fit? Drawing Lessons From Differing Labour Practices

## Richard B. Freeman

"While it is not possible to import any given practice or institution found in another country to the United States neither is it advisable to ignore practices that work well in other settings." Commission on the Future of Worker-Management Relations, U.S. May 1994 Fact-finding Report

"Foreign experience, particularly of succesful countries like Germany and Japan, is useful and appropriate. But partial transplantation from a different system is a dangerous thing. (We) should tread warily about adopting fully systems which have been devised in the context of other legal frameworks and cultures. A transplanted works council system would create difficulties for our system of exclusive bargaining representative status" William Gould IV, Chairman, National Labor Relations Board, 29 September 1994.

"We cannot import a (labour) model from another country whose tradition of industrial relations is different from ours. Neither can we say they have nothing to teach us." Bill Morris, General secretary TGWU union, U.K. *Financial Times*, 7 Sept 1994.

Analysts and decision-makers pay considerable attention to labour markets in other countries. Europeans look at the U.S. employment record, and wonder if deregulation of labour markets and flexibility, U.S. style, could reduce European unemployment. Americans wonder what Japan does right, and whether there is something to learn from European works councils or apprenticeships. Multinational firms ponder the effectiveness of the differing compensation and personnel practices in the countries in which they operate. Unions worry how labour practices and standards in trading partners will affect labour relations in their country. Members of the European Union debate the effects of the Social Charter on their labour relations systems.

We are attentive to labour practices in foreign lands, but, as the quotations above indicate, we are unsure about the lessons to draw from these practices. Will something that works "over there" work here or will it fail to "fit" our ways of doing things? Which practices will adapt or evolve into something different in a different setting? Which may catalyse forces that will change our entire system of labour relations?

This paper examines these questions regarding the fit or portability of labour relations across borders. My interest in this topic began with the National Bureau of Economic Research's Working Under Different Rules project - a four year cross-country study of labour outcomes and practices in advanced OECD countries designed to illuminate U.S. labour market problems and policies. Given the study's findings about what worked in other settings, what lessons could I, or anyone else, legitimately draw for the United States? The importance of the portability issue was reinforced for me during the 1993-94 deliberations of the Commission on the Future of Worker-Management Relations - a body set up by the Clinton Administration to recommend changes in American labour relations - on what the U.S. could learn from foreign experiences in order to assess potential reforms in American labour laws and regulations.

Analysing the interrelation of diverse labour practices within a country, much less across national lines, raises empirical and conceptual questions on the frontier of social science, if not beyond. There are issues about how national, company, or union policies actually operate at workplaces. There are issues about how to model the interactions among unions, firms, and the government agencies that regulate labour relations. In this essay I make no pretence to having "solved" these complicated issues. Rather, my goal is to highlight some important aspects of the problem and to begin to develop a framework for thinking about them. To keep concrete issues to the forefront, I first summarise the findings of the Working Under Different Rules study and the lessons I drew from this study. Then I explore the issue of whether foreign practices can change an entire labour relations system. Finally, I sketch out an abstract framework for thinking about how different practices and institutions fit into labour relations systems.

## 4.1.    WHAT WORKS OVERSEAS: THE WORKING UNDER DIFFERENT RULES PROJECT

The Working Under Different Rules project was developed in response to the difficult time that American workers had from the mid-1970s up to and including the mid-1990s. This was a period in which wage inequality grew, and the real earnings of less skilled American men plummeted to the point where fully employed workers in the lower parts of the earnings distribution had living standards below those of comparably situated workers in Europe (Freeman, 1994, chapter 1) and where many young men found crime more attractive than work. Child poverty rose, and the

U.S. developed a seemingly permanent underclass of the homeless and beggars. Unionism in the private sector declined, so that workers who believed their rights had been violated at workplaces flooded courts and regulatory agencies with suits and complaints.

While the U.S. avoided European levels of unemployment and durations of joblessness, the difficulties of American workers suggested that the country might have something to learn from the labour market and social policies of other advanced countries (just as those countries had something to learn from American experiences). The project sought:

1)    to determine whether other advanced countries had avoided some of the problems that faced workers in the United States, and if so, how;
2)    to see if their institutions and social protection policies affected labour market performance in important ways; and
3)    to assess which, if any, foreign experiences offered lessons for the design of U.S. policy and institutions.

For four years, members of the NBER's Program in Labor Studies and researchers in Europe examined labour markets and income maintenance systems in the major developed countries. The results are five books in a new University of Chicago Press Comparative Labor Market series and the "Working Under Different Rules" overview volume.

In summary, what did we find?

With respect to the first goal, we found that many problems of American workers in the late 20th century were not endemic to advanced capitalist economies.

### 4.1.1    Other countries did not experience massive increases in wage differentials and inequality, nor drops in the real earnings of the less skilled: their problems were in employment and unemployment

Wage inequality increased in Canada, Japan, and in some continental European countries as well as in the United States, but by much less than in the U.S. Inequality barely changed in France and Italy, fell in the Netherlands, and rose less in Sweden and Germany than in the United States. The only country where the relative position of less skilled men fell as much as in the United States was the U.K., but low paid British workers realised modest increases in earnings in the 1980s. Only low paid American men had sizeable decreases in real wages. Nowhere did the ratio of the earnings of college graduates to the earnings of less educated workers rise as much as in the United States. As is well-known, Europe's labour market problems were low employment-population rates and long durations of joblessness.

### 4.1.2   Loss of collective representation or employee voice was most severe in the United States

The drop in union representation of workers in the United States meant that most Americans lack any independent worker-run institution of collective voice at the workplace. The American move to a union-free private sector contrasts with the rough maintenance of union strength and continued role of collective bargaining in the country most similar to the U.S., Canada, and with the situation in continental Europe where, even in the face of falling union membership in several countries, workers maintain a collective voice within firms through legally mandated works councils or other institutions.

### 4.1.3   Persons in the lower parts of the income or earnings distribution had lower standards of living in the United States than in other advanced countries

The fall in the real earnings of low wage Americans produced the anomalous situation in the 1990s in which low paid Americans had lower living standards (using purchasing power parity measures of the value of foreign currencies) than low paid workers in other advanced countries, despite America's overall high standard of living. A tenth decile worker in the U.S. had roughly half the real compensation of a tenth decile worker in, say, Germany. Even compared to Canada, whose economic system is similar to the American, low income Americans did poorly. From the 1970s to the mid-1980s the poverty rate in Canada went from above the American rate of poverty to substantially below the American rate. Homelessness was hard to find in Canada while it pervaded major U.S. cities.

### 4.1.4   Changes in the relative supply of workers by education contributed to differing trends in wage inequality

In the United States, the growth of the college educated workforce decelerated greatly in the 1980s - a direct response to the falling return to college of the 1970s. By contrast, Canada and the Netherlands continued to expand the number of college graduates relative to high school graduates in the 1980s. As a consequence, Canada had only modest increases in the college-high school wage differential, and the Netherlands had modestly declining wage differentials. In general, changes in the relative supplies of workers with given levels of education in a country greatly influence relative wages: a faster increase in the proportion of workers with college degrees resulted in a smaller increase in earnings differentials by education in the 1980s.

In addition to differences in labour market outcomes, the Working

Under Different Rules project highlighted the variation in the institutions that govern the labour market. Per the project title, our research showed that, indeed, people work under different rules, with different modes of compensation, forms of representation, and job security in otherwise comparable capitalist economies. The American way of determining outcomes is characterised by the great reliance placed on the decentralised labour market and the low social safety net. As a result, market forces are more critical in determining the economic well-being of Americans than in determining the well-being of citizens of other advanced countries.

### 4.1.5   Institutional factors are important determinants of the change in wage inequality and in the skills attained and real earnings of low-paid workers

Countries with smaller increases in wage differentials than the United States had three characteristics. First, they placed more emphasis on wage-setting institutions and less on pure market forces in determining pay than the U.S. Whether it is peak-level collective bargaining between employer federations and union confederations; Ministry of Labour extension of contracts from collective bargaining to firms outside the bargaining set; or national minimum wages, virtually all European countries use some form of wage-setting institution to buttress wages at the lower part of the wage distribution. Second, many countries maintained the strength of unions or had smaller declines in unionisation than the United States. Unions kept a high membership in Germany, Canada and in Scandinavia; and unions in some countries with low density, such as Spain, or France, maintained sufficient support among workers to influence national policies. Third, some countries had more extensive training systems than the United States. Japan used job rotation to give its employees a broad set of skills, and linked its education system closely to employment in particular firms. Germany and Austria have extensive apprenticeship programmes for students who do not go on to university, with national skill standards.

### 4.1.6   Countries that give workers greater training within firms than the U.S. provide considerable institutional support for this training effort

Worker training differs across countries in many ways. Some countries base their training systems largely on the firm. Others rely more on government training programmes, or on school-based or individual training decisions. Estimated returns to training for individuals in the form of wages, and for firms in the form of productivity suggests that company-based training has the highest payoff. Presumably, this is because it is linked more directly to the skills needed at the particular workplace. The U.S. has a weak in-firm training system, with much of the training concentrated on high level workers rather than on raising the skills of the low paid. The experiences of Germany and Japan, the exemplars of within-firm training, show that considerable institutional structure is needed to induce firms to provide training to workers. In Germany, apprenticeship training is closely linked to schooling; employers pay much less for apprentices than for other workers; job security protection gives employers an incentive to train; unions and works councils play a role in determining the content of training; and trainees must pass national skill tests. In Japan, lifetime employment practices in large firms provide an incentive to train, consensual decision-making within firms and the devolution of certain decisions to the shopfloor enhances the need for a knowledgeable workforce.

### 4.1.7 Labour laws and regulations affect modes of employee representation and participation in enterprises

The development of works councils in Europe shows that labour laws can create socially accepted and workable institutions for employee representation within firms. The specific ways councils operate is largely driven by legal regulations: whether the council consists solely of worker representatives or includes management, whether different groups of workers have their own representatives; the power given to councils to affect outcomes differ depending on national labour laws. In addition, even the modest differences in labour laws between the United States and Canada - the United States requires secret ballot elections for representation, in which management is free to devote considerable resources to opposing unionisation, whereas Canada relies extensively on card checks that limit management's role and otherwise leave the decision to unionise more to workers - appear to influence union strength between the two countries. What goes on in national legislatures and courts has an important effect on labour institutions because both employers and employees seek to obey laws and because laws give a weapon to the side whose rights are transgressed at the workplace.

### 4.1.8 Differences in social protection policies affect poverty rates, at a major tax or budget cost

Low earnings contribute to high rates of poverty in the United States. But so too does the lower level of the American social safety net. Comparisons of the distributions of disposable income, which includes taxes and transfers and non-wage income, as well as labour market earnings, show that much of the higher rate of poverty in the United States than in other advanced countries is attributable to differences in social protection policies, particularly for children. The contrast between social protection programmes and poverty rates in Canada and the United States is a case in point. Canadian unemployment benefits, family income maintenance programmes, and other welfare state programmes are sufficiently stronger than American programmes to produce a lower after-tax and transfer poverty rate in Canada despite a higher before-tax poverty rate. The cost is a larger share of national output devoted to such transfers in Europe and Canada than in the United States, which in turn requires greater rates of taxation and/or budget deficits. Sweden is, in this respect, the extreme case. It has the lowest rate of after-tax-and-transfer poverty among OECD countries, and the most egalitarian distribution of disposable incomes. It also has the highest rate of government expenditures to GDP - averaging 60 per cent in the 1980s and 70 per cent in the 1990s following the economic crisis that began then.

### 4.1.9    Most social protection programmes have modest side effects on the labour market; their primary effect is on the well-being of the people they were designed to help

Many social observers, unfamiliar with the weak evidence on the disincentive effects of the widely studied American welfare system, blame the extensive income maintenance systems and employment regulations of Western Europe for high unemployment. There are examples of poorly constructed programmes, such as sick leave in Sweden, which adversely affected working time; and of unemployment insurance programmes that extend periods of joblessness. However, our study found that in general these programmes do not have major efficiency costs. One reason is that many programmes require people to work in order to receive benefits. In Sweden you must have a job to take advantage of the sick leave policy or to enjoy the benefits of extended vacation and holiday time or to receive child care subsidies or parental leave benefits. Another reason is that firms or individuals find ways around some programmes. In Spain, there is considerable non-compliance with high payroll taxes mandated to pay for health care; small firms evade those social security taxes. Since most Spanish workers have family members in a firm that pays the social security taxes, however, virtually all Spaniards are covered by the health care system.

The project also found that market forces present economies with apparent "trade-offs" between some outcomes:

### 4.1.10    The 1980s cross-country experience is consistent with two market-driven trade-offs: one between employment and real wages; and one between employment and wage inequality

Countries like the United States with poor productivity and real wage growth had better employment performance than countries with greater productivity and real wage growth. By contrast, European countries with strong real wage growth had poorer employment performances. Except for Japan, no country managed to do well on both of these levels; and even Japan had economic problems in the 1990s. In addition, countries that maintained stable wage distributions had worse employment records than the United States, which suggests a second possible trade-off - between income inequality and employment of low skill workers.

Put differently, countries that maintained the earnings of the less skilled seemingly "paid" in terms of high unemployment; while the United States "paid" for its growth of employment through falling real earnings. But the fact that low skill and low paid American men had relatively poor employment prospects despite falling real wages and that wages tend to be lower in local labour markets with high unemployment shows that the low wage problem goes beyond the simple "trade-off" analysis.

## 4.2. DRAWING IMPLICATIONS FOR THE U.S.

The final chapter of Working Under Different Rules draws lessons for the U.S. from these conclusions about foreign experiences. I found this to be a difficult exercise. It was difficult because economics has no established framework for analysing the portability of foreign experiences across borders, much less a body of knowledge about their potential fit to the U.S. Still, I had to draw some lessons.

At a broad level, the finding that other advanced countries avoided massive rises in wage inequality and declining real earnings for low paid workers, reduced poverty more than the United States, provided mechanisms for employee representation and cooperation with employers, and in some cases provided better within-firm training for less educated workers produced one important lesson: that the outcomes on which the U.S. did poorly were not inexorable. If every country had the same outcomes, despite different institutions, I would have been pessimistic about finding ways to improve results. There is no point in trying to accomplish the impossible, however desirable. Finding that other countries did better along some dimensions made it realistic to hope that the United States could do better also.

The finding that one reason for differences in outcomes were differences in institutions and policies further suggested that if the U.S. could alter its labour market institutions and social policies, it might be able to improve its outcomes in some areas.

But the evidence of trade-offs in outcomes implied that improvements in one area may be associated with worsened outcomes in others, raising the question of whether by adopting foreign practices, one would simply be trading one set of problems for another. If the U.S. added some elements of a European welfare state, for instance national health care, would it necessarily run into European employment problems, or could it find some way to avoid them? From the European perspective, would U.S. style flexibility necessitate huge income inequality, increased poverty, homelessness, and the urban pathologies that mar American society, or could Europe find ways to avoid them? These considerations naturally led me to wonder what happens when a country adopts foreign labour practices: do these practices work in the same way, or better, or worse than they do overseas?

History provides a mixed record of success in transferring labour practices across country lines. Despite American efforts after World War II to introduce U.S. style unionism in Japan and Germany, both countries developed their own distinct rules of the workplace and labour institutions. Canadian labour legislation partially copied the American Wagner Act, but with small differences that produced different levels of unionisation in the two countries half a century later. Japanese transplants to the United States or Europe have imported some Japanese personnel practices, but not others. European efforts to increase the flexibility of their labour markets have had, at best, marginal success.

Given the problem of transferability, I limited the remaining lessons to three broad principles for the direction of possible public and private policy:

### 4.2.1   Reversing the decline in the living standards of less skilled workers and reducing poverty rates would require the United States to supplement market forces in wage-determination and training as it has not done in the past

Other advanced countries maintained the real earnings of the lower paid workers through better training and/or some form of institutional setting of wages. While a "better training" solution would be more consonant with American reliance on the market than institutional interventions in pay setting or income determination, the training systems that are exemplary require considerable institutional support. And training was only part of the reason for the narrower earnings distributions and higher real earnings of low skill workers in Europe than in the United States. Wage-setting institutions such as national collective bargaining or minimum wages far above U.S. levels were important in maintaining the labour market position of the less skilled, albeit presumably at the cost of some employment, in Europe.

Some of the ways foreign countries place lower bounds on the real earnings of their workers seemed "alien" to the U.S.'s decentralised labour market. I found it inconceivable that European-style national collective bargaining or extension of labour contracts from some employers to their competitors would work in the United States, outside a mass mobilisation war environment. If the United States chose to raise the wages of the less skilled through interventions in wage-setting, the methods for doing so would be likely to differ from European practices. For example, the Earned Income Tax Credit is a U.S. intervention that supplements the pay of low wage workers with a negative income tax, consonant with a decentralised wage-setting system. Attaching additional social benefits to work, such as health insurance paid partly by general tax funds, is another way to buttress the living standards of the low-paid. Raising the minimum wage is another possible tool for intervention that fits U.S. wage-setting practices.

### 4.2.2    It is possible to reduce poverty through social safety nets that are largely complementary with work

Other countries have more extensive social protection systems than the U.S. which greatly reduce their poverty rates. In contrast to the American welfare system, moreover, some foreign systems of social protection complement work. These programmes offer an important lesson for designing policies to remove the welfare trap that reduces the work incentive for many Americans. At one time, some Americans viewed "workfare" as a conservative attack on income maintenance programmes, but in fact workfare is the essence of the best welfare state and social protection programmes in Europe. Programmes that provide benefits for workers, such as France's state-provided day-care for children of working mothers or Sweden's benefits that accrue to employees, show that it is possible to design social protection programmes that redistribute income and make work more attractive.

But, as with training and wage-setting, these programmes require greater intervention in market determination of outcomes than has been the experience of the United States, and even a welfare system that complements work would cost money, for instance for child care or to offer wage subsidies to employers for hiring low skilled workers. No foreign country provides an extensive social safety net without allocating a larger share of national output for social protection than does the United States. If the U.S. wanted to improve the situation of the poor, it would have to pay.

### 4.2.3    Providing collective representation and venues for participation for American workers will require new labour institutions and changes in labour law

European and Canadian experiences show that legal regulation is a key element in giving employees a collective voice in firms; and that such institutions can create cooperative and productive labour relations. Canadian labour laws limit management pressures in union organising, suggesting to some labour relations experts that these practices be adopted in the United States. But even Canada has moved in the health and safety area toward European-style works councils that cover non-union workers as well as union workers. One lesson from European experience is that intra-firm organisations should include all employees, not just the blue collar workers that are normally unionisable in the United States. Both Europe and Canada mandate councils, which suggests that such organisation must be legally required. A more conservative reading of the evidence is that voluntarily established committees that have some legal standing might better fit the American labour scene. Such committees would, however, need real power in, say, regulating occupational health and safety or dealing with grievances, obtaining information about company plans, or in joint consultation or decision-making on, say, training. European experience further suggests that such institutions should not have rights to engage in wage-bargaining or call strikes.

The reader will note that rather than offering specific policy recommendations I limited my lessons to pointing out areas in which new policies were needed if the U.S. were to resolve its problems. This is in keeping with the National Bureau of Economic Research charter, which forbids researchers from making policy recommendations in research studies. But even without that rule, I was uneasy about recommending any specific policy because of my uncertainty about how it would "fit" with other U.S. labour practices. I was troubled, for instance, by how European works councils would operate in the U.S. without industry-wide collective bargaining and a "social partners" tradition of decision-making. Perhaps, as many American unionists feared, anti-union management would use these organisations as "company unions" (employer-dominated organisations designed to avoid unionisation). Perhaps these organisations would prove incompatible with exclusive bargaining representatives, as in the Gould quote earlier. Or perhaps they would "mutate" into plant-level wage-bargaining organisations in the decentralised U.S. labor market, as many American businessmen feared.

Even in Europe, there are striking cases of the same policy having different effects in different settings. For instance, both Spain and Germany weakened employment protection laws in the 1980s, but whereas in Spain the legal change led firms to hire most new employees under temporary contracts, there was little change in German employment policies. The greater strength of unions and works councils and importance of apprenticeship in Germany meant that firms still chose to hire people under permanent contracts. Similarly, while all Western European countries (save for the U.K. and Eire) have some form of works council legislation, the mandated councils differ greatly depending on the national labour relations system into which they fit. In short, labour institutions and policies can work differently and produce different outcomes in different settings.

The title question of this essay, to which I had given only cursory thought when the Working Under project began, loomed large at the conclusion of the study.

### 4.2.4    The Effect of Foreign Practices on National Labour Relations

On 14-15 March 1994 the Commission on the Future of Worker-Management Relations[1] held a conference in Washington D.C. on "International Evidence". This conference and ensuing discussions impressed upon me that business and labour leaders were concerned with another issue regarding foreign labour practices - the possible effect that introducing such practices might have on the entire labour relations system.

As an example of this concern, consider what might happen to U.S. labour relations if, by magic, the European practice of extension of contracts were introduced into the U.S. American firms would probably not oppose union organisation as strongly as they do: why spend resources fighting unions if you are going to pay the going union wage in any case? But they would probably form stronger employer associations to bargain with unions in pattern-setting agreements. Unions might lose one of their organising appeals: why join a union if you are going to receive the going union wage in a non-union firm? They might also be more willing to strike in certain negotiations, since the outcomes would affect larger numbers of workers. Extension of contracts would reduce wage inequality among firms. But it might also induce growth of the underground economy. No one can say for certain what the ultimate effect of such a major innovation would be on the U.S. labour relations system.

The problem is that labour relations in a country are the product of complex interactions among many decision-makers: unions, various levels of management, employees, and government regulators, each of whom adapts behaviour to the changing behaviour of the other players. Without an understanding of these interactions - of the complex adaptive system that constitutes labour relations - no one can be sure of what might happen if a country introduces transplants from overseas. This leads both unions and management to be wary of foreign practices, or indeed, of any change in the status quo that does not clearly shift the balance of power in their direction. Since a major institutional innovation may alter a labour relations system in hard-to-predict directions, many participants in the Commission Hearings advocated caution, per the Gould quotation. Similarly, in the Hearings before the Commission, representatives of labour and management testified that no changes should be made in the Railway Labor Act that regulates railroads and air transportation and that no changes should be made in Section 8(a)2 of the Wagner Act law that prohibits company-dominated unions, despite this provision potentially making it illegal for companies to discuss wages and working conditions with groups of non-union employees. The reason management and labour preferred the status quo was not that they failed to recognise problems in each area, but that each feared that efforts to resolve the problems might open a Pandora's Box of changes, that could change the entire labour relations system to their detriment at some future date.

## 4.3.    TOWARD A FRAMEWORK FOR ANALYSIS

Standard industrial relations or labour economics analysis provides little guidance to answering questions about the fit of labour institutions across countries or about the effect of one institution on other institutions. While industrial relations experts have recognised at least since John Dunlop's Industrial Relations Systems (1958) that unions, management, and government agencies interact in complex systemic ways[2], they have produced almost no formal analysis of how a labour system fits together or how it changes over time. Labour economists have eschewed modelling systems in favour of analyses of individual decisions or outcomes.

In this section, I take a first step toward developing an analytic framework that should help us address the "does it fit?" issue. I formalise the concept of fit in a labour relations system and examine the relations among institutions within a system. The definitions and discussions are designed as prologue to a formal model of a labour relations systems as a complex adaptive system, *vide* the non-linear dynamic systems analysis associated with the Sante Fe Institute.

Consider a society with institutions X and a second society with institutions Y. For simplicity, let X and Y be vectors with N components, each of which can take on the values 1 or 0, where 1 means the institution is operative in the country (its cell fires "on" in a neural net) and 0 means that it is not. For instance, one component might be centralised collective bargaining: 0 for the U.S. and 1 for Austria. The vector of all the institutions produces an outcome defined by the function F, where higher values of F are more desirable. Now, assume institution I does not operate in X or Y, but can be introduced (turned on) at a fixed cost of $C_I$. With I = 1 output changes in both societies, say to X' and Y'. The absolute fit of I then depends on whether it raises or lowers F, given $C_I$.

**Definition:** I "fits" society X if $F(X') - C_I > F(X)$.

This makes fit depend on the net marginal product of I: if we rewrite F as output net of the cost of the additional institution, f, we have $f(X') - f(X) > 0$.

The relative fit of I in society X versus Y depends on whether I raises net output more or less in X compared to Y.

**Definition:** I makes a "better fit" in society X than in Y if $F(X') - C_I - F(X) > F(Y') - C_I - F(Y)$, that is if $F(X') - F(X) > F(Y') - F(Y)$.

Note that $C_I = 0$ in the society where I originated. Thus the gain from transplanting I to a foreign country must exceed the value of I in the original setting for I to be worthwhile. The imitator pays an entry fee for introducing the new institution whereas the initiator has already paid that cost.

The cost of introducing an institution aside, institution I makes a better fit in X than in Y if $F(X) < F(Y)$ - that is, if whatever I does, X was less able to substitute for it with existing institutions or mechanisms than was Y. Put differently, I fits X more than Y the greater the "hole" it fills in society X than society Y. Finally, I will better fit X than Y when $F(X') > F(Y')$ - that is, if I is a better absolute fit in X than in Y.

Since in this model the only difference between societies is in their vectors of institutions (I assume the same F for both), these definitions direct attention at how institutions interrelate as arguments in the output function. To illuminate the "does it fit?" question, we must examine the extent to which the contribution of one institution depends on the contribution of other institutions within a labour relations system.

At an abstract level Kauffman's (1989; 1993) NK model of rugged fitness landscapes offers a way to analyse the interrelation among elements in the X and Y vectors. His model, which builds on Sewell Wright's vision of biological fitness as represented by peaks and valleys in a fitness plane, analyses epistatic interactions among genes or proteins. Kauffman posits a system of N parts (institutions), each of which takes on a limited set of possible values and whose marginal product depends on the value of K other parts of the system. If $K = 0$, there are no interactions; independent innovations can bring the society to its peak. In this case, there is no value to a systemic analysis: it's every tub on its own bottom. At the other extreme, when $K = N-1$, every part of the system is linked to every other part, and it is not possible to say anything without a systemic analysis. The same institution might improve output in X but reduce it in Y, depending on what else is there. For example, a system of devolving enforcement of occupational health and safety to workplaces might work if employees have independent organisations - unions or works councils - to participate in the process but might fail in their absence.

The NK model treats all components or institutions similarly: no component has a larger or smaller effect than any other, though with $N < K-1$, neighbouring components may interact directly while distant components do not. To examine situations in which some institutions have larger effects than others, or in which some have special links to others, requires additional structure. Economists interested in "high performance workplaces", whose success appears to require a set of interrelated institutional changes (Milgrom and Roberts), have begun to analyse the latter issue within firms. To apply their analysis to societies as a whole, consider two separate institutions, $I_1$ and $I_2$, absent from society X. If X introduces the first institution, ouput rises from $F(X)$ to $F(X,I_1)$; if it introduces the second, ouput rises to $F(X,I_2)$. But neither of these institutions works to its full potential without the other, so that $F(X,I_1)$ and $F(X,I_2)$ are only modestly higher than $F(X)$. The real pay off comes from bringing them in together. Milgrom and Roberts use the concept of super-modularity of the production process to formalise this:

> **Definition:** F is super-modular when $F(X, I_1, I_2) - F(X) > F(X,I_1) -$ $F(X) + F(X,I_2) - F(X)$. Here $I_1$ and $I_2$ are labelled complementary institutions.[3]

As an example of complementary institutions, consider national collective bargaining and a strong employers' federation. You cannot have successful national bargaining without an employers' association on one side of the table, and a strong employers' federation may make little contribution to national output in the absence of centralised collective bargaining.

An implication of this line of argument is that a set of interrelated programmes will often have a greater chance of succeeding than a single programme designed to resolve a given problem. Multiple programmes can cause offsetting behavioural incentives, or can reinforce each other in ways that makes the effect of several programmes together differ from that of any programme alone. The coexistence of public day-care centres, time-limited welfare benefits, and general family child allowances in France creates a much greater chance for moving single-parents from welfare to work than would otherwise be the case. In the U.S. the combination of a miniumum wage and earned income tax credit may work better than either policy by itself.

One refinement of the super-modular notion may prove useful. In many situations of institutional change, changes in one institution or in one element of a given institution seem to reduce social output even though changes in the entire vector of institutions (all components of an institution) could lead the society to a higher peak in productivity space. The transition economies in Eastern Europe, for instance, have suffered major falls in output on their way to a market economy; New Zealand had trouble moving toward a freer market economy; and Sweden's effort to reform its welfare state and deregulate its economy has been more costly than anyone expected. It is not simply that complementary institutions produce a beneficial interaction or synergy, but that introducing them separately may be costly. I shall call institutions with this characteristic, partner institutions:

> **Definition:** $I_1$ and $I_2$ are partner institutions when $F(X, I_1, I_2) - F(X)$ $> 0 > F(X,I_1) - F(X)$ {and $F(X,I_2) - F(X)$}.

### 4.3.1    Malleable and Catalytic Institutions

Thus far, I have taken institutions as fixed discrete factors - 0-1 elements in a vector or on-off cells in a neural net. But unless they are extremely narrowly defined, institutions have internal structures that merit some attention. When we talk about the institution of an "employee involvement programme", for instance, we want to include quality circles, teams, whether committees of employees are elected, or not, etc. The internal elements of particular institutions, moreover, are likely to be adaptable or malleable to different environments and thus contribute to their fitting into the labour relations systems of different countries.

To formalise this notion, I represent an institution with a set of N elements, which for simplicity have values 0 and 1. Elements are defined so that the ideal or prototype institution would have a 1 for each element. Some of these elements must be 1 for the institution to function; they are hard components of the institution: if they are on, the institution is on. Other adaptable elements can be 1 or 0, depending on their environment, without turning I off. For example, for free unions to operate, workers must be able to control their representatives - this is the hard component. But the particular way they do so may differ across societies; this is an adaptable part of the union institution.  Formally:

> **Definition:** Element n of I is adaptable if changing n from 1 to 0 in the prototype institution leaves $I = 1$.

We can expand on this by examining the effect on I of making $n = 0$ when some other elements are 0.[4]

Since an institution consists of N components, the malleability of the institution depends on the number of components that can be off while the institution functions:

> **Definition:** The malleability of an institution is measured by the number of elements that can be 0 while $I = 1$.

Malleability tells us the extent to which an institution functions despite the "failure" of particular components: its redundancy, as it were. In a neural network, this would show up in the size of the basin of attraction of the institution. If vector $(1,1,1)$ is the prototype institution - leading to $I = 1$ but if vector $(1,1,0)$ also produces $I = 1$, the third component of the institution would be adaptable. The greater the number of vectors that differ from the prototype but yield $I = 1$ the greater is institutional malleability.

Since malleable institutions have many flexible or adjustable features, they should transplant readily to foreign countries and thus are likely to be found in many labour relations systems. As a case in point consider works councils, which are found in different guises in Europe, depending on the overall labour relations system. Management has a major role in works councils in France whereas unions dominate councils in Germany. In some countries, all employees elect councillors; in others, blue-collar and white-collar employees elect separate representatives. In Germany, councils have co-determination powers; in other countries, they have the right of consultation only. I can envisage works councils working in the U.K. and even in the U.S., where ten states have mandated health and safety committees. By contrast, extension of collective contracts to nonunion workers has fewer malleable components: either the government extends or it doesn't, and it seems unworkable in the decentralised U.S. or U.K. labour markets.

Note that by itself, malleability tells us nothing about the desirability of introducing an institution. Works councils might be malleable, but perhaps they would lower output in the U.S. Here we must go back to the fitness. Under plausible conditions, a more malleable institution may be a better fitting one as well, but the definitions are designed to allow the two characteristics to be orthogonal. Taken together, fitness and malleability are designed to capture what many analysts mean when they say "I does/does not fit" across national lines: the degree to which institution I can adjust to that other setting and its potential productivity in that setting.

Finally, neither fitness nor malleability addresses the possible effect of introducing a new institution on existing institutions. The concept I want to introduce here is that of the catalytic power of an institution - the extent to which that institution induces change in other institutions. An institution I may turn off/on another institution J or turn on/off some components of J. It may affect J directly - I comes in and J stops - or through a more complex set of interactions, by altering the long-term steady state of the labour relations system, for instance by affecting other institutions. These considerations dictate the following definitions:

> **Definition:** Institution I is directly catalytic with respect to J if $DJ/DI \neq 0$ - that is, if changing I from 0 to 1 or 1 to 0 causes J to change - or with respect to element n of J if $Dn/DI \neq 0$, where D is the difference operator, all other institutions held fixed.

> **Definition:** Institution I is ultimately catalytic with respect to J if $DJ/DI \neq 0$ - that is, if changing I from 0 to 1 or 1 to 0 causes J to change - or with respect to element n of J if $Dn/DI \neq 0$, all other institutions allowed to vary as well.

Looking at the entire labour relations system, a measure of the catalytic power of I would be the difference between the full vector of institutions when $I = 1$ and when $I = 0$.

In one sense, catalytic power is the flip-side of malleability: catalysis reflects the effect of the new institution on existing institutions whereas malleability measures the effect of existing institutions on the new one. One way of thinking about malleability and catalytic power is in terms of something with which we all deal daily: our mates. A marriage is more likely to succeed if one/both parties are malleable - that is, if they adjust to their partner. It may also succeed better if one partner has catalytic power and induces changes in the other. But a marriage is likely to experience trouble if both partners are catalytic and neither is malleable. My guess is that in any plausible model, catalytic power and malleability will be, as is implicit in this example, inversely correlated, but note that there is nothing in the definition to ensure this.

## 4.4. CONCLUSION

The definitions and discussion above are tentative first steps toward clarifying the meaning of a labour relations system and the fit of different institutions in a system -- issues that first struck me as important at the conclusion of the Working Under Different Rules project and were reinforced during the deliberations of the U.S. Commission on the Future of Worker-Management Relations. My hope is that one can develop the concepts of fitness, malleability, and catalytic power further in various ways, and use them in formal models of systems of institutions that will further illuminate the "does it fit?" title of this essay.

## NOTES

1　The Clinton Administration established the Commission to examine U.S. labour relations and make specific policy recommendations for 1) encouraging new methods or institutions for improving work place productivity through labour-management cooperation and employee participation; 2) changing the legal framework and practices of collective bargaining to enhance cooperative behaviour, improve productivity, and reduce conflict and delay; and 3) to seek ways to increase the extent to which work place problems are resolved by the parties themselves rather than through courts and regulatory bodies.

2　Dunlop defines an IR system as: "comprised of three groups of actors - workers and their organisations, managers and their organisations, and governmental agencies concerned with the work place and work community (who) ... interact within a specified environment comprised of three interrelated contexts: the technology, the product and factor markets or budgetary constraints and the power relations in the larger community, and the derived status of the actors. An industrial relations system and its larger setting create an ideology ... regarding the

interaction and roles of the actors that helps to bind the system together" (Dunlop, revised edition, 1993, p. 283).
3    In continuous functions, this is nothing more than requiring positive cross-partial derivatives.
4    There are various ways to expand this definition, for instance, in terms of the contribution of pairs of institutions to the institution remaining in operation: maybe it takes element 1 or element 2 to be on, and so forth.

# REFERENCES

Casti, John, *Alternative Realities: Mathematical Models of Nature and Man* (John Wiley, NY, 1989)
Commission on the Future of Labor-Management Relations, *Fact-Finding Report*, May 1994 (U.S. Department of Labor and U.S. Department of Commerce, Washington, D.C.)
Dunlop, John T., *Industrial Relations Systems* (Harvard Business School Press edition, 1993)
Freeman, Richard B. (ed), *Working Under Different Rules* (Russell Sage, 1994)
Kauffman, Stuart, "Origins of Order in Evolution: Self-Organisation and Selection" in Brian Goodwin and Peter Saunders, *Theoretical Biology: Epigenetic and Evolutionary Order from Complex Systems* (Baltimore, John Hopkins Press, 1989)
Kauffman, Stuart, *The Origins of Order* (New York, Oxford University Press, 1993)
Milgrom, Paul and John Roberts, "Complementarities and Fit: Strategy, Structure, and Organizational Change" Stanford mimeo, 1994

# PART II
# SPAIN: LESSONS FROM A FAILURE
# IN JOB CREATION

# 5. Job Creation In Spain: A Macroeconomic View

**José Viñals***

## 5.1. INTRODUCTION

The persistently high unemployment rates observed over the last ten years in the European Union member countries are a cause for serious concern, given the significant social and economic costs associated with them. In particular, the European economies' inability to create net employment in a sustained manner, and thus provide jobs for those citizens wanting to work, has meant a highly significant loss of these countries' human potential, and therefore of the output that would have been generated if these inactive resources had been gainfully employed. This unfavourable situation is aggravated by the highly undesirable effects that unemployment has on income distribution, by creating a dual social structure composed of the employment "haves" and "have-nots". Unemployment also has a negative impact on the public deficit, since it reduces tax revenues and, at the same time, increases social transfers to the unemployed. Finally, the persistence of high unemployment rates for prolonged periods is extremely damaging for society as a whole: it carries a high psychological cost for those workers who are unable to find a job, tends to be associated with increases in the crime rate and, ultimately, may erode the foundations on which social coexistence is based.

If the unemployment problem is serious in the European Union countries as a whole, it is even more so in Spain. Indeed, over the last ten years, the Spanish unemployment rate has averaged 19%, almost double that for the European Union countries as a whole, which has been 10%.

I argue in this paper that the main reason for the high unemployment rate in Spain is the economy's clear inability to generate net job creation for prolonged periods. Hence, any solution to the unemployment problem must necessarily include the reactivation of long-term employment.

In order to analyse future options for job creation in the Spanish economy, this paper has been structured as follows: Section 5.2 succinctly describes the main features marking employment and unemployment in Spain in the last few decades and identifies the major similarities and differences with respect to the situation in other countries. Section 5.3 explores the causes underlying the unfavourable behaviour of employment in the Spanish economy in the medium term, distinguishing between strictly internal causes and those also shared by other European countries, and specifying whether they originate in the public or private sector. The basic features of employment in Spain and the most decisive influencing factors having been isolated, Section 5.4. examines the incidence that a series of structural factors may have on the future behaviour of employment in Spain, the most important being those related to the process of European economic integration. Finally, Section 5.5. examines, in the light of the analysis and evidence presented in the previous sections, certain economic policies that could be implemented in Spain to promote sustained job creation.

## 5.2.　　BASIC　　FEATURES:　　EMPLOYMENT　　AND UNEMPLOYMENT

### 5.2.1　　The long term: trends

The unemployment problem reflects an economy's inability to create jobs at a high enough rate to absorb the growth of its labour force. Figure 5.1 shows the unemployment rate in Spain for the period 1964-94. The most interesting point here is that, in the last 30 years, the unemployment rate has increased from about 2.5% to the present rate of 24%, i.e., a tenfold increase. The increase continues to be striking even after the deduction of a few points from the current rate to take into account people employed in the informal economy. The other point shown by the figure is that once unemployment has increased, it shows an enormous reluctance to fall back to reasonable levels, even during periods of strong economic growth.

Before examining the economic causes underlying the extraordinary growth of unemployment in Spain, it will be useful to describe its evolution in terms of two basic components: labour force and employment. Table 5.1 and Figure 5.2 show changes in the labour force and in the number of the employed and the unemployed during the period under consideration. It is readily apparent that the increase in unemployment has been due to the economy's inability to create employment in a context of labour force growth. Specifically, while the labour force has increased by somewhat more than 3.5 million people during the period as a result of population growth and the increasing participation of women in productive activities, total employment has increased by barely 100,000 people.

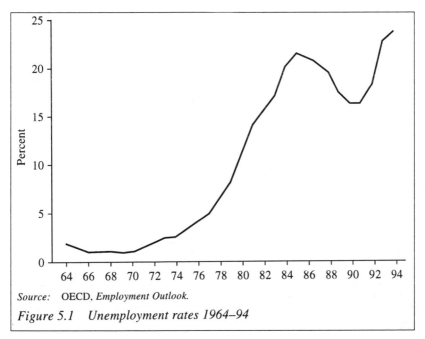

Source:     OECD, *Employment Outlook.*

*Figure 5.1     Unemployment rates 1964–94*

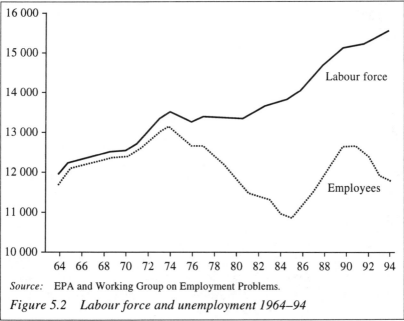

*Source:*     EPA and Working Group on Employment Problems.

*Figure 5.2     Labour force and unemployment 1964–94*

*Table 5.1   Labour Force Employment and Unemployment in Spain (1964 –*
*1994) (variations in thousands of people)*

|  | 1964–75 | 1976–84 | 1985–90 | 1991–94 | 1964–94 |
|---|---|---|---|---|---|
| Labour Force | 1 428 | 363 | 1 342 | 437 | 3 570 |
| Employed | 1 216 | –1 931 | 1 652 | –836 | 101 |
| Unemployed | 212 | 2 294 | –310 | 1 273 | 3 469 |

*Source*:   INE (EPA)

*Employment by Sector (data in thousands, variations except for 1994)*

|  | 1964–75 | 1976–84 | 1985–90 | 1991–94 | 1964–94 | 1994 (%) |
|---|---|---|---|---|---|---|
| Agriculture | –1 302 | –1 020 | –530 | –318 | –3 170 | 10 |
| Industry | 641 | –678 | 231 | –522 | –328 | 21 |
| Construction | 307 | –373 | 387 | –175 | 146 | 9 |
| Services | 1 569 | 140 | 1 565 | 179 | 3 453 | 60 |
| TOTAL | 1 216 | –1 931 | 1 653 | –836 | 101 | 100 |

*Source*:   INE (EPA)

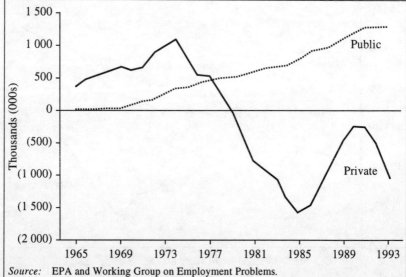

*Source:*   EPA and Working Group on Employment Problems.

*Figure 5.3    Spain: Private and public sector employment (cumulative*
*variation) 1964–94*

*Table 5.2   Private and Public Sector in Spain (1964 – 1994)*

|  | 1964–75 | 1976–84 | 1985–90 | 1991–94 | 1964–94 | 1994 |
|---|---|---|---|---|---|---|
| Employment | 1 216 | –1 931 | 1 652 | –836 | 101 | 11 743 |
| Private sector employment | 857 | –2 277 | 1 172 | –920 | –1 168 | 9 972 |
| Public sector employment | 359 | 346 | 481 | 84 | 1 269 | 1 771 |

*Source*:   INE (EPA)

In other words, the Spanish economy has shown a basic inability to expand employment in net terms, creating only about 3,000 jobs per year on average against the 117,000 jobs it would have been necessary to create in order to prevent the increase in unemployment.

However, the employment problem is even more serious than the above figures suggest as, in Spain, the total employment figures conceal a very different picture as regards public sector and private sector employment. Indeed, as Figure 5.3 and Table 5.2 show, the Spanish economy has not only performed extremely poorly overall in job creation but also, since the mid-1970s, it has embarked on a job destruction process in the private sector that it was able to counteract only by resorting to the public sector. This trend is closely linked with the progressively increasing share of public expenditure in the Spanish GDP, with the level currently standing at 50%.

No doubt, the lengthy restructuring process in the agricultural sector in Spain over the last few decades has been the cause of job losses in this sector, which have been estimated at 3.2 million jobs. However, as indicated at the bottom of Table 5.1, this trend has been just barely balanced by net job creation in the other private productive sectors (basically services). Consequently, one of the key questions to be asked is: What are the factors that are blocking the creation of non-agricultural jobs in the private sector in Spain?

It is readily understandable from the above that the unemployment problem and the private sector's inability to create employment are two sides of the same coin in Spain. Furthermore, if it is considered that the labour participation rate in Spain (58%) is the lowest of the EU countries; that the Spanish unemployment rate is the highest in the European Union; and that the percentage of chronic unemployed (slightly more than 50%) is one of the highest in the European Union, the dimensions of the unemployment problem become even more disquieting. In other words, there is a relatively small part of the population of working age that wishes to take part in the production process and, of that part, a relatively large number is unable to join this process, since they are unable to find jobs for long periods. This means that of all the Spaniards of working age, slightly less than half have a job. This gives rise to a marked underuse of the country's human resources, a serious threat to the financial feasibility of the Welfare State and, ultimately, a drag on Spain's economic progress vis-à-vis its European partners.

### 5.2.2   The short term: cyclical fluctuations

Any analysis of the nature of employment is incomplete without an examination of its cyclical course. Thus, Figure 5.4 shows the behaviour of employment and real GDP throughout the business cycle in Spain, showing the deviations of employment (non-agricultural private sector) and GDP with regard to their respective trends.[1] Thus, during periods of economic growth, employment and real GDP grew at rates above their trends (which is shown in the figure by both variables being above the horizontal line representing zero), whereas the opposite happens during periods of recession.

As can be seen from the figure, the Spanish economy has undergone acute cyclical fluctuations during the last 20 years, shown by the marked

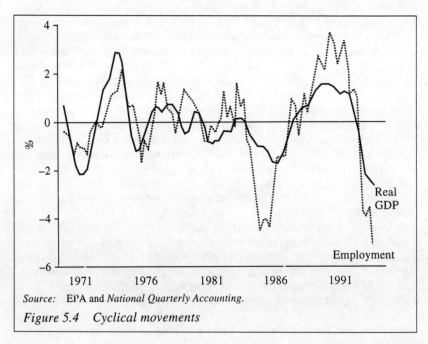

*Source:*   EPA and *National Quarterly Accounting.*

*Figure 5.4   Cyclical movements*

swings of real GDP against its normal or trend values. However, more interesting still is the high cyclical sensitivity of employment, as shown by the fact that fluctuations in employment are even more extreme than those of output (the variability of employment is 1.9% while that of GDP is 1.2%). This shows that adjustments in the labour market are mainly implemented through employment and not through wages, as would be the case in an economy that functioned more rationally.

Another intriguing feature of the cyclical course of employment is the fact that it has tended to grow at rates below those of real GDP in periods of economic expansion and drop more sharply in periods of recession. Thus, while a GDP growth rate of 1% has been associated with a positive response of employment of 0.7%, a drop in GDP of 1% has been associated with a 1.5% decrease in employment.[2] This is consistent with the suspicion that the existence of high firing costs is not sufficient to sustain employment during periods of recession and may even lead to extreme situations in many companies, where the workforce cuts finally implemented are more drastic than would have been the case if firing costs had been lower. At the same time, it is reasonable to assume that such a situation would tend to inhibit job creation in periods of economic growth, given the problems that may arise in the future when the business climate becomes less favourable.

### 5.2.3 Is Spain different?

The seriousness of Spain's employment and unemployment problems becomes immediately clear when the situation in Spain is compared with that of other economic areas, such as the European Union and the United States. This comparison is also useful to identify those aspects of employment and unemployment that Spain shares with its European neighbours and those that are specific to Spain.

#### 5.2.3.1 Unemployment

Figure 5.5 shows the joint evolution of unemployment in the three above-mentioned areas during the period 1970-93. The most salient point here is that, while the unemployment rate has ranged between 5% and 9% in the United States during this period, the unemployment rates in the European Union, and particularly in Spain, have tended to increase considerably. This becomes all the more apparent if one considers that, in the last 25 years, the unemployment rate has only increased from 5% to slightly more than 6% in the United States, while in the European Union, it has grown from 2.5% to 11% and, in Spain, from 2.5% to 24%.

Another significant feature is that the profile of Spanish unemployment is very similar to that of the European Union in the periods 1970-77 and 1985-94, but exhibits a clear departure during the interim period. Indeed, the difference in current unemployment levels between Spain and the

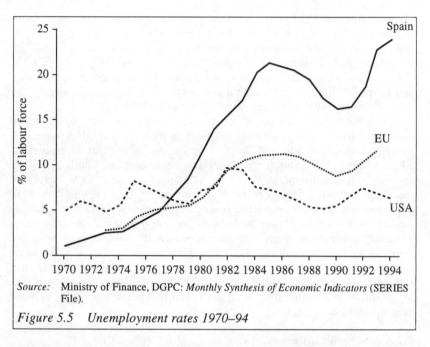

*Source:*   Ministry of Finance, DGPC: *Monthly Synthesis of Economic Indicators* (SERIES
           File).

*Figure 5.5    Unemployment rates 1970–94*

European Union is to be found in the marked increase of the
unemployment rate during the period 1978-83, which was particularly
severe in Spain. After the mid-1980s, the high unemployment rates
prevalent by then have shown a strong tendency to persist in Spain and the
European Union, in sharp contrast to the situation in the United States.

The evolution of unemployment over time in the three areas considered
can be understood more easily if we consider its relationship with
inflation,[3] as shown in Figure 5.6. As can be seen, the unemployment and
inflation rates in the three areas were fairly similar in the early 1970s. The
first significant increase in unemployment - matched by the increase in
inflation - occurs in the mid-1970s, mainly as a consequence of the supply
shocks resulting from higher oil prices on world markets. These shocks
recurred in 1979-80. Although it is true that the unemployment rates in the
late 1970s were fairly similar in Spain, the European Union and the United
States, such was not the case with the inflation rates, which had increased
significantly more in Spain than in the European Union, and more in the
European Union than in the United States.

The conviction that it was necessary to reduce inflation to more
reasonable levels led the economic authorities to implement economic
policies designed to contain demand in the 1980s. However, while the
greater structural rigidities in the European markets had previously led to
a more inflationary response by their economies to the supply shocks of

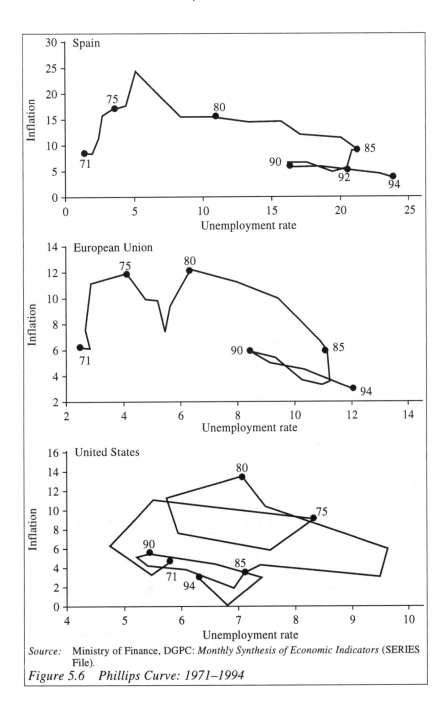

*Source:* Ministry of Finance, DGPC: *Monthly Synthesis of Economic Indicators* (SERIES File).

*Figure 5.6   Phillips Curve: 1971–1994*

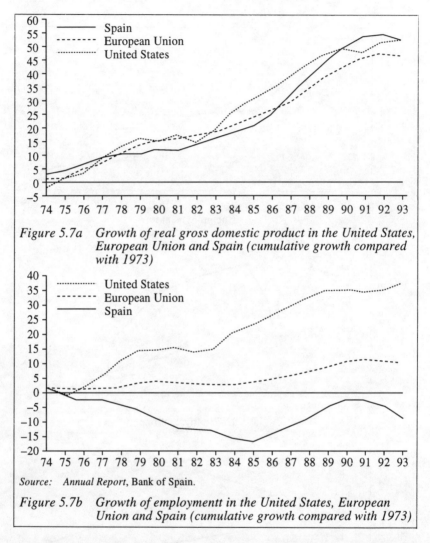

*Figure 5.7a    Growth of real gross domestic product in the United States,*
*European Union and Spain (cumulative growth compared*
*with 1973)*

*Source:    Annual Report, Bank of Spain.*

*Figure 5.7b    Growth of employmentt in the United States, European*
*Union and Spain (cumulative growth compared with 1973)*

the 1970s, these rigidities were now seriously hampering efforts to reduce
inflation. This meant higher increases in unemployment in Spain than in
the European Union, and higher increases in the European Union than in
the United States. Finally, the high unemployment rates attained in Spain
and in the European Union member countries as a whole in the mid-1980s
have shown signs of remarkable persistence since then, probably also as
a result of the existence of major structural problems.

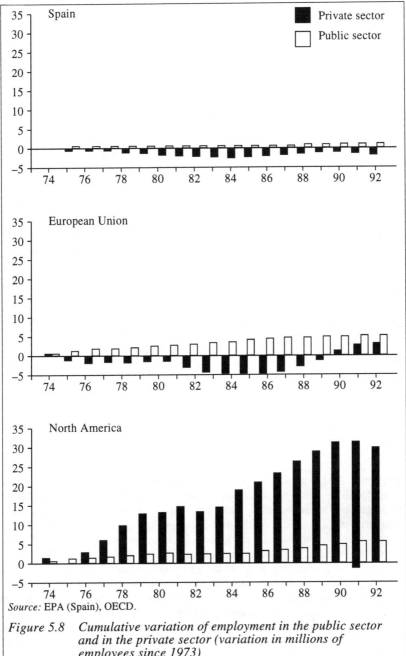

*Source:* EPA (Spain), OECD.

*Figure 5.8    Cumulative variation of employment in the public sector
             and in the private sector (variation in millions of
             employees since 1973)*

### 5.2.3.2    Employment

The increased unemployment in Spain, in comparison with the European Union and, particularly, with the United States, is matched by the behaviour of employment. Thus, Figure 5.7 compares the course of production and employment in the three areas during the period 1974-93.[4] The most noteworthy feature is that while the mean growth of real GDP has been very similar in all three areas - about 2-2.2% per year - employment has followed highly divergent courses. Thus, while the United States economy has created employment at an average annual rate of 1.6% during the period in question, in the European Union, employment has grown at a mere 0.5% and in Spain, employment has been destroyed at an annual rate of 0.4%.

Figure 5.8 compares job creation in the public and private sectors during the above period. Clearly, the North American economy's ability to create jobs is fuelled by the private sector's dynamism. However, in the European Union, and most particularly in Spain, the ability to generate net jobs is not due to the private sector - which rather tends to destroy jobs - but to the public sector.

To summarise, the Spanish economy shares with the European Union as a whole certain differential features in the behaviour of medium-term employment and unemployment that are clearly distinct from the US economy: in particular, the tendency for unemployment consistently to increase and its enormous downward rigidity during periods of economic growth; the lack of dynamism in employment; the negative contribution of the private sector to the job creation process; and the relatively significant and direct role played by the public sector in this process. However, all of these unfavourable features are much more marked in Spain than in other European Union member countries, probably reflecting the relatively greater importance of the structural problems affecting Spanish markets.

## 5.3.    CAUSES

The basic features identified in the previous section suggest that the "structural" level of employment in the Spanish economy is very low, as indicated by the fact that the "structural" unemployment rate is very high. The primary goal of this section is to ascertain, in the light of recent conceptual advances and the empirical evidence available in Spain, the economic reasons for this phenomenon.

So far, the analysis has addressed "quantities" (employment and unemployment), without making any special reference to "prices" (wages). However, both wages and employment and unemployment are variables that are jointly determined as a result of the equilibrating processes that take place in the goods and services markets and in the labour market. Consequently, this section will focus on the joint determination of "prices and quantities".

### 5.3.1    Conceptual framework

In the case of Spain, the existence of persistently high unemployment rates suggests that the economy does not return to equilibrium output and employment levels after cyclical disturbances that, initially, reduce output and employment and, consequently, increase unemployment. This suggests that the automatic macroeconomic adjusting mechanism does not operate satisfactorily in Spain, since a deterioration in the economic situation in general, and in the labour market in particular, does not lead, as would be expected, to a reduction in price and wage growth that would gradually restore output and employment to their initial levels. In other words, the key feature of the Spanish economy is the strong downward stickiness of prices and wages.

These arguments can be formalised in the context of the macroeconomic models that are most commonly used currently to account for changes in employment and unemployment.[5] In these models, the real wage (that is, wages in relation to the general price level) and employment are determined together as a result of the interaction between the pricing process of firms which operate in imperfectly competitive goods and services markets (on the one hand) and the wage bargaining process in an imperfectly competitive labour market (on the other). In these models, there are a series of real wage and employment levels which comprise a situation of "equilibrium" and which depend on the exogenous factors involved in price and wage-setting in the various markets. Associated with this equilibrium level of employment is an equilibrium level of unemployment, defined as the level at which the inflation rate is stabilised, generally known as NAIRU ("non-accelerating inflation rate of unemployment"). Consequently, the economy has an unemployment rate that tends to converge on the NAIRU. However, at the same time, the course of the NAIRU is affected by a series of exogenous factors over time. Thus, there are countries where the evolution of these factors leads to a relatively favourable situation, with a low NAIRU and a high equilibrium level of employment (as in the United States), and economies where the case is exactly the opposite (as in Spain).

Although it would of course be necessary to formalise the conceptual model in some detail in order to be able to analyse accurately the relationship between the different variables, for our purposes it suffices to state that the factors affecting the NAIRU and the equilibrium level of employment (and the equilibrium real wage) can be grouped under two categories: "price pressure" variables, that consider the more or less competitive nature of the goods and services markets; and "wage pressure" variables, which include all those items affecting wage pressure (such as the model of collective bargaining, firing costs, the unemployment benefit system, the taxes on earned income and the degree of regional, inter-sectoral and occupational labour mobility).

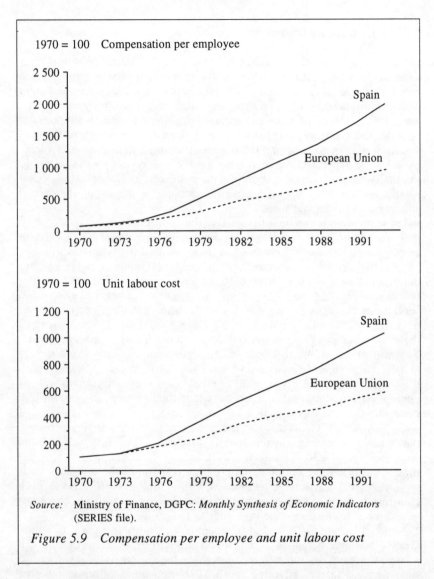

1970 = 100    Compensation per employee

1970 = 100    Unit labour cost

Source:    Ministry of Finance, DGPC: *Monthly Synthesis of Economic Indicators*
           (SERIES file).

*Figure 5.9    Compensation per employee and unit labour cost*

### 5.3.2    "Price pressure"

With regard to the "price pressure" variables, the empirical evidence and
recent experience in Spain suggest that certain parts of the goods and
services markets are plagued with rigidities. This is particularly so in
those markets that have been traditionally sheltered from competitive
pressures, either because the goods and services are not marketable

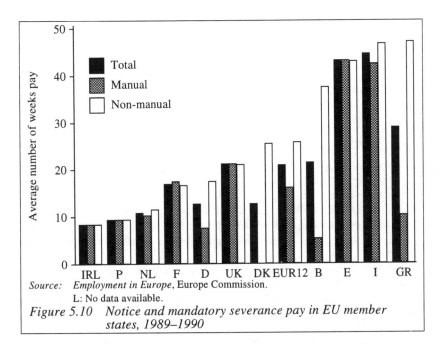

*Source: Employment in Europe*, Europe Commission.
L: No data available.

*Figure 5.10    Notice and mandatory severance pay in EU member
states, 1989–1990*

internationally or as a result of competition-limiting regulations or activities in these markets.[6]

In principle, the less competitive the structure of a goods market is, the higher the real wage level will tend to be and the lower the equilibrium level of employment. In Spain, the lack of any significant degree of competition in the services sector encourages companies to pass cost increases on to prices, as the demand curves for their products are relatively inelastic. If, furthermore, as seems to be the case in Spain, wages in the manufacturing industry are partially referenced to wages in the services industry, the upward trend in wages will tend to spread to the rest of the economy, with the resulting unfavourable effects on the overall level of employment.

### 5.3.3    "Wage pressure"

When examining the variables that determine "wage pressure" in Spain, on the basis of the evidence available, it appears that the behaviour of wages is governed by the following factors: indexing with inflation, relative insensitivity to downturns in the labour market, and wage structure rigidity when considered by sector and region.[7]

Admittedly, the various empirical studies of the Spanish labour market conducted recently, using a conceptual framework similar to the one described above,[8] have produced results that can only be considered preliminary. However, my interpretation is that these studies concur, in general lines, on the relatively significant role played in maintaining the currently low levels of employment in Spain by the following factors: the increase in labour costs caused by the "tax wedge", the lack of competition in the labour market as a result of the behaviour of employed and unemployed workers ("insiders-outsiders"), and the collective bargaining system by which the greater part of the working population's remuneration is decided.

### 5.3.3.1   Labour costs and the "tax wedge"

The econometric estimates of Spanish companies' aggregate labour demand suggest that, in the long term, this demand shows a significant degree of elasticity to variations in labour costs. However, as Figure 5.9 shows, these costs have increased considerably in Spain in recent decades. It is therefore reasonable to assume that the factors that have contributed to increasing the cost of labour have had an unfavourable effect on labour demand.

One factor that has stood out in recent empirical studies as a primary contributor to the wage costs borne by companies is the so-called "tax wedge"; that is, the difference between the total cost incurred by a company when employing a worker and the disposable income actually received by the worker. This wedge contains the employee's and employer's Social Security contributions, direct taxation of earned income and indirect taxation.

In Spain, the ongoing increase in the Social Security financing requirements and the increased tax burden recorded in the last 20 years, have led to a very rapid growth of the "tax wedge", placing it currently above that of other European Union member countries. For example, taking as a reference the difference between the total cost borne by firms when employing a worker and the worker's net wage as a proportion of the total cost, according to recent estimates, the "tax wedge" would amount to about 40% in Spain, above France (36%) and Italy (29%) but below Germany (48%).

### 5.3.3.2   Lack of competition in the labour market

Another factor that adversely affects the Spanish economy's ability to create employment is the behaviour of employed and unemployed workers. Or, to put it in more academic terms, the conduct of "insiders" and "outsiders". Indeed, the available empirical evidence seems to attribute a significant role to this type of behaviour when accounting for the downward stickiness of real wages during periods of declining employment.

To begin with the "insiders": the existence of highly protective labour legislation in Spain (see García Perea and Gómez, 1993), which makes it very expensive for firms to dismiss their workers (Figure 5.10), is an obvious factor in wage pressure. This situation, which has done very little to promote Spanish companies' competitiveness, has been aggravated in recent years as a result of the introduction of temporary contracts after 1984.

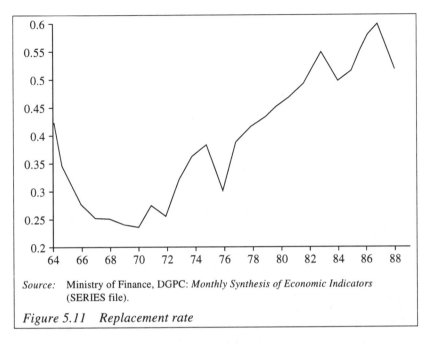

Source: Ministry of Finance, DGPC: *Monthly Synthesis of Economic Indicators* (SERIES file).

*Source:* Ministry of Finance, DGPC: *Monthly Synthesis of Economic Indicators* (SERIES file).

*Figure 5.11    Replacement rate*

Although it is true that temporary contracts initially tended automatically to moderate aggregate wage growth in Spain (as their level of remuneration was below that of the indefinite term or permanent contracts), over time they seem to have led to a "dualism" in the labour market which, paradoxically, has helped increase wage pressure and, thus, has had a negative impact on employment growth. In particular, as the studies by Bentolila and Dolado (1992, 1994) have shown, the conviction shared by workers on permanent contracts ("insiders") - who have the real power in wage bargaining - that demands for higher wages will lead primarily to the firing of workers on temporary contracts increases wage pressure and makes the employment adjustments more traumatic.

If we compare the power of the "insiders" in the Spanish economy and in the European Union member countries, this problem is particularly acute in Spain. Thus, the experience in Spain shows that the evidently desirable introduction of greater facility - that is, lower costs and less restrictive circumstances - to enable companies to adjust their workforces to changing economic conditions should be extended to all workers in the private sector, and not just to a specific group of workers, in order to avoid the development of a dual structure in the labour market, which ultimately tends to work against job creation.

As regards the role of the unemployed ("outsiders") in the functioning of the labour market, the Spanish evidence is less conclusive than the

European evidence, which seems to identify major problems arising from the insignificant role played by the unemployed in moderating wage growth during periods of recession.[9] However, evidence of the negligible influence of unemployed workers on wage growth is supplied by the fact that, empirically, the system of unemployment benefits; the lack of regional, sectoral and occupational mobility; and the mismatch between the qualifications offered by unemployed workers and companies' needs are significant contributors to the high unemployment rates in Spain.

In principle, it could be thought that the wage pressure exercised by the "insiders" would decrease considerably if the unemployed were prepared to compete with sufficiently low wages for the jobs that might become available. However, in Spain, there are a number of factors that work against such competition and, consequently, reduce the likelihood of a degree of wage moderation able to equilibrate the labour market around higher employment figures.

On the one hand, Spanish unemployment benefits are among the most generous in the European Union, considering their amount, duration and conditions required for eligibility. Furthermore, their amount related to the mean wage has increased significantly in Spain over the last two decades (Figure 5.11). This means that unemployed workers have less incentive than would be desirable to look for work.

On the other hand, it is a well-documented fact that the level of labour mobility in Spain is very low, both in absolute terms and compared with other countries, due to current labour legislation and regulations and other economic and institutional factors. Indeed, the data on inter-regional migration and job turnover show that geographical and inter-sectoral mobility have decreased in the last 20 years.[10] Although it is not easy to define the exact causes of the decrease in regional mobility, the evidence suggests that the nature of the unemployment benefits, and in particular, the regional schemes to protect the rural unemployed, the functioning of the National Institute of Employment (INEM) and the housing problem are, among other factors, responsible for the current low level of mobility. Likewise, the above-mentioned legislation protecting job stability, the limitations on certain types of employment contracts, and the marked mismatch between the professional qualifications of the unemployed and firms' needs also tend to limit labour mobility, reducing in turn the competition for the jobs available.

### 5.3.3.3   Collective bargaining

The wages of most Spanish workers are set each year by collective bargaining. This bargaining is organised by sectors and provinces, with the "minimum levels agreed" being binding for the firms belonging to each sector and province. Consequently, a minimum reference wage floor is established which tends to be exceeded in the agreements signed by the various firms.

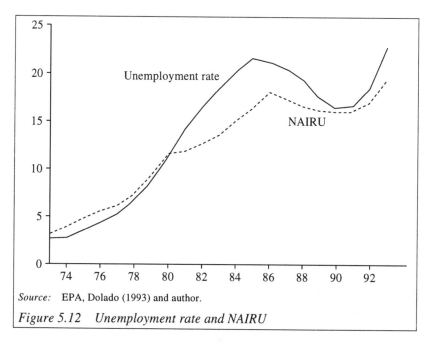

*Source:* EPA, Dolado (1993) and author.

*Figure 5.12 Unemployment rate and NAIRU*

It is likely that the wage-bargaining method used in Spain is the main cause of the insufficient degree of differentiation perceived in wage structure across sectors. As a result, real wage growth in a particular sector does not relate to any significant extent to the improvements in that sector's productivity. However, the bargaining model used does not seem to provide the benefits that would be expected from a relatively corporatist system: namely, greater wage moderation, since the unions would be aware that a lack of wage moderation would lead to a higher inflation rate without any positive effects on their members' purchasing power or on employment. In fact, according to the classic analysis performed by Calmfors and Drifill (1988), the Spanish economy would be situated in a clearly unsatisfactory position midway between the two extreme options: complete centralisation-synchronisation with nationwide bargaining, and complete decentralisation with bargaining at the firm level.

To summarise, this section has discussed the existence of a large number of structural rigidities in major segments of the Spanish goods and services markets and of the labour market which seriously limit competition and, consequently, reduce the downward flexibility of prices and wages during periods of economic downturn. This, in turn, interferes with the macroeconomic adjustment mechanism by which prices and wages automatically tend to moderate in such situations, favouring the return to initial output and employment levels. Clearly, then, an absolutely indispensable prerequisite for improving wage and price flexibility is to introduce a greater degree of competition into the goods and services market and the labour market.

### 5.3.4   NAIRU

By way of example of the adverse behaviour of Spanish markets, there follows an updated estimate of the Spanish economy's structural unemployment rate or NAIRU,[11] obtained by Dolado (1993) from the structural model estimated by De Lamo and Dolado (1991). As stated previously, the NAIRU is the unemployment rate at which the inflation rate is stabilised and which is basically determined by the variables affecting price and wage pressure. Thus, as the behaviour of these variables becomes more adverse and price and wage pressure increases, the economy's NAIRU will also increase, which means that the unemployment rate will have to remain at relatively high levels in order to avoid increasing inflationary pressures.

Figure 5.12 shows the combined course of the actual unemployment rate and the structural unemployment rate or NAIRU for Spain during the period 1973-93. The line representing the course of the NAIRU has been estimated by Dolado (1993) using a model that attempts to quantify the relative weight of the price and wage pressure variables mentioned in Section 5.2 of this paper. As can be seen, during the period 1973-93 the Spanish economy's structural unemployment rate increased at roughly the same rate as the actual unemployment rate, thus confirming the structural nature of the employment and unemployment problem in Spain.

In 1993, the estimated structural unemployment rate (NAIRU) was 19.5%, while the actual unemployment rate was about 23%. Even after allowing a certain leeway to take into account the uncertainty surrounding the estimation of the NAIRU, the sheer size of the NAIRU indicates that solving the problem of unemployment necessarily involves implementing structural economic policies that bring down the NAIRU. Otherwise, any attempt to reduce the unemployment rate using solely demand-expansion policies would be brought up short very quickly by the structural unemployment rate, giving rise to inflationary pressures.

### 5.4.   CHALLENGES FOR THE FUTURE

The analysis of the past and present situation of employment and unemployment in Spain in the previous sections of this paper has highlighted two phenomena. First, that the Spanish economy has a very limited ability to create employment in a sustained fashion; and second, that in the presence of unfavourable economic shocks, the adjustments finally fall - in spite of the laws protecting employment - on employment rather than on wages. Consequently, the employment situation is far from satisfactory in both the short and long term.

The situation is even more worrying when, taking into account the current high level of unemployment, we turn to examine the main structural factors that may affect the Spanish unemployment rate in the future, either as a result of the growth of the labour force or of the evolution of employment.

### 5.4.1 Labour participation

As regards the labour force, although it is true that population growth has progressively fallen in recent years and is presently very similar to that of other European Union member countries, it is also a fact that the participation rate of the working age population is still relatively low compared with most of the European Union member countries, due mainly to the lower participation of Spanish women. Consequently, it would not be unreasonable to suppose that, in the future, the participation rate of the female population, and thus of the population as a whole, will increase, bringing Spain closer to European levels. A recent study by Bover and Arellano (1994) finds that certain structural factors, such as the higher level of education and the lower birth rate, have a significant influence on the participation rate of the female population. It can therefore be inferred that as new cohorts of more educated women replace the older cohorts, and as the level of education improves in Spain, the participation rate and, ceteris paribus, the labour force will also tend to increase.

### 5.4.2 Agriculture

Another major structural factor is the likely continuation of the restructuring process in the agricultural sector. As was already discussed in Section 5.1, during the last 30 years rural employment has fallen considerably, with more than three million jobs lost in this sector. However, there is no evidence to support the belief that this process has run its course: the proportion of rural employment out of total employment is still 10% in Spain, which is almost double that of the European Union countries, excepting Portugal and Sweden. Consequently, it is reasonable to assume that agricultural employment will continue to fall in Spain in the medium term. Without doubt, the existence of a Common Agricultural Policy in the European Union is a factor that will have a significant impact on this trend.

### 5.4.3 Single market[12]

Another structural factor that will significantly affect the behaviour of the Spanish economy in the future, and of employment in particular, is the recent creation of the Single European Market, which considerably increases foreign competition in the areas of trade and finance. Indeed, according to recent studies, increased foreign competition will foreseeably cause a restructuring of the Spanish production system over the next few years.

In principle, this restructuring should lead to a transfer of resources (capital and labour) from the sectors producing internationally non-tradeable goods to sectors producing internationally tradeable goods, and from certain tradeable goods sectors to others. Likewise, the increasing financial integration between Spain and the rest of the world will not only help strengthen common links between financial conditions in Spain and abroad, but will also enhance the level of competition within the Spanish financial system.

It is therefore obvious that the recent creation of the Single Market is a factor of vital economic importance for Spain and is associated with a series of significant potential benefits in the medium and long term which may improve its capacity for economic growth and employment generation. These benefits are the result, on the one hand, of refocusing the Spanish production system in order to utilise more efficiently the country's comparative advantages and to exploit existing economies of scale and scope; and, on the other hand, of the improvement in the financial systems, level of efficiency.

However, the transition toward a more open economic system and the inter-sectoral reallocation of labour and capital also involves adjustment costs that may affect employment. Therefore, one of the main challenges currently facing Spanish society is the need to adopt behaviours that will enable it to minimise adjustment costs and lay the foundations for attaining the potential benefits associated with the creation of the Single Market.

Unfortunately, the inadequate functioning of the Spanish economy, as shown primarily by the downward rigidity of prices and wages and the unfavourable behaviour of employment, suggests that, unless certain reforms are implemented promptly, it will not be possible to achieve either goal.

First, the rigidities present in those goods and services markets that are still sheltered from competition may considerably hamper the desirable reallocation of resources from non-tradeable goods to tradeable sectors. This reallocation is necessary if the potential benefits from the expansion of the foreign market are to be attained. In particular, the existence of excessive prices and profit margins in services sectors is one of the obstacles impeding an efficient reallocation of resources within the framework of an increasingly open economy.

Second, the absence of a sufficient degree of wage moderation as a result of the inadequate functioning of the Spanish labour market may prevent the above-mentioned medium- and long-term benefits from materialising, by eroding the comparative advantage in labour costs that Spain still offers compared with most of its European Union partners, and by squeezing the profitability of industrial companies, thus impeding the foreign direct investment required to improve Spain's human and technological capital stock.

Third, the wage structure's high degree of inflexibility in following more closely the varying evolution in the productivity of different sectors and the low degree of inter-sectoral, occupational and regional mobility of labour may significantly hamper the transfer of labour from shrinking sectors to expanding sectors, thereby increasing adjustment costs through the resulting increase in unemployment and excess production capacity.

Finally, the efficiency of the Spanish financial system at financing at a reasonable cost the expansion of the production capacity of certain sectors and the restructuring of others is impaired by the high interest rates that are due to the high public deficit.

In sum, the creation of the Single Market will only have a positive impact on the Spanish economy and employment growth if the increased competition it brings to the tradeable goods sectors and to certain segments of the financial system is accompanied by suitable structural reforms aimed at increasing wage and price flexibility, and by macroeconomic policies aimed at increasing nominal stability. Otherwise, there is a serious danger of increasing duality between competitive and sheltered markets: a duality which would result in very high adjustment costs in terms of growth and employment and which might even prevent the potential medium- and long-term benefits the Single Market may bring to Spain from materialising.

### 5.4.4 Economic and Monetary Union

The final structural factor affecting the future growth of employment in the Spanish economy is the creation of an Economic and Monetary Union, whose legal principles are set forth in the Treaty of Maastricht. Generally speaking, Spain stands to gain considerable benefits from membership in the Economic and Monetary Union in terms of a greater degree of integration and a greater nominal stability. However, there are also potential costs arising from the impossibility of resorting to monetary and exchange rate policies to offset the negative effects that real asymmetrical shocks may have on the Spanish economy. Consequently, with increasing price and wage flexibility, the benefits of membership in the Economic and Monetary Union are also greater and the costs are lower. This greater flexibility will also help enhance, over the next few years, the effectiveness of macroeconomic policies designed to achieve convergence and thus prevent Spain from falling behind in the process of European integration, a situation that would be extremely undesirable in both economic and non-economic terms.

## 5.5. ECONOMIC POLICIES

There is no doubt that the factors described in the previous section pose a considerable challenge to which the Spanish economy is obliged to respond if it is to promote the future growth of output and employment. However, as discussed in Sections 5.1 and 5.2 of this paper, the unsatisfactory functioning of the goods and service markets and of the labour market, reflected in the high unemployment rates and the considerable degrees of price and wage rigidity, raise a considerable obstacle that must be overcome before the challenge can be faced.

On the basis of the above, the core ideas on which any job creation policy in Spain should be erected are the following. First, as the employment problem is closely linked with the existence of an inflationary bias in the Spanish economy, this bias must be eradicated in order to reduce unemployment. Second, as a consequence of the first point, job creation policies should go beyond the labour market as such and also address the goods market. And, finally, given the multiple causes limiting job creation in Spain, the measures required to attack these causes are likewise manifold and highly varied, addressing both the micro- and macroeconomic spheres.

In light of the conclusions obtained in the previous sections, there follows a description of a number of economic policy measures that might help improve the functioning of the Spanish economy and, in particular, increase its ability to attain sustained growth and employment creation.

### 5.5.1    Macroeconomic policy

The most important contribution that macroeconomic policy can make to the employment generation process is to focus firmly and credibly on achieving nominal stability, which is an indispensable prerequisite for achieving sustained economic growth.

With respect to monetary policy, the Bank of Spain's Autonomy Law unequivocally states that the primary goal of monetary policy is price stability. As regards fiscal policy, the high levels of public deficit and debt make the design of structural measures to control the deficit, founded primarily on the containment of public expenditure, the priority goal. Thus, the general lines of budgetary consolidation indicated by the authorities in the recent review of the Convergence Programme are encouraging; one can only hope that they are followed to the letter. The drive toward fiscal consolidation over the next few years is vital in order to lend credibility to the general framework of macroeconomic policy and make it more effective in achieving nominal stability, so as to enable fulfilment of the convergence condition established in the Treaty of Maastricht for membership of the Economic and Monetary Union.

In order to restore the health of Spain's public finances, the authorities should successfully control the growing weight of the regional governments in the Administration's overall deficit; added strength should be given to the legal and administrative resources available to reduce tax evasion; the current loopholes in budget discipline and control should be eliminated; and, finally, the Public Administration should be overhauled with a view to increasing its cost-effectiveness.

## 5.5.2   Structural policies

As the structural rigidities in goods and services markets and in the labour market are significant negative contributors to the job creation process in Spain, the necessary reforms should be undertaken promptly in order to increase price and wage sensitivity to periods of economic downturn.

In the goods and services markets, one vital task is to improve the degree of competition in a large number of economic sectors so as to make the pricing process more sensitive to competitive conditions. In order to achieve this goal, a large number of activities must be deregulated; the presence of the public sector, as producer or supplier of services in those areas (such as education, health, telecommunications, transport, etc.) where the private sector is able to offer similar services under satisfactory conditions, must be reduced; and the privatisation process should be selectively reactivated. Recent measures to liberalise the telecommunications sector and certain segments of air transport are steps in the right direction which should be continued in the future.

As regards the labour market, in recent months a package of reforms has been introduced and has already started to have favourable effects on employment. However, the scale of the employment and unemployment problem in Spain is such that further reforms are still required in certain areas:

1)   It would be desirable to re-examine the collective bargaining model in order to better adapt it to the varying economic conditions observed in firms. Thus, formulas could be considered that enable binding agreements to be reached at firm level, without having to accept, a priori, the minimum wage levels imposed by sectoral agreements. This would help eliminate the "inflationary bias" in wage growth, with its negative impact on labour demand, and improve economic efficiency by matching real wage growth to firms' real productivity.

2)   As the behaviour of "insiders" biases wages upward, with the resulting contractive effect on employment, it is important to reduce their bargaining power. The most direct way of achieving this would be to amend the legislation governing the termination of employment contracts with a view to lowering the monetary and administrative costs that firms must bear when implementing staff

cuts. The measures enacted a few months ago, which widen the range of situations under which companies may make such cuts, are a step in the right direction.

3)    Strengthening the disposition and ability of the unemployed to compete for the jobs available may help in the effort to eradicate the upward bias of wages. Consequently, it would be very desirable to review the duration, amount of, and eligibility for unemployment benefits in order to increase unemployed workers' motivation to find a job instead of subsidising their current status. These measures would complement those implemented in the recent labour reform, which have consisted of improving the efficiency of labour market agents and approving the apprenticeship and part-time contracts.

4)    It would also be advisable to lower labour costs by reducing the "tax wedge". One such desirable measure would be to lower Social Security contributions, using alternative sources of financing that have less disturbing effects on the job-creation process to recoup the lost income. The rate at which this reduction can ultimately be made will depend on the Spanish economy's inflationary trends, since increasing the VAT rate would affect, at least temporarily, the inflation rate.

Although this is by no means an exhaustive list of economic policy options to improve the functioning of the labour market, it includes, I believe, the most pressing. One could add others, such as improving the occupational training processes, removing the barriers to the creation of new firms and promoting Research and Development, that might, in the long term, favour the economy's employment creation and growth processes.[13]

Ten years ago, Spain was initiating an analogous process of recovery as that which is underway today, after emerging from a long and deep recession, and the fiscal consolidation and structural reform policies advocated at that time by numerous economists were in line, in general, with those currently proposed. However, the opportunity offered by the extraordinary period of economic growth in Spain in the second half of the 1980s to correct the underlying problems with the necessary diligence was lost - in part because economic growth hid, temporarily, the true scale of these problems.

Let us then heed the lessons of our recent past and not repeat the mistake of leaving for tomorrow what should have been done yesterday.

## NOTES

*    The opinions contained in this article are purely personal.
1.    The trends in GDP and approximate employment have been obtained using the

Hodrick-Prescott procedure.

2. It should be remembered, however, that the introduction of fixed-term employment contracts in 1984 has helped increase the degree to which cyclical changes in employment follow cyclical changes in GDP and reduce the asymmetry in the response of employment to periods of expansion and contraction.

3. Bean (1994) analyses in analogous terms the evolution of unemployment in the United States, the European Union, Japan and the EFTA.

4. See the Bank of Spain's 1993 Annual Report.

5. See, among others, Bean, Layard and Nickell (1987), Layard, Nickell and Jackman (1991) and Bean (1994).

6. Raymond Bara (1992) and Alvarez, Jareño and Sebastián (1993), among others, model the behaviour of the prices of industrial goods and services in Spain.

7. See Andrés and García (1992) and Viñals (1992).

8. The most interesting studies on this aspect are those of Dolado, Malo de Molina and Zabalza (1986), De Lamo and Dolado (1991) and Jimeno and Toharia (1992).

9. This problem is analysed in depth in Andrés and García (1992).

10. See, among others, Bentolila and Dolado (1991), Revenga (1991) and Bover and Antolín (1993).

11. My thanks to Juan José Dolado for providing the NAIRU estimate shown in the figure. See also Dolado (1993).

12. This section is based on Viñals (1993).

13. A detailed analysis of these macroeconomic policies can be found in the OECD report (1994).

# REFERENCES

Alvarez, L.J., Jareño J. and M. Sebastián (1993), "Salarios públicos, salarios privados e inflación dual", Working Paper No. 9320, Research Department, Bank of Spain.

Andrés, J.and J. García (1992), "Principales rasgos del mercado de trabajo ante 1992", in J. Viñals (ed.), *La economía española ante el Mercado Unico Europeo*, Alianza Economía.

Albi, E., (ed.) (1992), *Europa y la competividad de la economía española*, Ariel.

Bank of Spain (1993), *Annual Report*.

Bean, C. (1994), "European Unemployment: A survey", *Journal of Economic Literature*, June.

Bean, C., Layard, R. and S. Nickell (eds) (1987), *The rise in unemployment*, Oxford, Basil Blackwell.

Bentolila, S. and J.J. Dolado (1991), "Mismatch and internal migration in Spain, 1962-86", in F. Padoa-Schioppa (ed.), *Mismatch and Labour Mobility*, Cambridge University Press.

Bentolila, S. and J.J. Dolado (1992), "La contratación temporal y la formación de salarios en las empresas manufactureras españolas", *Boletín Económico*, Bank of Spain, December.

Bentolila, S. and J.J. Dolado (1994), "Labour flexibility and wages: lessons from Spain", *Economic Policy*, 18.

Bover, O. and P. Antolín (1993), "Migraciones regionales en España", *Boletín Económico*, Bank of Spain, May.

Bover, O. and M. Arellano (1994), "Female Labour Participation in the 1980's: the Case of Spain", Bank of Spain, mimeo.

Calmfors, L. and J. Drifill (1988), "Bargaining structure, corporatism and macroeconomic performance", *Economic Policy*, 6.

De Lamo, A. and J.J. Dolado (1991), "Un modelo del mercado de trabajo y la restricción de oferta en la economía española", Working Paper No. 9116, Research Department, Bank of Spain.

Dolado, J.J. (1993), "Análisis y determinación de la tasa de paro de equilibrio", in *El mercado de trabajo español: reforma y creación de empleo*, Círculo de Empresarios, Boletín 57.

Dolado, J.J., Malo de Molina, J.L. and A. Zabalza (1986), "Spanish industrial unemployment: some explanatory factors", *Económica, Supplement*, 53.

García Perea, P. and R. Gómez (1993), "Aspectos institucionales del mercado de trabajo español en comparación con otros países comunitarios", *Boletín Económico*, Bank of Spain, September.

Jimeno, J.F. and T. Toharia (1992), "El mercado de trabajo español en el proceso de covergencia hacia la unión económica y monetaria europea", *Papeles de Economía Española*, 53.

Layard, R., Nickell, S. and R. Jackman (1991), *Unemployment: Macroeconomic Performance and the Labour Market*, Oxford University Press.

OECD (1994), *The OECD Jobs Study*.

Raymond Bara, J.L. (1992), "La inflación dual en España: comportamiento de los precios en los sectores industriales y servicios", *Papeles de Economía Española*, 52/53.

Revenga, A. (1991), "La liberalización económica y la distribución de la renta: la experiencia española", *Moneda y Crédito*, 192.

Sebastián, C. (1994), *Como crear empleo en una economía competitiva*, Círculo de Empresarios, Monograph.

Viñals, J. (ed.) (1992), *La economía española ante el Mercado Unico Europeo*, Alianza Economía.

Viñals, J. (1993), "El reto europeo: riesgos y oportunidades para la economía española", *Papeles de la Economía Española*, 57.

# 6      Creating Employment in Spain: Labour Market Imperfections

## Carlos Sebastián

---

## 6.1.   INTRODUCTION

The Spanish economy has the highest unemployment rate in Western Europe (see Figure 6.1). Statistical problems aside - and they should be neither ignored nor magnified (the Active Population Survey, or EPA, is an excellent survey) - the high unemployment rate in Spain is due to two largely unrelated factors: the jump in the active population during the eighties and the Spanish economy's inability to generate a high rate of employment growth (see Figure 6.2).

The strong active population growth, in turn, has two causes: the baby boom in the sixties and the increasing presence of women in the labour market from the late seventies onward. However, the high unemployment rate is not due so much to this as to the second factor. Simply by way of illustration, if we were to project the growth in active population, ironing out the jump in the eighties, the unemployment rate would still be higher than those recorded in the other industrialised countries (see Figure 6.3).

On the other hand, the active population could have grown further if labour demand had pulled harder, as the participation rate has been shown to be dependent on job supply.

## 6.2.   THE INABILITY TO GENERATE EMPLOYMENT

The Spanish economy's inability to generate jobs at any significant level - a direct consequence of which is the fact that the level of employment did not exceed 1974 levels at any time during the period of growth during the latter half of the eighties - can be adequately illustrated by comparing, on the one hand, the growth of the GDP to unemployment and, on the other,

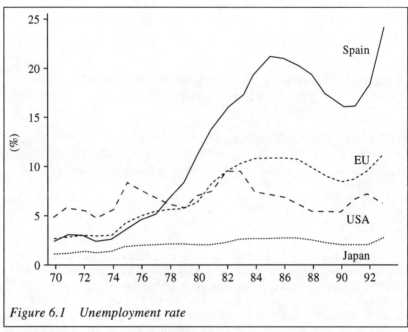

*Figure 6.1    Unemployment rate*

*Figure 6.2    Labour force and employment in Spain*

*Figure 6.3   Labour force and employment in Spain*

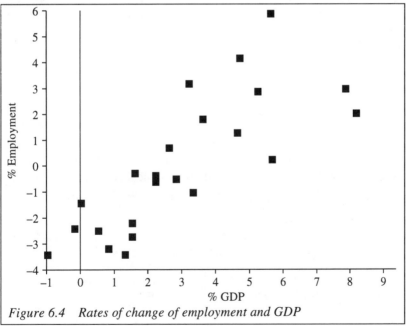

*Figure 6.4   Rates of change of employment and GDP*

the experience in Spain to that in other industrialised countries. The first comparison (Figure 6.4) shows that there was no net job creation in any year during the period 1971-93 with a GDP growth rate of less than 3% (with the exception of 1985, when the GDP growth rate exceeded 2.5%). The second comparison (Table 6.1) shows that the relationship between GDP variation and employment variation is significantly less favourable in Spain than in the United States, France and Germany in all the periods reviewed. Particularly striking is the fact that between 1974 and 1990, Spain's GDP grew by more than 47% but employment actually fell by 0.4%. This situation is just the opposite of what occurred in the United States and differs from what occurred in both European countries as well.

The reason for this poor employment growth in Spain is to be sought in the high level and strong growth of the user cost of labour, together with certain structural problems in the Spanish production system.

The excessive protectionism and high degree of interventionism that marked the Spanish economy during the Franco regime, even during the period of rapid growth (1960-74), gave rise to a fairly inefficient production structure which the traumatic experience of the seventies (oil crisis and high wage increases) made all too apparent by showing how certain industries directly and indirectly employing a large number of people had increased to unsustainable proportions. The drastic reduction in these industries' size meant the destruction of a large number of non-viable jobs that had been created under the wing of State protection. The inter-industry changes that took place in the Spanish economy between 1970 and 1982, due to changes in relative prices and the gradual dismantling of barriers to foreign trade, have led to a gradual drop in labour requirements per unit of aggregate output. Although this is not the main cause of the slow employment growth, it has compounded other factors which we will analyse in the following.

## 6.3.    THE USER COST OF LABOUR

Given a stock of active capital, a certain technological level, and prices for other production factors in real terms, labour demand will depend on user labour cost in real terms, that is, the cost of using the labour factor divided by the price of the goods produced.

There are situations in which labour demand is affected by other factors, giving rise to what are known in economic analysis as shifts in the labour demand curve. Other situations arise in which, due to market imperfections, producers cannot find their place on the demand curve: that is, they would like to employ more hours of work than they actually can.

The former situation is caused by changing uncertainty, as perceived by corporate decision-makers, and by changes in a company's financial circumstances. Both factors, whose significance for real corporate decisions (production, employment and investment) is not always sufficiently stressed,[1] exhibit a markedly cyclical behaviour, which means that the labour demand curve undergoes major shifts during periods of economic fluctuation. This type of situation may also be triggered by productivity "shocks" which, according to the real business cycle theory, are the cause of fluctuations.

The second type of situation is seen to occur in two cases. The first arises when the prices of goods and services are rigid, leading to situations of excess supply - more common in recessions - and companies are unable both to sell the desired quantity of goods and to employ the desired quantity of labour hours. The second case arises when, with current wages, there is no labour supply to meet the demand. This is caused by imperfections in the labour market, usually supply rigidities and geographical and occupational mismatches (between labour supply and demand). Normally, these situations exert upward pressures on wages but do not manage to eliminate the excess demand; they typically occur during the upward phase of business cycles. The graphs in Figure 6.5 clearly illustrate the three situations just discussed.

The user cost of labour consists of three components: wage costs, non-wage labour costs and implicit labour costs. The level and growth of all three of these have clearly worked against employment generation.

### 6.3.1   Wages

We propose initially to discuss the growth of wage costs in Spain. The first point to remember is that these costs increased drastically during the political transition of the late seventies, to such an extent that we can safely say that the Spanish economy experienced not so much an oil shock as a wage shock (see Table 6.2).

During the eighties, not only did the economy fail to regain the ground lost in the political transition, but labour costs grew at a rate that was excessively high in view of the growth in productivity and the trends in our competitors' costs. Figure 6.6 shows that the Spanish industry's unit labour costs (labour costs per unit of production) increased 75% more over a 12-year period (1981-92) than the US industry's costs, and almost 40% more than those of the countries which were EEC members at the beginning of the decade.

As Table 6.3 shows, this has been caused by both a greater wage growth and a less favourable course taken by the other elements that make up the unit labour cost (other non-wage labour costs and productivity).

The fact that, as stated earlier, labour demand shifts and the occurrence of greater job destruction in Spain during the 1974-84 recession was not concurrent with the greater growth in real wages (job destruction increased significantly after 1979 and the period of greatest real wage growth was between 1974 and 1978) have led some authors to deny the existence of a

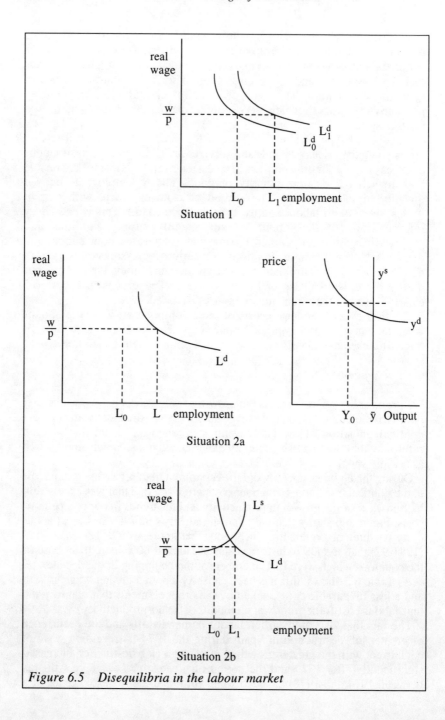

*Figure 6.5   Disequilibria in the labour market*

Table 6.1    Change in GDP and Employment 1974 – 1990 (per cent)

| 1974–85 | GDP | Employment |
|---------|-----|------------|
| Spain   | 18.5 | −18.3 |
| USA     | 31.8 | 24.4 |
| Germany | 23.1 | −5.0 |
| France  | 25.5 | 0.1 |

| 1985–90 | GDP | Employment |
|---------|-----|------------|
| Spain   | 24.5 | 16.1 |
| USA     | 14.0 | 10.1 |
| Germany | 17.0 | 11.9 |
| France  | 17.1 | 4.6 |

| 1974–90 | GDP | Employment |
|---------|-----|------------|
| Spain   | 47.6 | −0.4 |
| USA     | 50.2 | 36.8 |
| Germany | 42.8 | 6.3 |
| France  | 46.9 | 4.7 |

Table 6.2    The Oil Shock 1974–81 (per cent)

| | SPAIN | GERMANY | USA |
|---|-------|---------|-----|
| Oil price ($) | 228.8 | 228.8 | 228.8 |
| Real oil price * [a] | 25.2 | 109.9 | 78.3 |
| Nominal wage ** | 280.6 | 57.1 | 72.1 |
| Real wage ** | 41.7 | 28.7 | 1.9 |
| Inflation * | 214.1 | 37.8 | 84.4 |
| Money supply * | 181.7 | 53.9 | 82.9 |
| Gross domestic product ** | 9.8 | 17.6 | 19.3 |
| Employment * | −11.8 | −2.6 | 18.9 |

* 1974–81
** 1975–81
[a] Price in national currency deflated by CPI

*Table 6.3   Unit Labour Cost in Industry (1981–92)*

|  | ULC % | Wage % | Differentials * SPAIN Versus | |
| --- | --- | --- | --- | --- |
|  |  |  | ULC % | WAGE % |
| Spain | 94.5 | 175.1 | – | – |
| USA | 15.3 | 55.3 | 68.7 | 40.0 |
| Germany | 41.5 | 81.5 | 37.4 | 19.8 |
| France | 43.7 | 95.5 | 35.3 | 11.3 |

* The differences between the wage differential and the ULC differential are due to differences in the rate of change of other labour costs and productivity.

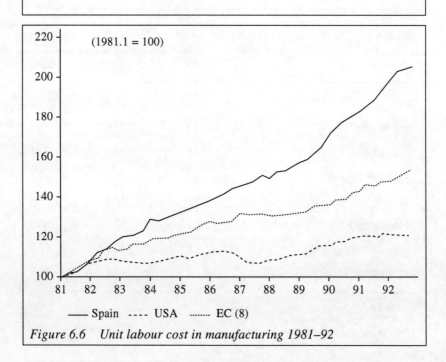

*Figure 6.6   Unit labour cost in manufacturing 1981–92*

negative relationship between employment and real wage. However, the evidence in support of the negative relationship is fairly conclusive, both in Spain and in other economies. In Spain, the elasticity of (long-term) labour demand with respect to labour cost in real terms ranges between -0.5 and -1.0.[2] Thus, the growth of labour costs is a highly significant factor, in the medium and long term, for accounting for the poor growth in employment.

The mid-seventies recession can be more easily understood in light of an explanation of the behaviour of wages and employment during that period which, in fact, only serves to confirm the negative relationship between wages and employment. Job destruction was limited during the early years of recession, in spite of great wage increases. Indeed, destruction of industrial employment did not start until 1978, and, even then, the rate of destruction was initially slow. Companies kept their staff numbers virtually unchanged, in spite of the wage increases and decreased output, for several reasons: 1) high redundancy costs, due to the restrictive labour legislation then in force and to the climate of sociopolitical uncertainty; 2) the existence of negative real interest rates; 3) the likely presence of highly inelastic expectations regarding the course of factor prices, that is, the idea (common when an unexpected jump occurs in a variable) that the increase in factor prices (energy and labour) was not permanent. These three reasons combined explain the considerable lag in the adjustment of employment levels.

In 1979, two new events served to exacerbate an already serious situation. On the one hand, there was the second oil crisis, which doubled again the price of crude oil; on the other, the implementation of a stricter monetary policy after 1978, with the result that in 1979-80, real interest rates became increasingly positive. Since a higher energy bill was not financed by monetary expansion measures, and, moreover, since the oil price increase was not passed on in full, corporate profits were squeezed still tighter. The change in monetary policy and its effect on interest rates brought to the surface the financial difficulties affecting companies due to their lower output and internal imbalances (labour, energy and financial). The need to accept drastic employment adjustment, together with the associated costs, then became urgent. The new environment and, probably, the changed prospects, in the sense that the increase in wage and energy costs were now perceived as a more permanent situation, led many companies to suspend payments or go bankrupt. These two facts - staff cuts in the companies that survived and the disappearance of the less fortunate ones - account for the marked job destruction that took place in Spanish industry between 1979 and 1984.[3] The delay in making this adjustment - caused by high redundancy costs in tandem with negative interest rates - is the main reason why Spain lagged behind other countries with respect to economic recovery.

Returning to more recent experiences, the growth in compensation per worker has increased above the wage levels agreed upon in collective

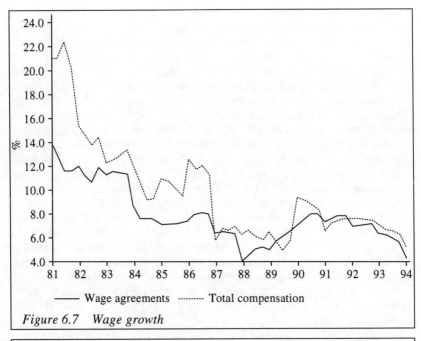

*Figure 6.7    Wage growth*

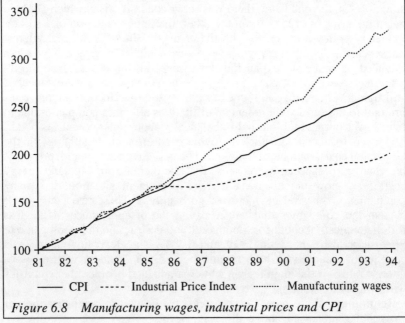

*Figure 6.8    Manufacturing wages, industrial prices and CPI*

bargaining. However, this "wage drift" has levelled off in recent years (see Figure 6.7). Wages in Spanish industry have grown at a higher rate than industrial prices, and this trend has become more marked in recent years (1988-92), due to the overvaluation of the peseta. Therefore, the real wage levels affecting labour demand have increased considerably. Real wages in terms of consumer prices have also increased, albeit not to the same extent (see Figure 6.8).

The explanation of the dissimilar behaviour of industrial and consumer prices is to be found in the changes in the tax wedge and in the phenomenon of dual inflation, which has become very pronounced in Spain in recent years. The prices of services have evidenced a more inflationary behaviour than those of industrial goods, and even those of the consumer price of industrial goods (measured from the industrial price component of the CPI). This is due to the greater weight of labour costs in services - hence the significant role played by wages in price increases - and the lower degree of competition in the services sector, both because of the non-tradeable nature of their products (which protects them from foreign competition) and because of the regulations governing these sectors.[4]

A particularly prominent feature of wage behaviour in Spain is a lack of sensitivity to the dynamism of the labour market. A series of studies carried out in the mid-eighties, summarised in Dolado and Malo de Molina (1985), provides comparable estimates for several countries of the rigid response of real wages (in terms of consumer prices) to the unemployment rate, mostly referring to the period 1968-84. These studies show that wages are more rigid in Europe than in other OECD countries, and that wage rigidity in Spain is greater than in most European countries. Empirical evidence presented by Layard, Nickell and Jackman (1991) confirms this impression.

The situation did not improve between 1982 and 1992. In European countries, and particularly in Spain, wages grew without regard to labour market developments. Thus, wage growth was acyclical as opposed to the markedly cyclical behaviour of employment. This is in sharp contrast to the United States; Figure 6.9 shows how the nominal wage growth rate in the American economy was higher (with a small timelag) when employment was growing and lower when employment growth began to taper off. This impression is fully confirmed when the phenomenon is analysed econometrically. Wages in the US follow a strikingly cyclical pattern.

On the other hand, as illustrated by Figure 6.10 - which plots the same variables in Spain - Spanish wages follow no cyclical pattern, and their growth has no apparent bearing on the growth of employment. The same phenomenon is observed in other European economies.

Another important feature of wage-setting in Spain is the narrow wage spread, both horizontal (by fields of activity) and vertical (by job category). The wage spread narrowed drastically between 1973 and 1977,

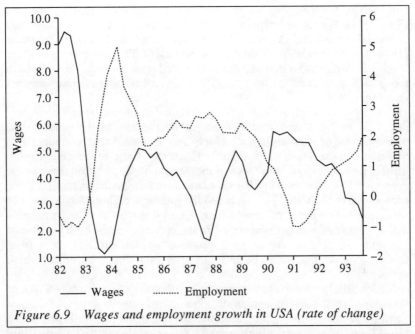

*Figure 6.9   Wages and employment growth in USA (rate of change)*

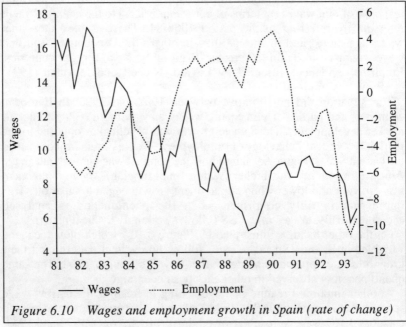

*Figure 6.10   Wages and employment growth in Spain (rate of change)*

although it widened slightly again in the eighties.[5] The data on wage distribution, published by the INE (National Institute for Statistics) for 1988, show that wage differences hinge mainly on sex and type of employment contract, and only to a very minor extent on the branch of activity.[6] The minimal wage spread between different branches is a consequence of the wage slides brought about by occupational reclassification and changes in the composition of employment. The spread by job category is likewise narrow. The (minor) increases in the indicators of vertical spread are basically due to increases in the compensation of higher-ranking positions, which are often excluded from the collective bargaining process.

A striking feature of the wage structure is the contrast between the great proportion of fixed remuneration and the small proportion of performance-related remuneration. This trend, which is currently growing more pronounced and which illustrates the low priority given to productivity incentives, runs completely counter to the practice prevailing in other European countries, where the variable component - governed by corporate productivity and performance - is increasingly gaining in significance.[7]

The cause of this divergence between Spain and the rest of Europe is to be found, as we will discuss further on, in the degree of centralisation of collective bargaining. In those European countries where compensation schemes have been linked most closely to productivity and profitability benchmarks, a progressive decentralisation of the collective bargaining process has ensued, increasingly occurring at company level.

The concurrence of labour supply and unsatisfied labour demand is due not only to the lack of geographical mobility and the unemployment protection system - both these issues are addressed in later pages - but also to the poor performance of the official agency in the labour market. Until the recent reform, this activity was the monopoly of the inefficient state employment agency (INEM) and access to private companies was vetoed. This unfavourable situation not only affected corporate productivity and employment levels but also hampered the translation of the pressure of unemployed workers into wage moderation.

Another factor affecting wage rigidity is the low intensity of job-seeking by the unemployed. For almost half of the jobless in Spain, registering themselves as unemployed at INEM is the only search activity undertaken. The large number of long-term unemployed and the high level of unemployment benefits could be behind this lacklustre attitude.

Finally, in a technologically changing world, training plays a vital role in matching professional skills to production requirements. There is a certain consensus in Spain that the public training system is inadequate, not only because of the relatively small budget allocation but also because an excessively centralised management is no help in matching teaching with real needs.

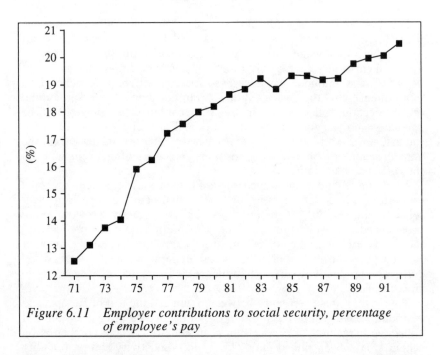

*Figure 6.11    Employer contributions to social security, percentage of employee's pay*

### 6.3.2    Non-wage costs

The other items comprising the cost of labour use are non-wage labour costs and implicit labour costs.

The former basically consist of Social Security contributions. In Spain, these are very high in comparison with other countries and have increased still more over the last 20 years. Figure 6.11 plots the course of employers' Social Security contributions as a percentage of employees' pay (obtained from National Accounts). The impression gained from less aggregate data is one of a much larger percentage of employers' contributions. Data obtained from the Central de Balances for the period 1983-87 indicate that employers' contributions represented, on average, 28% of total wages and salaries paid by companies; the figure most often reported by companies (the sample's mode) was 33%. Figure 6.11 gives an idea of the evolution over time of this major item of wage costs: it increases significantly between 1974 and 1983, then levels off and starts to rise again in recent years.

### 6.3.3    Implicit labour costs

Implicit labour costs represent an economic valuation of the limitations imposed on companies, which prevent them from making optimal use of the labour factor.

There are three types of limitations, which give rise to three types of implicit labour costs: those that operate on the decisions to modify the quantity of labour used, those that operate on the decisions to vary the conditions under which workers provide their services and those that operate on the terms of employment contracts.

The first type of implicit labour cost basically consists of redundancy costs. These include not only the total severance payments that must be made to the redundant employee but also the conflicts and disruptions of the company's production activity that may arise as a result of the announcement to terminate a certain number of contracts. Within a context of uncertainty, the higher these costs are, the lower the company's labour demand will be. It is true that their presence may mean that employment reduction is less in "bad times" but this may lead to the company's bankruptcy or suspension of payments, as in the early eighties.

High redundancy costs strengthen the "insider-outsider" structure responsible for greater wage pressures. Moreover, the higher the redundancy costs, the lower the investment in new production lines. Finally, high redundancy costs decrease labour turnover and, hence, increase the duration of unemployment.

The second type of implicit labour costs is the consequence of regulations that limit the company's decisions about the way work is organised. These range from the prohibition against employing workers for fewer hours than the legally established number to limitations, present in some legal systems such as the Spanish one, on a company's internal reorganisation (transfers to other jobs, relocation, etc.). In the event of a change in demand conditions or in the technological context within which the company operates, these limitations mean a loss of productivity for the company. It is reasonable to assume that the employer, being aware of these constraints, will consider this likely loss of productivity to be a cost of labour use. Such restrictions will increase labour costs and decrease labour demand. In some cases, the price of overcoming such restrictions will become tangible, in the form of payments or other allowances that the employer is obliged to make, or in the extra wages he must pay to employ the worker for a greater number of hours than necessary.

The third type of implicit labour costs is more difficult to gauge: namely, the restrictions imposed on the parties in order for them to freely establish the contractual terms of their professional relationship, matching them to the nature of the job and to both parties' expectations and perceived risks. Obviously, there must be a general framework regulating labour relations, but what is open to discussion is the amount of detail contained in this framework, considering the undesirable restrictions that may be imposed on production organisation.

We turn now to discuss implicit labour costs in Spain. In the Spanish legal system, and in the practical reality of labour relations, redundancy costs have been - and remain - very high.

We have already explained that high redundancy costs were one of the reasons why the major wage increase during the period 1975-79 was offset by a relatively mild reaction in terms of employment reduction during those years and that the coincidence of these two circumstances was the cause of the drastic cuts in the workforce made between 1979 and 1984.

Some authors have attempted to gauge the impact of labour rigidity on employment and productive investment decisions. Rogerson (1990), using plausible parameters for Spanish industry, has carried out simulations to assess the effects of varying labour reduction costs on investment and employment. He reached the intriguing conclusion that imposing adjustment costs which roughly approximate the situation of the Spanish labour market causes a siseable reduction in employment, due to the contractive effect on investment, and that this effect is greater than the one operating directly on employment decisions given a stock of capital.

After the reform of the Workers' Statute generalising the use of temporary employment contracts at the end of 1984, the existence of high redundancy costs led to an extensive use of this form of contractual relationship as it meant that, upon termination of the contract, an employee could be dismissed at very low cost.

This fact had positive effects on employment and has facilitated the major workforce adjustments that have been carried out since the beginning of 1992. Some studies confirm the positive effect on employment of the flexibility achieved by the generalisation of temporary contracts after 1984 (Mateos and Sebastián, 1990; Bentolila and Saint-Paul, 1992). The latter study considers that the existence of temporary contracts helps accelerate job creation during periods of economic recovery but facilitates and accelerates job destruction during recessions. The same result was also foreseen by Rogerson (1990). However, on the basis of recent experience, it has been observed[8] that, in early 1992, unskilled labour employed under indefinite-term contracts was the first to be laid off. This is a consequence of the wage structure of permanent labour with its narrow wage spread. After the fourth quarter of 1992, the majority of the jobs lost were those of workers employed under temporary contracts.

However, in many ways, the temporary contract does not appear to have been the best solution. The fact that it is so common in Spain, which has the highest percentage of temporary contracts in the EC, is a consequence of the high cost of terminating normal contracts (also one of the highest in the EC). But the flexibility gained through temporary contracts has a negative impact on both the "insiders-outsiders" structure and incentives to employees.[9] The duality created by the coexistence of permanent and temporary contracts further strengthens the "insiders-outsiders" structure, because a high real wage defended by "insiders" (employees with permanent contracts) is not only protected from pressures by the unemployed ("traditional outsiders"), but also would affect more jobs of temporary workers (workers belonging to a new class of "outsiders") than "insider" jobs. Therefore "insiders'" wage excesses would negatively affect other people's jobs. Bentolila and Dolado (1993) find evidence of higher wage demands by "insiders" in companies with a higher proportion of temporary contracts. The temporary contract, on the other hand, does not contribute to the development of the worker's skills, nor does it necessarily stimulate a greater effort on the part of the employee (who knows that he is more likely to lose his job than the permanent worker, regardless of his relative effort). The temporary contract therefore has negative effects on productivity.

Redundancy costs in Spain are some of the highest in Europe (together with Portugal and Italy) and much higher than those of the North American members of the OECD.[10] They are higher by law, but even more so in practice, mainly because the odds are against a company's being granted a sentence of justified dismissal in the case of individual dismissals. According to current legislation, if the dismissal is declared wrongful, the employer must pay the dismissed employee the so-called interim wage payments (wage payments that have accrued between the date of dismissal and the date of the court sentence), and therefore prefers to pay the dismissed employee a higher severance payment than what is legally required. On the other hand, collective layoffs require government authorisation, which is not usually granted without the approval of the trade unions; this also leads to higher severance payments than the law requires. Finally, the act of submitting to the discretionary action of the government, dependent on a decision that ensues after a fairly lengthy process (about two months), considerably increases the degree of uncertainty for a company in an ailing condition - which is what led it to request authorisation for the layoffs in the first place - with the resulting negative effects on the company's position vis-à-vis suppliers, credit institutions and customers.

As mentioned, high redundancy costs produce a low labour turnover, contributing to the long duration of unemployment and to a low degree of job searching by the unemployed.

These high redundancy costs, with such harmful effects on wages, investment, production efficiency and employment, have not prevented the Spanish production system from destroying employment during recessions, to an even greater extent than countries with lower dismissal costs. This is shown all too clearly in Figure 6.2.

Table 6.4 shows the evolution of employment and GDP in Spain, France, Germany and the United States during the last two recessions. The first recession covers the period 1979-82 for countries other than Spain and the period 1979-84 for Spain. Recall that the recession at the end of the seventies lasted longer in Spain than in other industrialised countries, in part precisely because of the absence of adjustment in employment (and energy). Consequently, the comparison has been extended to 1984 in

*Table 6.4    Change in GDP and Employment, 1979 – 1993 (per cent)*

|  | 1979–82 * | 1992–93 ** |
|---|---|---|
| Spain |  |  |
| (a) Employment | –10.2 | –4.6 |
| (b) GDP | 6.6 | –1.3 |
| (1+a)/(1+b) | 0.84 | 0.97 |
| Germany |  |  |
| (a) Employment | –2.7 | –1.2 |
| (b) GDP | –1.5 | –3.1 |
| (1+a)/(1+b) | 0.99 | 1.02 |
| France |  |  |
| (a) Employment | 0.0 | –1.1 |
| (b) GDP | 4.7 | –1.0 |
| (1+a)/(1+b) | 0.96 | 1.00 |
| USA |  |  |
| (a) Employment | –0.6 | –1.0 |
| (b) GDP | –1.5 | –1.2 |
| (1+a)/(1+b) | 1.01 | 1.00 |

\* In Spain, 1979–84      \*\* In USA, 1990–91

Spain's case. The American economy started to pull out of recession earlier; therefore, the comparison refers to the period 1990-91, instead of 1992-93. In both instances, the Spanish economy has destroyed a greater proportion of employment, in spite of having higher dismissal costs.

However, until the recent reform, Spanish labour relations have suffered from other significant rigidities. On the one hand, little use has been made until now of the part-time contract, which implies a greater flexibility on both the supply and the demand side. Its weight in total employment recruitment is significantly less than in the other European countries. In this respect, it was also necessary to regulate the temporary employment agencies, which might help flexibilise recruitment by facilitating the immediate availability of suitably qualified workers, in the quantity required for a preset period of time.

On the other hand, the so-called Labour Ordinances (the National Labour Regulations in the previous political regime) still persist in labour legislation. These Ordinances can only be characterised as an anachronism that adds to the system's rigidity. The Ordinances, which are written separately for each sector, dictate a series of rules that severely limit the organisation of production. One of their most striking (although not most harmful) features is the detailed definition of job categories in each sector, so that each worker employed is allocated to one of these categories.[11] The Ordinances impose restrictions on worker mobility, both between production centres (regardless of whether geographical movements are involved) and between jobs. Thus, for example, there are restrictions on allocating a worker to a job in a category other than the one he has been assigned to. There are also strict limitations on changes in compensation systems. The imminent disappearance of these Ordinances is one of the positive consequences of the recent reform.

To summarise, the implicit labour costs are higher in Spain than in most industrial countries, have fallen insufficiently and have moved in an unsatisfactory direction. These costs impose a non-monetary penalty on labour use, contribute to excessive growth of wage costs and are one of the causes of the lack of sensitivity of real wages to changes in the labour market. These implicit costs, therefore, not only exert upward pressure on costs; in a context of uncertainty about business results, the presence of high implicit labour costs strongly discourages business investment and, hence, employment growth.

## 6.4.    MARKET REGULATIONS AND IMPERFECTIONS

The high level of the various components of the user cost of labour and their excessive growth are, to a great extent, the result of both a set of regulations present in the Spanish labour market and a series of imperfections in this and other markets. These regulations and imperfections refer to the following aspects: 1) labour contracts; 2) financing of the pension system; 3) collective bargaining and wage-setting; 4) work organisation; 5) protection of unemployment; and 6) imperfections in the labour and other related markets.

### 6.4.1    Labour contracts

We have already seen that Spanish regulations in this respect have evolved from the existence of indefinite-term contracts, with high dismissal costs, to the advent of temporary contracts, coexisting with the former. As stated, this situation has negative effects on labour demand, wage rigidity and labour productivity. On labour demand, because it implies a higher user cost of labour and because, in a context of uncertainty, it discourages productive investment, and therefore future employment creation; on wage rigidity because it reinforces the "insiders-outsiders" structure, given that high redundancy costs protect wage demands from pressures by the unemployed, and because wage excesses by "insiders" negatively affect other employees' jobs and not "insiders'" jobs; and, finally, on productivity because it discourages effort both on the part of employees with indefinite-term contracts and those with temporary contracts. High redundancy costs, finally, contribute to the long duration of unemployment and, hence, to low-key job searching, another cause of wage rigidity.

On the other hand, the limitations placed on the use of part-time contracts until the recent reform, reduced labour demand, hampered efficient human resources management - with negative effects on productivity - and diminished the workforce's potential to exert downward pressure on wages.

The optimal recruitment model is the indefinite contract with lower dismissal costs. Such contracts could be full- or part-time, depending on a company's requirements and an employee's preferences.

### 6.4.2    Financing of the pensions system

In addition to financial viability problems, if a change takes place in the population pyramid, as has occurred in Spain, a pensions system based on the principle of distribution rather than on that of capitalisation may amount to levying a tax on employment, if the main contributors to the distribution system are the employers. Such is the case of the public pensions system in Spain, which is financed to a great extent by a veritable tax on employment.

Given the predominance of Social Security contributions among labour costs which, in Spain, are some of the heaviest in the industrialised world, some have raised the possibility of partially replacing this cost with an alternative tax such as, for example, VAT. Zabalza (1988) considers that the positive impact of labour cost reduction on employment would be offset to a large extent by the wage increases obtained as a result of the higher consumer prices generated by the increase in VAT. However, as Servén indicates (1990b), this would depend on the degree to which VAT increases were transferred to the CPI, as well as the degree to which nominal wages affected prices. This author believes that the net effect could be clearly positive and would be even more so if companies were to reflect in their prices the reduction achieved in labour costs. If this did not happen, inflationary tensions would be generated which could ultimately erode the gains obtained from the reduction in Social Security contributions. The reduction in employers' contributions affects both marginal labour costs (with the resulting effects on labour demand) and average costs. If the decrease in the latter were not passed on in prices, not only would inflationary tensions be generated but there would be a transfer from taxpayers as a whole to employers, with virtually no effect on employment decisions. Therefore, Servén (1990b) proposes that the reduction in Social Security contributions which would be financed by increases in VAT be limited initially to contributions linked to net employment creation. This proposal, while ideal from a theoretical viewpoint, suffers from obvious operational problems.

In any case, Servén (1990b) concludes that, in the medium term, replacing the revenue lost by a one-point reduction in employers' Social

Security contributions with increases in direct taxation would increase labour demand by about 0.5%.[12]

Finally, a further point to bear in mind is the positive effect that the replacement of Social Security contributions by VAT would have on the competitiveness of exporting companies.

### 6.4.3    Collective bargaining and wage-setting

The rigidity of wages, the narrow wage spread and the small proportions of the flexible component in the remuneration structure are in part the result of the nature of collective bargaining in Spain.

An interesting starting point to consider is how the prevalent bargaining model - specifically, the degree of centralisation - affects wage growth.

The impact of collective bargaining on wages depends on two factors that operate in different directions: the clout of trade unions and the effects of wages on prices. The former increases when bargaining is centralised. A union that represents all the workers in an industry has greater market power. In such a context, on the other hand, the employers may pass on to prices (particularly in the case of non-tradeable goods) the wage increase agreed upon, since competing companies will face identical wage increases and, consequently, will have fewer objections to the unions' claims. If the bargaining is at company level, not only will the unions' market power be less, the employers' resistance will be greater, due to the uncertainty regarding the result of transferring wage increases to prices.

However, the greater the degree of centralisation, the greater the unions' awareness will be of the fact that the wage increases they pursue may lead to price increases, which would reduce workers' purchasing power. Consequently, more wage moderation might be expected when bargaining is carried out at a national level.

It may be inferred from this discussion that the extreme cases of centralisation (on both a corporate and a national scale) are those that generate the greatest wage moderation. The most inflationary model seems to be the intermediate model. On the other hand, if the pressure of the unemployed on wage-setting is less than desired, one should wonder which collective bargaining model is most capable of taking unemployed workers into consideration. The answer is once again the extreme cases. A nationwide agreement would be more likely to take into consideration the interests of all workers. On the other hand, if the bargaining were carried out at company level, the workers involved in the bargaining process would take the unemployed workers into greater consideration to the extent to which they consider it likely that the colleagues they work with every day (or they themselves) might become unemployed.

The transnational studies that have sought to provide evidence on the relationship between the degree of centralisation of the bargaining process and wage growth are not conclusive. They fail to take into account other factors that may affect this relationship, such as the type of monetary policy present in various countries, the degree of regulation of various economies and the prevalent labour legislation. Any differences in these three factors (and major differences do exist among the industrialised countries studied) would alter wage growth and its relationship with the bargaining model used. These drawbacks could account for the studies' lack of definition.

A fairly obvious consequence of centralised wage bargaining, whether at the industry or national level, is the tendency to index wages, and therefore to determine wage increases without reference to the actual situation and performance of the companies that have to pay these wages. This tends to worsen the financial difficulties of companies that are viable but experiencing temporary difficulties; it also tends to limit the use of compensation schemes to motivate productivity, with negative effects on worker effort.

Centralised bargaining tends to reduce wage spread. This has a negative impact on productivity and makes it harder for certain groups to find employment. Narrowing the wage band makes it difficult to find the right economic incentives for a highly changeable production situation. On the other hand, the establishment of a minimum wage, which is one of the factors causing the reduction in the spread, works against young people and other groups of those looking for their first job. Employers have no incentive to employ these people if they are forced to pay them the same wage as experienced workers.

The rigidity of the Spanish (and European) labour market is related to the collective bargaining process and the role of unions in that process. The bargaining model used in Spain has an intermediate level of centralisation, with a proliferation of industry and regional agreements. We have already noted that this intermediate level of centralisation in bargaining is doubtless what generates the greatest wage rigidity. It is true that when national-level bargaining was discontinued between 1987 and 1993, wage pressure was slightly greater than in previous years; but it is the significant presence of agreements with an intermediate level of centralisation throughout this period that has contributed most to wage rigidity. Between 1984 and 1991, most of the workers affected by collective bargaining were included in industry agreements, whereas only 15% of workers were covered by company agreements.[13]

Figure 6.12 shows how the percentage wage increases bargained for in industry-wide collective agreements were systematically higher than those arrived at in company-wide agreements.

We have already discussed the reduced wage spread in Spain and the small proportion allocated to variable remuneration in wage schemes. As we have already suggested, both phenomena are the result of the way in which collective bargaining has been carried out and the degree to which it has been centralised.

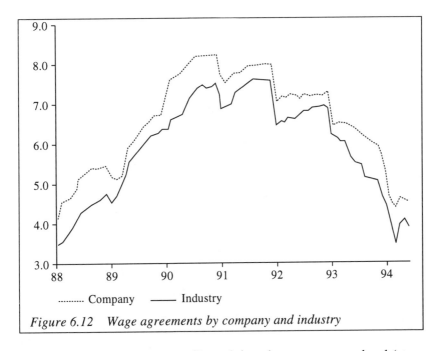

*Figure 6.12   Wage agreements by company and industry*

The negative consequences of bargaining above a company level (at an industry or regional level) are aggravated in Spain by the fact that the Workers' Statute conferred a general validity on collective agreements within their area of application, so that the conditions contained in an agreement were applied to all companies in the agreement's area of application (sector or province), regardless of whether these companies took part in the negotiations. This rule only serves to widen the gap between wage agreements and corporate reality. In most European countries, no such rule exists. Spain's recent reform includes the possibility of a wage release clause, as we will see further on.

Another consequence of the collective bargaining procedure in Spain is the lack of an incentive for companies to recruit young people seeking their first job. By setting a minimum wage level in the agreements, one which was considerably higher than the legal minimum wage - and given the availability of a sufficient supply of adult workers with previous work experience - companies had no incentive to recruit young people with no work experience.[14] This being the case, it is not surprising that the various programmes to promote employment of young people have had such poor results.[15] From these reflections we may infer that a more efficient system would have to articulate a structure for collective bargaining in which national framework agreements coexist with company-wide agreements, with the contents of the latter going beyond mere wage-setting issues.[16]

### 6.4.4    Work organisation

Until the recent reform, work organisation in Spain was conspicuous for its extreme rigidity. Internal, functional and geographical mobility, the definition of job categories, the determination of working hours, the modification of working conditions, the payment of overtime, and other aspects of work organisation were all governed by highly restrictive legislation. This led to losses in productivity and increases in labour costs (the latter because companies often had to resort to wage hikes to placate the workers covered by the existing restrictive legislation).

The most representative example of this overregulation are the National Labour Regulations, which changed their name but not, in the least, their contents with the advent of democracy. The reform of the early eighties provided for the supersedence of the Regulations but, since it was established that a Regulation would not be abolished until an agreement on the same issue was in place, the result has been that over a period of more than 13 years, of 144 existing Regulations only 15 have been abolished, all of them in marginal sectors except for the steel industry. We will discuss the recent reform's approach to this matter further on.

### 6.4.5    Protection of unemployment

The availability of generalised unemployment relief causes an increase in the opportunity cost of being employed, which pressures wages upward. Moreover, it encourages low-key job seeking, which contributes to wage rigidity. Studies for different countries confirm these relationships.[17] In times of growth, the unemployment benefit causes shortages in labour supply, which become more marked at lower skill levels.

Generalised unemployment relief systems encourage clear instances of "moral hazard", that is, situations that encourage non-compliance and dishonesty by the beneficiary.

This effect, which is at the root of the upward pressure generated on wages by these benefits and their contribution to the lack of sensitivity of wage growth to the unemployment rate, must be considered in all its depth and juxtaposed to the equity arguments that can be made in favour of these systems of protection.

The reform of unemployment protection systems should aim to strike a balance between the "moral hazard" they cause and its consequences, on the one hand, and equity, on the other. The recent changes in these systems, in Spain and in other European countries, are due solely to financial considerations and not to any effort to achieve such a balance.

Any such reform should be guided by two principles: first, an integration of the unemployment benefit with active occupational training measures, so that the beneficiary is required to participate in training activities. This requires a more efficient management of the training activities financed by public funds. Second, the protection system should be given a markedly non-cyclical character, so that its duration is shorter in times of economic recovery and growth than in times of recession.

### 6.4.6    Other imperfections in the labour and related markets

We have already noted that the lack of geographical mobility, the poor performance of the state agency in the labour market and the considerable deficiencies in occupational training are, together with the unemployment protection system and wage rigidity, the causes of the simultaneous persistence of a large number of unemployed workers with a certain number - which in some phases of the cycle can become quite large - of unfilled vacancies. This has negative effects on wage growth.

The lack of geographical mobility in Spain is certainly extreme. According to the EPA, and in spite of an unemployment rate exceeding 24%, only 29% of unemployed workers would be prepared to take a job outside the province they currently live in. This percentage has remained relatively stable during the last few years. To a great extent, this is a cultural problem but, in order to overcome it, changes will have to be made in the labour market's institutional framework (reform of unemployment insurance and enhanced efficiency of the employment agencies); it will also be necessary to remedy major shortcomings in other markets, particularly the property and mortgage markets.[18] The reform of these markets would not only have direct positive effects on the economy's cost structure but would also contribute significantly to increasing geographical mobility.

Imperfections in other markets are also affecting the growth of wage costs. Specifically, as we have already mentioned, the difference between real consumption wage and production labour costs, a difference which is known as the "wage wedge", is due to fiscal factors and the different evolution followed by the prices of tradeable goods and nontradeable ones (mainly services). This divergence is caused in part by imperfections in the services sector, a sector which is noted for its lack of competitiveness and excessive regulation. A deregulation of this sector would contribute to lower inflation and wage growth.

The other components of the "wage wedge" are taxes (the so-called "tax wedge"). We have already discussed what is probably the most important of these: Social Security contributions. Other fiscal components are the indirect taxes levied on wage-earners' purchases and the direct taxes levied on their income: these affect labour supply decisions and, therefore, the real wage demanded. An excessive tax burden - necessary to finance a certain conception of the State's role in the economy and society - undoubtedly exerts upward pressure on the cost of labour.

The labour market has other imperfections, besides those that derive from the factors we have discussed so far. These other imperfections are caused by the difficulties experienced by those seeking and offering work in gaining access to information. The liberalisation of employment agencies included in this year's reform must help flexibilise the market by reducing information costs.

On the other hand, an efficient occupational training system would also help avoid the mismatch between vacancies and unemployed workers and would, moreover, have a clearly positive impact on productivity. Along with sufficient funding, a prerequisite of any efficient system is decentralised management.

## 6.5.   THE 1994 LABOUR REFORM

The recently approved labour reform has taken a few timid steps in the right direction with regard to the regulation of issues 1, 4 and 6 of the previous section. As to the regulation of issue 3, while the evidence points to good intentions, these are as yet quite hazy.

There are two important aspects of the regulation of labour contracts: the type of contract and the conditions under which it is to be terminated. A number of changes have been made in both of these.

In the former, the most important change has been the liberalisation of the part-time contract, with an expansion of the concept of "part-time". As noted, the flexibilisation of the number of hours that an employee may work in a company has positive effects on the organisation of production, increases labour demand and stimulates labour supply. Flexibility could also help reduce the pressure on wages. On the other hand, the reform provides for the phasing out of temporary contracts by discontinuing the so-called "employment promotion contract", which was the most popular form of temporary contract.[19] We have already pointed out that the generalisation of temporary contracts that began at the end of 1984 is far from an optimal form of recruitment, although at that time it introduced a greater flexibility, given the recruitment options available. The crucial complement to this phasing out of temporary contracts would have been a significant reduction in the costs of dismissing permanent employees; but this, unfortunately, has not happened. Finally, training contracts have been reformed, by the creation of the "hands-on" and apprenticeship contracts. The most positive aspect of that reform is the lowering of the minimum wages to be paid under these contracts. Although many doubt that these hiring procedures will prove successful, they can hardly be viewed as a distorting factor.

With regard to the conditions for contract termination, the labour reform has made little progress. The existence of three types of dismissal is ratified: individual termination for disciplinary reasons, termination of an individual or of several for justified causes, and collective termination, also for justified causes. In the first case, there are virtually no changes:

the concepts of lawful and wrongful dismissal are upheld. In the other cases, payment of interim wages is retained, together with severance pay equal to 45 days per year of service, with a maximum of 42 months, if the company declines to readmit the worker(s). In reality, it is very rare for a dismissal to be declared lawful. Consequently, companies avoid individual dismissals whenever they can or settle for higher compensation than legally required in the event that they do decide upon such dismissals. The recent reform's retainment of this system of individual dismissal, which encourages non-compliance by workers on permanent contracts, is disappointing.

The causes for justified dismissals have been expanded: economic justifications have been introduced. This may be considered a significant advance, since if implementation matches the legislator's intention, it will make possible a much more flexible management of labour resources throughout the business cycle, and in companies in the process of restructuring. Collective dismissals continue to require government authorisation, although the time allowed for the government to notify a company of its decision has been shortened somewhat and, furthermore, the meaning of absence of official communication has been reversed, so that silence is deemed to convey authorisation, not refusal. Government authorisation, which has been eliminated in countries such as France, is unjustified, since it merely adds bureaucratic weight and creates uncertainty in companies that are already suffering difficulties (which is what led them to consider the collective dismissal in the first place) and which are obviously now in a weakened position vis-à-vis credit institutions and suppliers. A company with 100 employees whose demand has fallen by 15-20% due to cyclical factors or loss of competitiveness, will be forced to apply for government authorisation whenever it wishes to lay off even 10 workers, with the logical consequences on its standing with its sources of finance.

It remains to be seen how non-collective dismissals for justified causes will be settled if the employees in question subsequently take the matter to court. If the situation proved the same as the one observed in cases of individual dismissal, the administrative procedure might be the lesser evil. Obviously, the advisability of requiring a court sentence in case of conflicts concerning individual or collective dismissals needs to be reassessed. The alternative of generalising an independent arbitration procedure (something very different from the current bureaucratised system "IMAC") to settle interpretation conflicts in cases of dismissal seems preferable.

The severance payment for dismissals with justified (non-disciplinary) cause is unchanged at 20 days per year worked with a maximum of 12 months' pay. This is high, although comparable with several European countries. The problem, again, is that the likelihood of obtaining government authorisation is considerably increased if the agreement of the workers' representatives is secured in the course of necessary hearings while the Administration is studying the application. Consequently, in order to obtain this agreement, companies will still tend to settle for severance payments higher than the ones legally required.

To summarise, the reform has taken steps in the right direction with respect to labour recruitment, but is still a long way from a more efficient model in which, together with part-time contracts, a prevalent form of contract would be the indefinite term contract, but with a reduction in dismissal costs. Furthermore, this reduction should take into account that the actual costs are significantly higher than those established by law. To this end, it would be necessary to study settling dismissal processes out of court. Recall that high dismissal costs have not prevented sharp drops in employment (they have even helped increase them in the medium term), have pressured wages upward, discouraging productive investment, and have acted as a barrier to improved productivity.

With respect to the organisation of labour (regulations concerning issue 4), the reform flexibilises some aspects: functional mobility, determination of working hours, payment of overtime and significant changes in working conditions, inter alia. The most common recourse is to include in the collective bargaining process the regulation of many aspects of work organisation which were previously regulated by government ordinances. This will allow a more flexible management of human resources. It may also help to amplify the content of collective bargaining, limited until now to wage setting. Of particular significance in this area is the proposal to abolish the archaic National Labour Regulations, replacing some of them with clauses to be included in the collective agreements. This time, in a departure from the reform in the early eighties, a deadline has been set by which these regulations will cease to exist, regardless of whether a new agreement has been reached. The consensus regarding this aspect of the reform is clearly favourable, although the question remains of how the parties will set about negotiating so many aspects that were previously regulated (such as the contents of the Regulations). However, although this may initially be a source of conflicts, it is a path that must be trodden.

As to the regulations affecting the functioning of the labour market - matching labour supply and labour demand - the reform takes a few steps. These basically consist of the elimination of the INEM's monopoly, the authorisation of private placement agencies, and also the regulation of temporary work agencies. Both measures are wise, although doubts remain regarding the operation of the latter. However, occupational training, one of the basic issues related to the matching of supply and demand, is not addressed - although Spain's is palpably inadequate. Nor is any mention made of action to encourage the geographical mobility of the active population; this is deemed to be beyond the scope of the labour market reform.

As mentioned, the collective bargaining process in Spain is grossly unsatisfactory for several reasons. It rarely addresses anything beyond the setting of wages and working hours. The wage levels decided upon rarely contain a variable component linked to an employee's productivity and the company's performance. Many agreements, moreover, are negotiated at the most inefficient level (at branch, sector, province or regional level). All this, together with an insufficiently developed corporate culture on the matter, accounts for the extremely low level of employer interest in collective bargaining.

The labour reform addresses this unsatisfactory situation with a certain lack of conviction about which path to follow. There are positive elements, such as the inclusion of the wage release clause in the agreements signed beyond the company level, and the referral to the collective bargaining process of many aspects that were previously regulated (including the contents of the Labour Regulations). It is not certain how the collective bargaining process will evolve. Much will depend on the social agents themselves, who will have to act within a more deregulated context than the accustomed one. As mentioned earlier, the coexistence of nationwide framework agreements with company-wide agreements would be the most appropriate structure for collective bargaining, but the reform does not appear to have considered the implementation of measures to help this structure become a reality. It is not even clear whether this is the model advocated.

Finally, in the discussion of the draft 1995 Budget (subsequent to the labour reform) another important aspect of the regulations affecting the user cost of labour was studied: the employers' Social Security contributions. The replacement of employers' contributions by indirect taxation is defensible. The choice of the specific tax whose rate would be increased to offset the drop in Social Security revenues is not insignificant, but it would be overshadowed by any decision to reduce employers' contributions. If we were asked to give an optimal solution, we would prefer that the lost revenue be offset by a decrease in public expenditure. The choice between VAT and fuel tax is not an easy one: both have their pros and cons. The significance of the drawbacks depends on the extent to which the increase in VAT is passed on to final consumer prices (and how that increase affects wage setting) and the extent to which the increase in energy costs affects production costs. The decision to use an increase in VAT to offset the decrease in employers' Social Security contributions would be particularly advantageous to companies exporting to non-EC countries.

As mentioned earlier, a reduction (even a substantial one) in marginal contributions (those associated with net employment creation) would have highly positive effects on employment creation; the tax offset required would be very small and, consequently, the above-mentioned disadvantages would scarcely be applicable. In this case, the drawbacks are of a more operational nature, in that they could encourage fraudulent practises.

In any case, the extremely modest figures used to date reveal a certain lack of faith in the wisdom of the decision to replace employers' contributions with another type of taxation. A reduction of less than a percentage point seems clearly insufficient, given the current high level of employers' contributions.

In the end, then, the labour reform is a step in the right direction, but its measures to reduce redundancy costs have been very timid; the unemployment protection system - whose reform was driven only by the system's financial crisis in 1993 - is retained intact; there is no clearly defined objective in the reform of the collective bargaining and wage-setting system; and, finally, it fails to address a number of important issues, particularly the ones surrounding occupational training. A certain continuation of the reform was seen in the 1995 Budget Act, with its modest reduction in employers' Social Security contributions, but this, too, exudes a considerable lack of confidence and conviction.

## 6.6.  THE POSSIBILITY OF A MACROECONOMIC EMPLOYMENT POLICY

The implementation of policies aimed at stimulating demand in order to reduce the unemployment rate has always had its champions, among both politicians and academics, particularly in Europe.

Any consideration of the possibilities of such a policy in Spain must begin with a discussion of the likely size of the "Keynesian unemployment", or NAIRU. Two studies[20] carried out using different methodologies in the latter half of the eighties estimated that only five or six percentage points of the unemployment rate between 1980 and 1985 could be attributed to deficiencies in demand. Interestingly enough, subsequent historic experience seems to have corroborated these estimates: the unemployment rate, which had reached 22% in 1985, fell to 16% with the strong growth during the period 1986-90. In other words, the substantial reduction (or even the elimination) of the restrictions on demand only reduced the unemployment rate by the six points that had been estimated in these studies.

After limiting, to a significant degree in our opinion, the action of the demand policy, the next step would be to consider the problems involved in implementing a policy of this nature, and some of its consequences.

The problems of an expansive fiscal policy in Spain derive, first of all, from the considerable size of the public deficit, which has led to a high level of government debt. The weight of public debt (measured, for example, as a percentage of the GDP, a percentage which has grown from 8% to 62% in 12 years) affects the interest rate, widening the gap between Spanish and international rates. Therefore, a public expenditure programme financed with public debt will probably have permanent effects on the level of interest rates.

Financing by taxation seems undesirable, both because of the impressive growth of the tax burden in the last ten years and the distorting effects of the Spanish tax system, some of which have already been discussed with reference to the size of the tax wedge. Other distortions operate on savings and on productive investment.

In addition to their long-term inflationary consequences, the problems of an expansive monetary policy include the difficulty of controlling long-term interest rates. The level of real interest rates, a reduction of which is advocated to stimulate demand, is determined in large part by the international markets and by the spread demanded by international holders of financial assets. An isolated attempt to achieve a substantial and permanent reduction in Spanish rates would be doomed to failure in the long term. A coordinated attempt by all the European countries, which would be a necessary prerequisite for reasons to be discussed further on, has only a slight chance of achieving a permanent reduction in real interest rates. Any success will hinge on the international markets' perception of the effects of such a policy on inflation in European countries.

On the other hand, the external balance may limit the implementation of an expansive macroeconomic policy. Such a constraint would be mitigated considerably if the expansive policy were adopted in a coordinated effort by all the European countries.

Finally, a demand policy may be inadvisable unless it is completely credible to the agents and generates no uncertainty in them. Increases in uncertainty have real contractive effects. The history of macroeconomic policy is full of cases in which government actions have given rise to increased uncertainty among the agents concerned.

In sum, then, a macroeconomic employment policy has a relatively small margin of action, since the "Keynesian" unemployment - the only unemployment that can be reduced by stimulating demand - may not be very large.

Furthermore, any such implementation, which can only be considered in a coordinated fashion at EC level, may suffer from operational problems and lead to undesirable consequences. Given the degree of integration of financial markets, the notable mobility of capital and the high levels of debt of European governments, it is no easy task to design such a policy.

An expansive fiscal policy would have long-term effects on interest rates and an expansive monetary policy might not be accepted by the international markets. If the policies are not credible, they will only have negative effects and will produce a rise in uncertainty which may in turn have contractive consequences.[21]

## NOTES

1.  Managers of risk-averse companies with asymmetrical information on the capital markets generate this type of factor demand function (see the studies published by the research team led by Professor J. Stiglitz; e.g., B. Greenwald and J. Stiglitz, 1988 and 1990; and J. Stiglitz, 1992).
2.  Raymond, García and Polo (1989) find an elasticity of -0.5 using time series. Dolado and Malo de Molina (1987), also using time series for the period 1964-83, obtain an elasticity of - 0.95. Using panel data from 820 companies for the period 1981-85, Servén (1990b) obtains an elasticity of -0.6. It should be pointed out that real wage growth was relatively moderate during the latter study's sample period. In the MOISEES model, estimated elasticity is greater than 1 in absolute terms, - 1.2 in the medium term, and -1.6 in the long term (see Molinas et al., 1990).
3.  Sebastián and Servén (1986) formulate a model simulating the behaviour of Spanish industry between 1975 and 1984, analysing the impact that the increased factor costs, the existence of adjustment costs, the fluctuations in interest rates and the inelastic expectations had on employment. This model generates a trend in employment and bankruptcies and suspensions of payments that is similar to the one actually recorded.
4.  The study carried out by Alvarez, Jareño and Sebastián (1993) provides evidence that private sector wages have pressured prices upward, with increased impact in the long term, and that the dual nature of inflation is explained by the upward push of wages and the different market positions of the industrial and service sectors, which, in turn, is accounted for by the differences in the degree of exposure to foreign competition. These authors find that private sector wages respond weakly to growth of (service) prices.
5.  See García Perea (1993).
6.  See García Perea (1993) and García Perea and Gómez (1993).
7.  See García Perea and Gómez (1993).
8.  See García Perea and Gómez (1993).
9.  See Jimeno and Toharia (1993) and Bentolila and Dolado (1993).
10. For an analysis comparing them with the EC countries, see García Perea and Gómez (1993).
11. In spite of the fact that, in many cases, the functional difference between categories is minimal.
12. This result is not very different from the one obtained recently by M. Fernández, J.M. Ponz and D. Taguas (1994).
13  In a recent study by Jimeno (1992), which defends, on both theoretical and empirical grounds, maximum centralisation of the collective bargaining process, the analysis of the Spanish experience (1984-91) shows that the response to the unemployment rate is greater in company-wide agreements than in sector-wide agreements, and that the inclusion of productivity clauses in the former reduces the wage increases agreed upon, whereas this does not happen in the sector agreements. During the years in which there were nationwide agreements (the

model advocated by the author), wage increases were lower but, on the other hand, the impact of the unemployment rate on wage bargaining was significantly lower than the one estimated for the years in which there was no nationwide agreement.

14. During 1987 and 1988, the minimum wages set in a broad sample of sector-wide agreements were equivalent to between 155% and 225% of the minimum inter-professional wage for young people aged 16 and 17.

15. See Mateos and Sebastián (1990).

16. The recent British experience, in which the adoption of a totally decentralised bargaining model has not managed to reduce the rate of wage growth, in spite of the positive results achieved, confirms the advisability of devising an articulated structure.

17. See, for example, the excellent survey by S. Nickell (1990) and the book by R. Layard, S. Nickell and R. Jackman (1991).

18. Enabling private individuals to carry out "property leasing" operations, with the consequent deduction of interest expenses, would help flexibilise the housing market.

19. The draft 1995 Budget considers the restoration of the temporary employment promotion contract, but only for people who have been unemployed for more than one year.

20. See J. Andrés, J.J. Dolado, C. Molinas, M. Sebastián and A. Zabalza (1990) and L. Servén (1990a).

21. An anti-cyclical macroeconomic policy must seek a neutral stance with regard to the allocation process and not surprise the agents: an anti-cyclical budget, with surplus during growth and deficit during recessions, so that debt does not increase during the cycle; explicitly stated monetary policy rules; a tax system that is as neutral as possible, etc.

## REFERENCES

Alvarez. L.J.; Jareño, J. and Sebastián, M. (1993): "Salarios Públicos, Salarios Privados e Inflación Dual", Documento de Trabajo, nº 9320, Servicios de Estudios del Banco de España, Madrid.

Andrés, J.; Dolado, J.J., Molinas, C.; Sebastián, M. and Zabalza, A. (1990): "The Influence of Demand and Capital Constraints on Spanish Unemployment", in J.H. Drèze and C.R. Bean (eds.), *Europe's Unemployment Problem.*, The MIT Press, Cambridge, Mass.

Bentolila, S. and Dolado, J.J. (1993): "La Contratación Temporal y sus Efectos sobre la Competitividad", Bank of Spain, *Boletin Económico*, July-August 1993.

Bentolila, S. and Saint-Paul, G. (1992): "The Macroeconomic Impact of Flexible Contracts: and Application to Spain", *European Economic Review*, 36, pp. 1013-47.

Calmfors, L. and Drifill, J. (1988): "Centralization of Wage Bargaining and Macroeconomic Performance", *Economic Policy,* nº 6, pp. 13-61.

Dolado, J.J. and Malo de Molina, J.L. (1985): "Desempleo y Rigidez del Mercado de

Trabajo en España", *Boletín Económico* del Banco de España, September, pp. 22-40.

Dolado, J.J. and Malo de Molina, J.L. (1987): "Un Modelo de Demanda de Trabajo con Expectativas de Output Aplicado a la Industria Española", *Cuadernos Económicos de ICE*, nº 37, pp. 59-69.

Dolado, J.J.; Malo de Molina, J.L and Zabalza, A. (1986): "Spanish Industrial Unemployment: Some Explanatory Factors", *Economica*, Vol. 53, pp. S313-34.

Fernández, M., Ponz, J.M. and Taguas, D. (1994): "Algunas reflexiones sobre la fiscalidad del factor trabajo y la sustitución de las cuotas a la Seguridad Social por imposición indirecta", Dirección General de Planificación del MEH. Documento de Trabajo D-94004.

García Perea, P. (1991): "Evolución de la Estructura en España desde 1963", in *Estudios de Economía del Trabajo en España III: El problema del paro*. Ministerio de Trabajo y Seguridad Social, Madrid.

García Perea. P. and Gómez, R. (1993): "Aspectos Institucionales del Mercado de Trabajo Español, en Comparación con Otros Países Comunitarios", *Boletín Económico* del Banco de España, September, pp 29-47.

Greenwald, B. and Stiglitz, J.E. (1988): "Money, imperfect information and economic fluctuations", in M. Kohn and S.C. Tsiang (eds.), *Finance Constraints, Expectations and Macroeconomics*, Oxford University Press, Oxford.

Greenwald, B. and Stiglitz, J.E. (1990): "Macroeconomic models with equity and credit rationing", in R.G. Hubbard (ed.), *Information, Capital Markets and Investments*, University of Chicago Press, Chicago.

Jimeno, J.F. (1992): "Las Implicaciones Macroeconómicas de la Negociación Colectiva: El Caso Español", Documento de Trabajo 92-08, FEDEA, Madrid.

Jimeno, J.F. and Toharia, L. (1993): "The Productivity Effects of Fixed-Term Employment Contracts: Are Temporary Workers Less Productive than Permanent Workers?", Documento de Trabajo 93-04, FEDEA, Madrid.

Layard, R.; Nickell, S. and Jackman, R. (1991): *Unemployment. Macroeconomic Performance and the Labour Market*, Oxford University Press.

Mateos, B. and Sebastián, C. (1990): "Los Programas de Fomento y la Evolución del Empleo", in, *Estudios sobre Participación Activa, Empleo y Paro en España*, Several Authors, nº 7, Colección Estudios FEDEA, Madrid.

Molinas, C.; Ballabriga, C.; Canadell, E.; Escribano, A.; López, E.; Manzanedo, L.; Mestre, R.; Sabastián, M. and Taguas, D. (1990): MOISEES. *Un Modelo de Investigación y Simulación de la Economía Española*, A. Bosch and Instituto de Estudios Fiscales.

Nickell S. (1990): "Unemployment: A Survey", *Economic Journal*, vol. 100, July.

Novales, A. and Sebastián, C.: "Tasa de Paro y Necesidades de Empleo, 1986-1996." in, *Estudios sobre Participacion Activa, Empleo y Paro en España*, Several Authors, nº 7, Colección Estudios de FEDEA, Madrid.

Raymond, J.L.; García, J. and Polo, C. (1989): "Factores Explicativos de la Demanda de Empleo", *Papeles de Economía Española*, nº 26, pp. 180-95.

Rogerson, R. (1990): "Restricciones al Despido, Inversión y Empleo, con una Aplicación a la Industria Española", in, *Estudios sobre Participación Activa, Empleo y Paro en España*, Several Authors, nº 7, Colección Estudios de FEDEA, Madrid.

Sebastián, C. (1994): *Cómo Crear Empleo en una Economía Competitiva*, Círculo de Empresarios. Madrid.

Sebastián, C. and Servén, L. (1986): "La Evolución del Empleo Industrial 1973-84: Un Análisis de Simulación", in C. Sebastián and L. Servén, *Análisis de Simulación en la Industria Española*, nº 3, Colección Estudios FEDEA, Madrid.

Servén, L. (1990a): "La Evolución del Desempleo en España: un Análisis de Desequilibrio", in, *Estudios sobre Participación Activa, Empleo y Paro en España*, Several Authors, nº 7, Colección Estudios de FEDEA, Madrid.

Servén, L. (1990b): "La Sustitución de Cotizaciones Sociales por IVA: Una Evaluación", in, *Estudios sobre Participación Activa, Empleo y Paro en España*, Several Authors, nº 7, Colección Estudios de FEDEA, Madrid.

Stiglitz, J.E. (1992): "Capital Markets and Economic Fluctuations in Capitalist Economies", *European Economic Review*, 36.

Zabalza, A. (1988): "Efectos Económicos de las Cotizaciones a la Seguridad Social", in *La Fiscalidad en la Empresa*, nº 2, Colección Debates de FEDEA, Madrid.

# PART III
# CULTURAL VALUES AND LABOUR
# MARKET INSTITUTIONS

# 7. The Institutional Structuring of Firms' Strategies

**Richard Whitley**

## 7.1. INTRODUCTION

The rise of new forms of capitalism in East Asia, expansion of the Italian industrial districts and other forms of "flexible specialization" (Piore and Sabel, 1984; cf., Hirst and Zeitlin, 1991; Kenney and Florida, 1993) and the relative decline of the US form of "Fordism" have stimulated interest in the variety of forms of effective economic organisation found in capitalist societies and the reasons for their differences. Several recent contributions to the analysis of economic systems have identified different kinds of capitalism, such as "alliance" (Gerlach, 1992), "innovation mediated" (Kenney and Florida, 1993), proprietary, managerial and collective (Lazonick, 1991), competitive managerial, personal and cooperative managerial (Chandler, 1990), as well as a number of distinct business systems (Whitley, 1992a).

While some of these writers have claimed to discern an evolutionary path of economic superiority in these different forms of economic organisation, others have focused on the reasons for the distinctive characteristics developing in particular institutional contexts and their continued effectiveness in those contexts. Rather than one form being seen as inevitably more effective than other ones, the ways in which economic activities are organised and controlled are increasingly coming to be seen as embedded (Granovetter, 1985) in particular institutional contexts which encourage certain patterns of organisation and action at the expense of others. The nature of firms, markets and dominant industrial sectors in different market economies developed interdependently with major social, political and cultural institutions such that where these latter were significantly different then the type of capitalism that became established also varied.

It is also important to note here that concepts of economic efficiency and rationality are themselves socially constructed to a significant extent. What counts as economic success depends greatly on the context in which firm performance is assessed. Where, for example, there is a highly liquid capital market and a strong market for corporate control (Lawrisky, 1984), firms are much more likely to be evaluated in terms of quarterly profitability and growth in earnings per share, and to focus on maintaining a high share price than in an economy where firm size and market share are the dominant standards of performance because of high levels of interdependence with financial institutions and other major economic actors (Clark, 1979; Fligstein, 1990; Fruin, 1992; Ingham, 1984). Economically rational strategies and actions in the one situation would be ineffective in the other.

These variations in forms of economic organisation and dominant performance standards across market economies are linked to significant differences in patterns of employment and the labour management strategies adopted by leading firms. Each kind of firm-market configuration, or business system, institutionalises distinctive sets of employment relations and ways of managing human resources as the result of differences in their interrelated political, financial, labour and cultural systems (Whitley, 1992a; 1992b). Such differences affect firms' responses to state employment initiatives and macroeconomic policies so that standard recipes for, say, full employment can have widely varied results across different kinds of market economy. It is therefore important to understand how and why patterns of employment differ between countries, and the processes governing changes in them, when considering the effectiveness of state policies on employment and why the rate and type of unemployment vary. How firms decide to recruit particular kinds of people, how they train, organise, reward, promote and dismiss them, are clearly central to the development of an adequate understanding of employment patterns in any market economy, and, equally clearly, reflect dominant labour market institutions in each country.

Furthermore, they are also closely connected to the kinds of firms that have become established in different market economies as leading economic actors, and the general growth patterns and strategies they adopt. Variations in labour management strategies reflect broader differences in firm type and priorities that are linked to dominant institutions which structure risks and performance standards. The Anglo-Saxon diversified large corporation, for example, is quite a different kind of firm, and follows a different strategic logic, from most large Japanese kaisha and Korean chaebol, largely because of major differences in their institutional environments, and this has a significant effect on their employment practices (Clark, 1979; Dore, 1973; Whitley, 1992a). It is necessary, then, to consider variations in such practices as part of a general comparative analysis of firm type and behaviour.

In this paper I present a framework for comparing and contrasting some key aspects of employment relations in different business systems in terms of their institutional contexts. Business systems are here seen as distinctive forms of economic coordination and control which organise economic resources and activities in different ways in different economies. They are constituted by three components which deal with the following three issues: a) which activities and resources are coordinated and controlled by organised economic actors - as distinct from ad hoc market exchanges, b) how do these actors cooperate and compete through markets of different kinds, and c) what are the prevalent ways in which work is coordinated and controlled within such organisation? Thus, the first component consists of the nature of leading economic actors, or firms, in an economy which coordinate and allocate activities and resources. The second focuses on the ways that markets are organised, while the third is concerned with the "internal" system of work organisation, including employment practices (Whitley, 1992b).

In analysing employment patterns across market economies, then, characteristics of both firms as economic actors and the prevailing ways in which they recruit, organise and reward employees are important. The most significant of these will be outlined in the next section, together with their likely a priori interconnections. The following section describes the critical institutional features which help to explain variations in these business system characteristics, and the third suggests the critical ways in which these features encourage particular kinds of employment patterns to develop, and their implications for changes in these patterns.

### 7.1.1    Firms' Strategies and Employment Policies

In considering the most important characteristics of firms for employment policies and outcomes, summarised in Table 7.1, it is helpful to distinguish between general aspects of firms and their preferred growth strategies, on the one hand, and their specific employment policies and practices, on the other hand. Focusing initially on the general nature of firms and their priorities, there are three particularly important characteristics for employment policies: their specialisation or diversification, their preference for discontinuous or incremental growth patterns, and their pursuit of growth goals subject to only weak profit constraints.

Specialisation here refers to the different kinds of resources and capabilities that firms coordinate and control, and of the managerial skills they contain. In discussing variations in the structure of industries, Richardson (1972) has distinguished activities that are similar and use the same "capability" of a firm, from those that are complementary and utilise dissimilar capabilities. By capabilities he means any combination of knowledge, experience and skill that provide some competitive advantage for firms, and suggests that these capabilities tend to be specialised since firms will, ceteris paribus, prefer to expand in directions where their

---

*Table 7.1     Key Characteristics of Firms' Strategies and Employment
Policies*

A.   *Firm Type and Priorities*

1.   Degree of specialisation or diversity of activities and capabilities.

2.   Extent to which growth is radically discontinuous.

3.   Extent to which growth is pursued as dominant goal with only weak profit
     constraints.


B.   *Employment Policies*

1.   Extent of employer-employee mutual dependence and commitment.

2.   Extent to which employees are rigidly differentiated and segmented in terms of
     recruitment, contractual conditions, rewards and development.

3.   Task and role specialisation.

---

particular capability generates comparative advantage. Complementary
activities are those which represent different phases of a production
process - and so need to be coordinated - but draw on separate skills and
competences.

For example, ceramic manufacturers usually specialise in fabricating
porcelain insulators rather than these being made by electrical engineering
firms, and retailers often focus on distributing a wide range of different
products rather than being integrated with manufacturers of a particular
product sector, such as clothing. However, the extent of firm
specialisation, and the means by which coordination of complementary
activities is achieved, differ between market economies, as the contrast of
postwar Japan and the USA clearly demonstrates (Clark, 1979; Gerlach,
1992).

The crucial point about specialisation here is the extent to which
managerial and technological capabilities - in a broad sense, including the
service sector - vary significantly so that economic actors authoritatively
coordinate different kinds of expertise and knowledge within the same
organisation. It is diversification of capabilities which is the key
characteristic here, rather than of products, so that firms are more
diversified and varied in the kinds of activities and resources they control
when they combine different skills and knowledge which enable them to
carry out dissimilar - and sometimes non-complementary - activities.

These skills and knowledge include, of course, marketing and distribution programmes, so that moving into radically different markets with novel kinds of customers and methods of reaching them requires the development of new capabilities and so diversification. Even more dissimilar capabilities are involved when manufacturing companies move into quite different service sector activities, as when Hong Kong cotton spinning companies developed surplus land and became active in property development (Nishida, 1991; Wong, 1988).

A basic contrast can be drawn, then, between economies which encourage and manifest a high degree of diversification of capabilities and activities within economic actors - understood as Penrosian firms - and those where firms specialise more in particular, closely related capabilities. In those latter economies, complementary activities are coordinated through various forms of cooperation or through arm's length market contracting, and so the typical size of leading firm tends to be lower than in the former case. Japanese car manufacturers, for instance, are much smaller in terms of employees than their US counterparts because of the extensive use of sub-contracting (Cusumano, 1985; Fruin, 1992, Sako, 1992). Vertical integration may involve the development of new capabilities - as when Ford integrated backwards into steel manufacturing - but is often the result of technological developments which enable complementary activities to be coordinated more effectively internally than through cooperation with suppliers or customers. It may not always involve diversification of capabilities, although full integration of an entire production and distribution chain is likely to require considerable variety of skills and knowledge.

This first characteristic of firms to be considered here can be summarised, then, as the degree to which economic actors coordinate diverse activities and capabilities. The small, specialised production units found in the Italian industrial districts clearly represent one extreme, while the highly diversified conglomerate operating in heavy industry, light industry, construction, retailing and financial services - such as some of the largest Korean chaebol (Amsden, 1989; Steers et al, 1989; Whitley, 1992a; Zeile, 1991) are at the other end of the continuum. In between are the relatively specialised Japanese kaisha, the vertically integrated German enterprise and the Anglo-Saxon diversified multinational.

Specialisation is important for employment policies because it is related to the willingness of firms to take on new staff, and the ways they do so. Typically, the narrower the range of managerial and other skills in leading firms, the less likely are they to recruit large numbers of new employees at short notice, and the more discriminating they are likely to be when doing so because they have to make sure that recruits will fit into the dominant culture and have appropriate skills. Diversified firms operating in varied markets, on the other hand, are likely to be able to recruit different kinds of staff more easily, not least because one of their managerial skills lies in coordinating separate kinds of activities and resources.

This dimension is related to the second characteristic which deals with the preferred pattern of growth of economic actors in different economies. Growth can either be incremental and closely tied to current capabilities, or more radical and discontinuous involving the acquisition or development of quite different skills. While many firms may prefer to expand through developing their particular capabilities, in some economies it may be easier to size growth opportunities through acquiring new expertise by buying other firms and/or recruiting different kinds of skills from the external labour market. Kagono et al (1985), for example, contrasted US and Japanese firms in terms of their strategic or incremental patterns of change and, in general, it is worth comparing economic actors' ability and willingness to alter their capabilities radically. This characteristic can be summarised as the extent of radical discontinuities in activities and capabilities controlled by economic actors over time.

Although associated with the variety of capabilities managed within firms, such that narrowly specialised firms are unlikely to consider rapid qualitative shifts in their activities and skills, the example of some Chinese firms in Taiwan and Hong Kong shows how specialisation can be combined with rapid shifts from wig production to plastic flowers to toys (Redding, 1990, 219-222). These small firms avoid being tied to a particular product line or technology by concentrating in sectors wih relatively simple and labour intensive machinery, which can either be rapidly adapted to new products, such as sewing machines, or can be amortised over a short period so that they can be scrapped when better opportunities arise in novel areas. In a sense, these Chinese family businesses specialise in flexibility and adaptiveness, rather than in a particular technological capability or product sector, and so can change activities quite radically and quickly. Conversely, firms that are vertically integrated and combine complementary, different capabilities may be firmly committed to a single sector and reluctant to shift resources and activities to quite unrelated and novel ones. It is useful, then, to separate these two dimensions for contrasting the variety of activities and capabilities coordinated by economic actors over time.

This characteristic of firms has quite strong implications for employment policies and practices because it affects the willingness of firms to change the mix of skills and capabilities they coordinate radically, and so the speed and frequency with which they hire and fire staff of different kinds. It is also related to the kinds of staff they may prefer to employ, since flexibility can become a key feature of the most valuable employees in economies where firms compete through implementing rapid shifts in products and markets. Where, on the other hand, firms prefer incremental growth strategies, they are unlikely to change employment practices at short notice, and will often build on existing skills and personnel in developing new markets and technologies rather than relying on the external labour market. This does, of course, depend on other characteristics to be considered, as well as on the broader institutional environment.

The third characteristic of firms to be analysed here deals with the preference for growth goals over profits. In the traditional theory of the managerial firm (e.g. Marris, 1964), growth goals were seen as dominating profit maximization ones, usually on the grounds of salaries and other rewards being tied to firm size. An additional factor encouraging the pursuit of large size in capital market based financial systems was its connection with increased security for top managers, although this safeguard appears to be less convincing after the merger booms of the 1980s.

In practice, growth is typically pursued by most firms, subject to a profits constraint, both for competitive reasons and because managerial skills develop and generate increased resources for new activities (Penrose, 1959). However, the extent and type of growth goals do differ across market economies, as does the significance of the profits constraint. For example, in South Korea, and perhaps postwar France and Italy, the dominant role of the state and the high level of business dependence on the state have, together with other factors, encouraged the pursuit of very large size and dominant position in a variety of markets, with only a very limited profits constraint (Amsden, 1989; Janelli, 1993; Whitley, 1992a). In Japan, on the other hand, firms pursue market share goals and seek to grow in size within their sector, partly because of the hierarchical nature of the 'society of industry' (Clark, 1979), and also as a result of the complex networks of mutual dependence between firms, suppliers, customers, banks, employees and other organisations which restrict unrelated diversification but lead to strong collective interests in expansion (Abegglen and Stalk, 1985; Fruin, 1992; Gerlach, 1992). Profit constraints may be more significant here than in Korea, but they are less strong than in the Anglo-Saxon economies because of the weakness of the market for corporate control.

In other kinds of bank dominated economies where firms are closely tied into large banks but are not so embedded in sector specific obligational networks as in Japan, growth goals are likely to be dominant because increased size implies greater demand for banks' services (Zysman, 1983), although profit constraints obviously are strong enough to ensure that loans can be serviced. Such growth may be more diversified than in Japan, but where employees have a strong influence, as in Germany, growth through radical diversification is unlikely if it is perceived to be a threat to current skills and capabilities.

In contrast where firms are much more isolated, and owners operate as portfolio holders and/or managers at arm's length from the companies they invest in, the pursuit of growth goals - and hence managerial rewards and power - is limited by the market for corporate control and the need to meet the targets and expectations of the capital market. Dividend payouts and growth in share prices are here more significant measures of corporate performance than growth per se, and those financial objectives are indifferent as to how profits are made. Effectiveness in these sorts of firms, then, is more a matter of achieving financial objectives than market share goals, and large size without sufficient rates of return on capital employed to pay significant dividends is unlikely to appeal to shareholders. Because the owners of these companies do not have any other connections to them, and so only benefit from the direct rewards of holding their shares, they have a very narrow interest in them, and one which, furthermore, is typically easily traded in the securities market.

Finally, family owned and controlled businesses may limit growth because of a reluctance to share control and a desire to increase family wealth rather than firm size. Where firms are viewed more as the means to enhance family prestige through the acquisition of wealth than as separate organisations, profits may well be more important than growth per se, especially if owners feel politically insecure and large size is seen as attracting the unwanted scrutiny from the state, as in Taiwan and many other countries (Gold, 1986; Greenhalgh, 1984; 1988; Redding, 1990). This does not imply that all family controlled firms will restrict growth, but that, in particular circumstances, they may do so more than other kinds of firms and will concentrate on areas where direct personal control can be maintained.

These examples suggest that a simple way of comparing and contrasting dominant objectives of economic actors is in terms of their pursuit of growth and large size with varying degrees of profit constraints. While the preferred direction of growth also varies significantly across market economies, especially with regard to its focus on a particular sector, it is the extent to which growth goals are subject to strong profit constraints which summarises many of the important differences in firms' objectives discussed above. Thus, the third dimension considered here can be summarised as the extent to which growth and size are dominant objectives with weak profit constraints.

Generally, we can assume that preferences for fast growth and increasing market share over profitability and increasing earnings per share are likely to encourage a positive attitude to recruiting staff, but this does depend on the other characteristics mentioned above, as well as on their general pattern of employer-employee commitment. Japanese firms in the postwar period, for example, have tended to focus on growth and market share goals because of a variety of institutional pressures and relationships, but their relatively specialised nature and development of high levels of employer-employee commitment have inhibited their rate of recruitment and encouraged sub-contracting instead in meeting the growing demand for their products (Clark, 1979; Whitley, 1992a).

Turning now to consider employment policies and practices more specifically, there are three major characteristics which have important implications for state policies and actions: a) the overall level of employer commitment to employees, b) the degree to which employers differentiate between different groups of employees, and c) the degree to which tasks and roles are specialised and allocated to individuals.

Employer-employee commitment refers here to the extent that firms and workers are effectively locked into each other, as in the long term employment system of major Japanese firms in the postwar period (Clark, 1979). This is the key aspect of the distinction between organisation and market based employment systems made by Dore (1973) and Whittaker (1990) in their contrast of British and Japanese employment policies. The former systems are characterised by long term and diffuse commitments to the bulk of the labour force who are rigorously selected and frequently trained for a wide variety of tasks. Rewards are linked to seniority rather than market rates and promotions are internal in these systems, so that intrafirm mobility is greater than interfirm movements. Given this stability of the workforce, and hence its becoming more of a fixed cost than a variable one, personnel management becomes a crucial function and is usually integrated into corporate planning activities.

Market based employment systems, on the other hand, rely on external labour markets for recruiting specialist skills and treat labour costs as variable in the short to medium term so that turnover is much higher. Training is here carried out externally too, and skills are less firm specific. Rewards tend to be based on the market "rate for the job" and mobility is more between firms than within them. Obviously commitment to individual employers tends to remain low in such circumstances and firms are less cohesive and distinctive in their core competencies than in organisation-based employment systems.

Clearly, this dimension has strong implications for employment policies in that economies where organisation-based employment systems are prevalent are going to be less flexible in terms of external labour markets, but probably more flexible internally. Thus state policies which assume high rates of labour mobility between employers will be ineffective in these societies compared to those where markets in skills are more "efficient" in conventional economic terms. Furthermore, skills themselves are more firm specific in the former societies and less likely to be standardised across employers and industries - though this does of course depend on the general system of education and training.

Secondly, a related characteristic which also affects the degree of internal cohesion is the extent of differentiation of employees and of their conditions of employment. The traditional division of the labour force has been between white collar technical, clerical and managerial staff, on the one hand, and blue collar manual workers, on the other hand. However, the growth of the service sector, part-time labour and increasing "white collarisation" of skilled manual workers in some countries, notably Japan, have made this distinction less dominant. Instead, firms and economies can be distinguished more generally in terms of the rigidity and extent of employee segmentation in terms of entry routes, contractual conditions and work organisation and promotion opportunities. Some employers prefer to recruit particular kinds of staff for specific jobs under conditions which inhibit internal mobility, while others may recruit a broad range of staff for a variety of posts under similar terms and conditions. Similarly, in some economies access to particular hierarchical levels in large firms is closely tied to the hierarchy of formal educational credentials so that internal labour markets are segmented by qualifications, while others are much more fluid and permit considerable internal upward mobility. Allied to this differentiation of types of employment is the differentiation of rewards between employee categories and the relative gap between operatives and supervisors, skilled workers and technicians, manual and non-manual workers. As Maurice et al have shown (1986), these vary considerably between France and Germany and are linked to the overall division of labour within firms and job flexibility.

A key aspect of the division of labour in organisations is, of course, the degree of task and role specialisation. Firms vary in the degree to which they narrowly specify tasks, allocate them to specific individuals and evaluate performance of those particular tasks on an individual basis according to specific and detailed procedures. A high degree of division of labour implies that employees are assigned individually to narrow and distinct activities which are usually coordinated through elaborate and formal procedures to constitute a relatively rigid system of work organisation and control. Low specialisation implies broader specification of tasks and roles which are not always allocated to specific individuals, sometimes overlap, and which can change frequently and easily.

Employee segmentation and specialisation affect the recruitment and reward policies of firms, as well as their general labour management practices. Economies where labour markets are highly segmented by employers obviously require employment policies that are adapted to the specific situations of the different groups involved. Equally, where firms prefer to hire generally qualified staff who can undertake a variety of tasks, rather than specialist people for a specific role, public systems of training in narrow skills are unlikely to be attractive to employers. Of course, over the longer term, state policies and organisations can change firms' practices, but in the short run, they have to recognise employers' preferences if they are to have a distinct effect on employment patterns.

Before continuing to identify the key institutions which structure variations in these characteristics, it is worth considering some of their interrelationships since certain combinations are inherently unlikely to be stable, as has been indicated above. Focusing first on the degree of specialisation or diversification, firms which combine many different kinds of skills and capabilities - such as large diversified, divisionalised companies in the Anglo-Saxon economies - are more likely to pursue discontinuous and radical growth patterns than those preferring to specialise in particular sectors or skills because they are not so committed to specific competences or fields of activity and they have developed an ability to manage different kinds of resources which facilitates, in turn, the acquisition or divestment of individual business units. Consequently, diversified firms are not likely to concentrate on growing incrementally through internal development of their core skills and capabilities as much as by acquisition of different kinds of skills and businesses.

Relatedly, diversified firms are less likely to develop long term commitments with key groups of workers since they depend less on particular capabilities in specific sectors than do their more specialised counterparts. Similarly, it is more difficult for such firms to develop a strong common culture and "common community of fate" with the bulk of the workforce because of their diverse skills, production systems and markets, they will therefore tend to differentiate more between groups of employees than companies focused on a particular sector and/or capability. Lastly, more specialised firms are more likely to emphasise flexibility and broad firm specific skills than are diversified ones because they have to manage market risks by adapting to external change through internal shifts in capabilities rather than by diversifying against it. Thus, role specialisation is likely to be relatively low in more sector focused and dependent firms.

Similarly, firms that grow discontinuously by radically changing their resources and capabilities are obviously not likely to develop strong connections to employees, and will usually not be able to establish a strong common culture among the bulk of their staff. Additionally, those that prefer to grow incrementally will be reluctant to institutionalise high levels of role specialisation because this would inhibit flexibility and their ability to respond rapidly to market changes. Since this pattern of growth implies an unwillingness to change human and material resources quickly, it follows that effective adaptation to external demands involves internal flexibility in the use of those resources.

In a similar manner, the pursuit of growth and market share goals with weak profit constraints facilitates higher levels of employee commitment, and, in the case of Japan, it has been explained partly by the institutionalisation of long term employment commitments in the 1950s (Clark, 1979). Conversely, where firms face severe profit constraints - as has been argued in many capital market based finance systems (Zysman, 1983) - long term commitments to employees are difficult to develop because of the need to meet short term financial pressures. For similar reasons, such companies are unlikely to develop strong common identities and employment policies among their employees.

Considering next the connections between employee differentiation and commitment, highly segmented labour forces and reward policies seem unlikely to be associated with high levels of employer-employee commitment, except perhaps around the inner core group with strong personal attachments to the owning family as in the Chinese family business or the Korean Chaebol (Redding, 1990; Whitley, 1992a). Conversely, homogeneous conditions of employment and reward policies are likely to engender a stronger sense of collective identity - as in many of the "permanent" staff of large Japanese firms (Dore, 1973; Whittaker, 1990). Relatedly, high levels of employer-employee commitment will be difficult to develop in organisations where the division of labour is highly specialised and rigid, so that few firms are likely to combine these characteristics. Finally, for similar reasons, firms that establish common patterns of recruitment, training and rewards among the bulk of their employees seem unlikely to develop highly specialised roles and tasks, although the reverse in not necessarily true, as the examples of the Chinese family businesses and the Korean Chaebol again demonstrate.

These interconnections highlight the existence of a number of distinctive patterns of employment policies and practices, especially those exemplified by firms in the Anglo-Saxon and Japanese economies. The former tend to be quite diversified and able to change their key resources, markets and skills relatively quickly in response to shifts in profitability. Growth and market share goals here are quite constrained by profit rates and firms rarely develop long term commitments to employees, or a strong common culture and homogeneous employment policies among them. The latter - at least in most of the postwar period - are quite focused on particular sectors and capabilities, prefer to grow incrementally and internally, develop long term commitments to the core male employees and a strong common culture which precludes a strict division of labour and role specialisation. Firms in other economies, such as the Korean, German and Scandinavian, tend not to exhibit such a clearcut pattern but do reflect distinctive institutional environments, and it is the key features of these institutions which will now be explored.

## 7.2.    MAJOR INSTITUTIONAL FEATURES STRUCTURING FIRMS' STRATEGIES AND PRACTICES

These characteristics of business systems developed interdependently with dominant social institutions during and after industrialisation in different market economies so that distinctive kinds of employment relations and labour management practices became established in particular institutional contexts and only change when central features of those contexts change. The crucial institutional arrangements which guide and constrain these characteristics are those governing access to key resources, especially labour and capital. Also important are the ways in which different kinds of labour power are developed, both in terms of technical skills and individuals' attitudes and values. Differences in the norms and rules controlling the terms on which private property rights' holders can acquire and use human and material resources, and exchange inputs and outputs, additionally have major consequences for firms' policies and structures, as do variations in social structures which differentiate individuals' capabilities and develop particular kinds of competences at the expense of others.

These institutions can be very broadly characterised and compared across market economies in terms of four major systems of norms and rules: cultural, political, financial and labour. These deal with both the kinds of resources - especially human ones - that are available to privately owned economic actors in any particular market economy, and the terms on which they are available, as well as, of course, with the sorts of people who become private property rights' owners. To some extent, the location of particular features in one of these "systems" is a matter of convenience - so that, for example, the degree of state regulation of labour markets can either be seen as part of the overall level of state regulation of markets or as a specific feature of the training and occupational system - but together they do summarise the key aspects of the institutional context which impinge most on forms of economic organisation.

Considering first the cultural system, the critical features influencing the nature of firms and employment policies are those conventions and norms which regulate trust relations, foci of commitment and loyalty and superordinate-subordinate relations. These are crucial because they structure exchange relationships between economic actors, and between employers and employees, as well as the nature of collective identities and ways of eliciting compliance and commitment within authority systems. They therefore affect governance structures of firms, the ways in which they deal with each other and other organisations, and the prevalent patterns of work organisation, control and employment.

The ways in which trust is granted and guaranteed are especially important influences on the level of interfirm cooperation and tendency to delegate control over resources in an economy. While there are significant variations in how competence, contractual and goodwill forms of trust (Sako, 1992) are developed in different cultures, the key feature here is the strength of the social institutions generating and guaranteeing trust between relative strangers. In particular, the extent to which property rights' owners, and the economic actors they control, feel able to rely on institutionalised procedures when making business commitments is a crucial factor in the establishment of collaborative relations within and between firms, and in the perception and management of risk (Zucker, 1986). Where such procedures are weak or judged unreliable, personal and particularistic-connection become especially important in organising exchange relationships (Hamilton et al, 1990; Redding, 1990).

Foci of social identity and loyalty are often discussed in terms of the individualism-collectivism, or "communitarianism" (Lodge and Vogel, 1987), continuum, but another significant distinction is that between family, or kinship based, units of identity and those based on broader collectivities. Cultures where the family is the dominant focus of identity, commitment and loyalty, to the extent that little or no responsibility or loyalty to extra-familial and non-kin groupings is regarded as an important component of moral worth, will inhibit the development of organisational loyalties among large numbers of employees. The establishment of a distinctive corporate personality and culture which is not tied to the characteristics of particular individuals is clearly much easier in a culture where collective loyalties are not highly concentrated on families and family-like personal linkages (Hamilton and Kao, 1990; Numazaki, 1992). Similarly, cultures which encourage commitment and loyalty to collective entities, such as political parties, unions and associations, that generate group identities as well as individual ones may develop higher levels of organisational commitment than those which emphasise individual rights and interests. Overall, then, the key feature of the cultural system here is the extent to which there are strong norms and conventions encouraging the development of extra-kin, non-personal collective commitments and obligations so that people feel responsible for the fates of collectivities they join.

Superordinate-subordinate relations are typically governed by a number of different norms and rules, as Eckstein and Gurr (1975) have shown, so that a considerable variety of authority patterns has developed across cross-cultures and political systems. Some of the key dimensions which affect subordination relations in work organisations are: a) the extent to which superordinate discretion is governed by formal rules and procedures, b) the degree of reciprocity expected of supervisors in return for deference and obedience, c) the appropriate social and moral distance between leaders and led, d) the autonomy and independent status of subordinates (d'Iribarne, 1989), e) the mode of legitimising access to superordinate positions such as elections or formal credentials, and f) the extent to which common interests can be invoked successfully in claims for compliance with superiors' instructions.

These dimensions can be combined in a large number of different ways in different empirical situations, but one far-reaching distinction can be drawn between cultural and political systems which, on the one hand, a) restrict superordinate discretion through formal rules and procedures to a fairly narrow range of issues and actions, b) acknowledge the independent and autonomous status of subordinates as individuals able to make rational decisions, and c) involve subordinates in the choice of superordinates and in decision making to some extent, from those that, on the other hand, do not. The former can be considered to institutionalise predominantly formal authority relations, while the latter develop more paternalist hierarchical relations.

Paternalism in turn can be divided into two major kinds: remote and reciprocal. Remote paternalism implies a high degree of social and moral distance between leaders and their followers with little direct reciprocity expected of superordinates in return for subordinates' deference. Common and shared interests are rarely invoked as the basis for compliance and superiors often claim a moral superiority which requires no further justifications, as in the virtuocracies of Confucian China and Korea (Pye, 1985; Silin, 1976). Reciprocal paternalism, on the other hand, involves much closer links between superordinates and subordinates, with reciprocal services expected of superiors through direct patronage and a strong belief in both leaders and led sharing a common community of fate, as in modern Japan (Rohlen, 1974; van Wolferen, 1989).

Formal authority can also be further subdivided into a number of different kinds, but perhaps the most significant contrast is between contractual and communal forms of authority. This distinction focuses on the extent to which authority rests upon widespread and diffuse appeals to common interests as opposed to highly specific and narrow agreements between discrete and separate contractors. Communal forms of authority imply relatively high levels of mutual trust and commitment, with shared understandings of priorities and interests, and often rely on expertise as a key quality of superordinates, while contractual authority tends to presume more adversarial relationships and a dominant pursuit of self-interest. The former seems to have become institutionalised in some Scandinavian and continental European countries, while the latter is found more in Anglo-Saxon societies (Lodge and Vogel, 1987). D'Iribarne (1989) suggests the prevalent form of authority in France constitutes a further kind of authority - the quasi-feudal - in which reciprocity is low and social distance high between superior and subordinate, but the autonomy and rationality of the latter is emphasised.

Turning to consider the political system, and especially the state, there are, of course, many features of state structures and policies which influence firms' policies and employment patterns, but four summary ones are particularly significant. First, the overall cohesion, prestige and autonomy of the state executive and bureaucracy is an important variable characteristic of all market economies. Sometimes referred to as the 'strength' of the state vis-à-vis social interest groups, landed elites, etc., this aspect clearly affects the development and implementation of economic policy, and the independence of business owners and managers. Second, states vary greatly in their commitment to coordinate economic development and willingness to share investment risks with private economic interests, as opposed to remaining aloof from firms' decisions. Some, such as many Anglo-Saxon states, have neither the wish to, nor the capability of, actively coordinating economic processes. Others, like perhaps the post-1950s Japanese, pursue 'developmental' (Johnson, 1982) policies but do not commit large resources to sharing private sector investment risks, while a few do both, such as the post-1961 South Korean state (Amsden, 1989; Wade, 1990). Clearly, where the state is both 'strong' and actively risk sharing, then private firms become quite dependent upon it and have to invest considerable resources in managing political risks.

A third significant feature of political systems is the extent to which there are important intermediary associations of organisations and groups between individuals and the state, particularly in the economic sphere. Some European states, for instance, appear unable to tolerate such groupings while others, like the Germans and Austrians, seem to positively encourage their formation and to develop quite strong corporatist forms of intra- and inter-sectoral organisation. Clearly, interfirm cooperation, alliances and cartelisation will be easier in the latter sets of states than in the former. Finally, there are significant differences in the extent to which states formally regulate market boundaries, entry and exit, as well as set constraints on the activities of economic actors. Product, capital and labour markets are variously regulated and this affects their segmentation, intensity of competition and mobility of resources and flexibility of firms.

Financial systems also vary on a number of dimensions, but the critical feature here deals with the processes by which capital is made available and priced. In particular, is it allocated by capital markets through competition, so that lenders and users remain relatively remote from one another, or is it provided by some set of intermediaries which deal directly with firms and become locked into their particular success? Capital market based financial systems, as characterised by Zysman (1983), mobilise and distribute capital largely through large and liquid markets which trade and price financial claims through the usual commodity market processes. Because many, if not most, investors and fund managers deal in portfolios of shares that can be readily traded on secondary and tertiary markets, they are only weakly committed to the growth of any single firm they own shares in, and so have only a relatively short term and narrow interest in its fortunes. This encourages a strong market for corporate control in capital market financial systems as ownership rights are easily traded and owners have little incentive to retain shares when offered considerable price premiums for them by acquisitive predators.

Credit based financial systems, on the other hand, typically have weak and fairly illiquid or thin capital markets which play only a minor role in mobilising and pricing investment funds. The dominant institutions here are either large, 'universal' banks as in Germany or a combination of commercial banks and long term credit banks coordinated by state agencies and ministries, as in France, Japan and some other countries (Cox, 1986). Because of capital shortages during high growth periods, and/or state control of interest rates to support economic development, demand for investment funds often exceeds supply to a considerable degree in these systems and so banks and/or the state allocate capital through administrative processes to particular sectos and activities, such as export industries or the heavy manufacturing sector. Since shares are not easily traded, owners, bankers and trust managers become locked into particular borrowers' fates and so have to be more involved in decision making and the detailed evaluation of investment plans than they do in capital market based systems. This, in turn, means that they have to deal with a considerable amount of information about their customers' businesses and develop considerable expertise in them. Once that expertise has been developed by financial intermediaries, they have a vested interest in using it to provide new services and play a more active role in firms' growth planning. They thus become even more committed to particular enterprises and develop a common community of fate with them. Although some financial systems do not fit neatly into this broad dichotomy (cf. van Iterson and Olie, 1992), and there are other important features of financial systems to be considered in analysing particular economies, this basic contrast between two major kinds of financial systems has strong implications for firms and markets and is a critical feature of the institutional context of labour management strategies

Considering finally the labour system, there are two broad, interrelated sets of institutions that are crucial to the kinds of employment patterns that become established in market economies. First, there is the system that develops and certifies competences and skills: the education and training system. Second, there are the institutions which control the terms on which the owners of those skills sell them in labour markets and how those markets are organised.

Of particular importance in comparing education and training systems is the extent to which practical skills are publicly organised and certified and combine practical learning in firms with formal learning in educational institutions. In their comparison of work organisation and control practices in France and Germany, Marc Maurice and his colleagues (1986) drew a contrast between unitary and generalist education systems, such as the French and Japanese, and dual, specialist ones, such as the German and some other Continental European ones. In the former, children are successively filtered by academic examinations in the general educational system and only "failures" enter state practical training organisations which are often poorly funded and have low social prestige. In the latter, practical skill training integrates theory and practice, as well as employers, unions and state education, and is seen as a different, but not greatly inferior, form of education to the grammar school system leading to university entrance. The specialist training system, at least in Germany, combines some elements of traditional apprenticeship with college based formal instruction and is cooperatively managed by representatives of labour, capital and the state. While the specialist-generalist contrast is too simple to summarise all the important differences between education and training systems, the central feature here is the extent to which they develop publicly certified, relatively standardised, broad practical skills which combine currrently usable capacities with more general knowledge and aptitudes which facilitate future learning and improvement in an integrated way involving all three major sets of organisations: employers, unions and the state. This can be termed the extent to which the training system develops broad, cumulating, publicly examined and certified skills through cooperation and collaboration.

The organisation and control of labour markets can be analysed on a considerable variety of dimensions but the critical features here are the extent to which the availability of skills and capabilities are controlled by trade unions and professional associations, and on what organisational bases, and the way that bargaining is structured. The overall power and significance of trade unions is obviously an important factor in employers' ability to change strategic priorities, technologies and markets as well as affecting their labour management strategies. Relatedly, the extent to which unions and other forms of collective representation are organised around craft skills and professional expertise, as opposed to being based on industries or enterprises, has strong consequences for the internal organisation of work process and the division of labour, as the history of demarcation disputes and professional specialisation in Britain illustrates (Child et al, 1983). Where, on the other hand, they are industry or sector based, employers are also likely to develop strong forms of intra-industry collaboration, as in Germany, and employer-employee cooperation across the industry may be easier to develop, as it is when enterprise based unionism is prevalent. Similarly, where bargaining is centralised, both unions and employers develop greater internal cohesion and coordination than when it is fragmented among firms and plants. In order to be effective representatives of collective interests, union and employer federations gain control over constituent members in centralised bargaining systems and usually firms develop interdependent linkages with each other in dealing with industrial relations issues.

These characteristics of the cultural, political, financial and labour systems are summarised in Table 7.2. Two aspects of these systems need to be emphasised before considering their connections and interdependence with the characteristics of business systems discussed earlier. First, the extent of integration and cohesion of these institutional features varies significantly across market economies. Second, the relative importance and influence of particular institutions on forms of economic organisation can differ greatly between societies, so that their effects on particular components of national business systems can also differ.

The degree of interdependence and mutual reinforcement of dominant political, financial, labour and cultural institutions in market economies varies between those which seem to constitute a seamless web of tightly coupled obligations and benefits between the major actors and

---

*Table 7.2    Key Features od Dominant Institutions Affecting Firms'
Strategies and Employment Practices*

A.  *The Cultural System*
1.  Strength of formal institutions governing trust relations.
2.  Strength of norms developing extra-familial obligations and commitments.
3.  Dominant expectations governing superordinate-subordinate relations:
     Remote paternalism
     Reciprocal paternalism
     Contractual authority
     Communal formal authority

B.  *The Political System*
1.  Cohesion, prestige and autonomy of the state.
2.  State commitment to economic development and risk sharing with private
    interests.
3.  Encouragement of intermediary organisations.
4.  Extent of market regulation.

C.  *The Financial System*
1.  Extent to which the financial system is credit based.

D.  *The Labour System*
1.  Extent to which the public training system develops broad, cumulative, certified
    skills on a collaborative tripartite basis.
2.  Strength of labour organisations.
3.  Extent to which unions and occupational associations are organised around craft
    skills and professional expertise.
4.  Centralisation and integration of bargaining.

---

organisations, as in, arguably, postwar Japan (Clark, 1979; Whitley, 1992a; van Wolferen, 1989), and those which seem much more loosely coupled and pluralistic, such as the Anglo-Saxon economies (Hollingsworth and Streeck 1993; Lane, 1992). In the latter, economic relations and activities have developed more autonomously and are less embedded in particular political, religious and social arrangements, and these institutions are themselves more independent in their patterns of development, selection and training of élites and dominant beliefs, than in the more integrated economies. Incremental change in prevalent economic relations and structures is less likely in the more tightly coupled economies, and depends more on interrelated changes in proximate institutions, than in the more fragmented and partitioned ones.

   The relative centrality of individual institutions to the kind of economic organisation that develops and is reproduced in a market economy also varies. For example, the postwar German system of skills training and industrial relations has had a major impact on patterns of work organisation and labour management strategies in German companies, to the extent that these are relatively homogeneous and distinctive when compared to those prevalent in, say, the UK (Maurice et al, 1986; Lane, 1992). In contrast, the variable and changing training system in the Anglo-Saxon economies has had much less impact on patterns of work organisation and control, which in consequence are less homogeneous and standardised across sectors. Similarly, cultural heterogeneity and the lack of strong, standardised norms and values throughout a society may be so great that their influence on, say, authority relations will be less marked than in societies where cultural uniformity is high and standards of behaviour are reproduced consistently and strongly through the family and educational system. In explaining the characteristics of any one business system, and changes in them, then some institutional features may be more important than others, and more significant in one economy than in different ones.

## 7.3.   INTERDEPENDENCES BETWEEN INSTITUTIONS AND EMPLOYMENT PATTERNS

In considering how social institutions structure forms of economic organisation it is important to bear in mind two points. First, the most direct connections between institutional features and business system characteristics often occur when institutions display particularly strong features at extremes of the dimensions being considered. Relatedly, the connections are often not reversible in the sense that the negative relationship may not hold to the same extent. Second, interdependences between single institutional features and forms of economic organisation are only tendencies which, in practice, are modified by other features and historical contingencies.

   The effects of particular political, financial, labour and cultural institutions on the characteristics of employment relations that become established and change in a market economy are often most marked when they exemplify a particular characteristic. For example, the link between a strong, developmentalist state and the prevalence of growth goals is not a continuous one but rather is particularly significant - and dominates other factors - when the level of business dependence on the state is especially high, as in postwar Korea (Amsden, 1989; Whitley, 1992a; Woo, 1991). Similarly, the effect of weak institutions governing trust relations on inter-firm alliances and sector organisations is mostly likely to be evident when formal institutions are very weak and/or widely regarded as unreliable, as in many expatriate Chinese economies (Redding, 1990; Silin, 1976). Additionally, these direct influences do not apply in cases when institutions exemplify the reverse features. Where, for instance, the state is relatively weak and/or does not pursue developmentalist policies, firms' strategies may or may not follow growth goals. The postwar federal German state appears less strong and cohesive than its French equivalent, but this has not led German companies to behave like Anglo-Saxon ones, not least because of the major differences in financial systems and other factors encouraging cooperation (Lane, 1992). Similarly, the existence of an effective legal system governing contractual trust does not necessarily lead to extensive delegation of control to salaried managers by owners, although the lack of such formal institutions is likely to encourage strong owner control.

This point highlights the interdependence of these institutional features in structuring employment patterns. In any particular market economy, the prevalent form of economic organisation will reflect the influence of all dominant institutions as they have developed in conjunction with each other during and after early industrialisation. The explanation of particular employment practices, and changes in their characteristics, then, clearly depends on an analysis of all the key institutions and how they interdependently structured the specific form of economic organisation that developed. The peculiarities of the prevalent business system in Britain, for example, cannot be adequately understood without taking into account the role of the interconnected pre-industrial state and financial system, and their links with the development of the training "system" and organisation of labour markets, not to mention the pervasive and long-established cultural norm of individualism (Macfarlane, 1978).

Focusing initially on the relationships between institutions and firms' strategies, I shall outline the major interdependences between features of the cultural, political, financial and labour systems and the degree of diversification, discontinuous growth and preference for growth goals of leading firms. Analysing first the diversity of activities and capabilities coordinated by leading economic actors, this usually increases as a result of internalising risk and of difficulties in developing linkages with other economic actors. Thus, highly diverse economic actors tend to develop in economies where the state remains aloof from economic coordination and risk sharing, and the banks likewise are remote from the activities of particular firms. In other words, economies characterised by arm's length relationships between major institutions and essentially adversarial relations between organisations are likely to encourage higher levels of diversification than those with more integrated and interdependent institutions. Conversely, where it is easier to develop obligational relationships between enterprises and reciprocity is a strongly established norm, firms are more likely to restrict their radical diversification into unrelated fields.

Credit based financial systems, where banks and other financial institutions develop close links with particular firms as they become locked into them, are also likely to limit unrelated diversification. This is because risks are shared and because banks invest in the development of knowledge of, and skills in, the particular industries of their clients and so will be reluctant to undertake further investment in unrelated areas. Banks may also be unlikely to believe that firms can manage quite different kinds of activities and will exercise more veto power over such moves than over expansion in present or related business areas. Additional constraints on unrelated diversification arise when firms are embedded in strong sector specific associations and linkages. Thus, where bargaining, training and similar activities in labour markets are governed by strong institutions at the sector level, firms will find it more difficult to pursue high levels of diversification than when such institutions are weak or non-existent, as in the Anglo-Saxon economies. Similarly, state support for intermediary trade associations, employers' federations and tolerance of interfirm coordination and cooperation will limit diversification because sectors are more likely to be governed by industry associations and formal and informal conventions limiting both entry and exit.

There is, however, one situation in which state coordination and risk sharing may well increase diversification. This is when business dependence on the state is very high and the dominant risk for firms is to lose state support. Here, firms may undertake considerable unrelated diversification as a way of limiting the risks attached to failure in any one area of business, especially where they are subject to state targets and sanctions. This is particularly probable when the state has encouraged investment in new areas and provided much of the capital required, as in South Korea (Amsden, 1989). Although risks may be shared with the state in this instance, they are still considerable and dominated by the fear of losing access to cheap credit and other political favours. Thus, unrelated diversification is most likely to be a feature of market economies in which: a) state support is either very low or else dominates large firm strategies, b) there are few strong intermediary associations, c) financial institutions are remote from particular firms and d) sector based institutions governing labour market activities are likewise weak.

Similar factors affect the degree of radical change in activities and capabilities coordinated by economic actors. The more embedded are firms in particular networks of mutual dependence with other employers, banks, unions and other major institutions, the less easy will it be for them to alter their major sector of activity, divest resources and acquire new ones. Contrarily, the more autonomous they are from trade associations, sector based bargaining and training institutions and employers' federations, the more straightforward is it to change business areas and core competences. Additionally, strong trade unions are likely to inhibit radical shifts in resources and skills since they will resist the devaluation of their members' expertise. In economies where institutions and organisations are interdependent and develop close ties of mutual obligation, then economic actors are likely to focus on specific sectors of activity and not engage in radical changes of direction. Rather, strategic development will be incremental and closely related to current strengths and capabilities, as in Japan (Kagono et al, 1985). Similarly, firms in the more "corporatist" European states are unlikely to operate as portfolio holders, buying and selling subsidiaries for short term gains, because they are members of complex networks which cannot easily be changed, and, often, because there are legal barriers to rapid entry and exit.

Flexibility in resources and skills, on the other hand, is likely to be encouraged when both capital and labour are highly mobile and there are few, if any, strong institutions linking firms together. State indifference to economic coordination and development needs, together with antagonism to interfirm cooperation and collaboration, will emphasise the isolation of economic actors and adversarial, predatory relations between them. Large, liquid capital markets, weak trade unions, fragmented bargaining and training systems and weak intermediary associations such as trade associations and chambers of commerce, together facilitate flexible and rapid responses to changing market pressures by radically changing the nature of resources and skills coordinated by economic actors (Campbell et al, 1991; Lane, 1992).

Considering next the dominance of growth goals with weak profit constraints, high levels of political risk encourage strong growth goals because firms compete for state support and attention and size is a major factor in both gaining assistance and in limiting the likelihood of withdrawal of support. Growth is also often facilitated by a strong state role in coordinating economic development and in sharing investment risks because of the preferential access to subsidised credit provided by the state, as well as such coordination reducing uncertainty about the pay offs from major investments. Thus rapid expansion can be achieved through cheap loans without risking family capital and existing assets. This typically requires a credit based financial system in which the state plays the leading role in allocating scarce capital (Zysman, 1983).

Credit based systems encourage growth goals as well because banks and other intermediaries become locked into particular customers and develop a multiplicity of linkages with them. Since they are interdependent with particular firms, it is in their interests to encourage growth so that they can provide more loans and other services on the basis of their initial commitment. If they own shares themselves, or act as trustees, the return on these investments is only part of the total return from all the services they provide, and so share price growth and dividends are not so crucial to them as they are to portfolio managers in capital market based financial systems. Additionally, banks have to develop specialist expertise in particular fields and markets in order to judge investment proposals and demands for loans competently. Once acquired, these skills have to be used so that further growth is encouraged. Similar arguments apply to strong trade unions where their interests also imply an emphasis on growth goals, especially where the workforce is effectively locked into particular employers and employer-employee interdependence is high, as in postwar Japan (Clark, 1979).

Turning now to consider more direct relations between institutional features and employment policies of firms, the impact of particular norms and values on employer-employee commitment and interdependence is quite marked. Low levels of trust and collective loyalty beyond family members inhibit the development of mutual trust and confidence between employers and employees who do not have personal ties and obligations, as Redding (1990) suggests is the case in many Chinese businesses (cf. Deyo, 1989; Silin, 1976). Similarly, authority claims based on the personal moral superiority of superordinates are unlikely to encourage close, reciprocal commitments between owner-managers and employees.

Mutual risk sharing and confidence building between employers and employees are also difficult to establish in economies where the state and the financial system do not share private sector investment risks and firms are forced to focus on short term market pressures. Especially where labour markets are weakly regulated and unions are also weak, this adversarial, anomic environment limits employers' ability and wish to develop long term cooperative relationships with employees, and leads them to pursue numerical rather than functional flexibility labour strategies (Friedman, 1977; Lane, 1989; 1992).

On the other hand, reciprocal paternalist patterns of authority as well as communal ones linked to shared skills and expertise are likely to encourage interdependence and reciprocal commitments, if not always to the extent found in large postwar Japanese firms (Aoki, 1988; Koike, 1987). Superordinate interest in, and commonality with, subordinates and their task performance skills and development facilitate the establishment of mutual commitment and trust, as does the experience of collaborating in training programmes and certifying skills. Centralised bargaining systems also enable firms and unions to develop routines facilitating cooperation and long term trade offs by providing a framework for repeated negotiations and mediating the pressures to pursue short term advantages. A strong labour movement also encourages employers to seek common ground with employees to reduce disruptions and ensure flexibility in responding to technological and market change, although this will be mitigated if unions are primarily structured around narrow craft skills which control access to particular jobs. Here, strong unions may inhibit flexibility of jobs that are tied to specific technologies and expertise so that employees limit change which threatens the current division of labour and their posts. Where employers are able to rely on the external labour market to recruit new skills and discard the owners of old ones, as in Britain (Gospel, 1992; Lane, 1989), they may prefer to manage change through numerical rather than functional flexibility and unions may encourage this by protecting the current skills of their membership rather than trying to extend their control to new skills and expertise, as in Denmark (Kristensen, 1992).

Differentiation and segmentation of employment conditions between manual, technical and managerial employees - and other groups within firms - are easier and more marked when trust levels are low, because employers then concentrate on binding a particular group to the destiny of the enterprise, typically through the reward system. This is easier when authority is predominantly contractual rather than communal because institutionalising sharply differential rewards does not contradict prevalent authority principles, or an emphasis on the common membership of the community of fate.

It is less likely to be widely institutionalised when unions are strong and employers are used to collaborating with them in the training system. A strong labour movement limits employers' ability to implement divide and rule strategies, and encourages them to pursue integrated employment policies for all employees, especially when the unions are sector or enterprise based. Similarly, a strong, jointly controlled system for developing broad, cumulating publicly certified skills reduces both the incentive and the feasibility of sharply differentiating between managerial, technical and skilled manual employees, since many will share training backgrounds and such a strategy would be divisive and conflict with this collaboration.

Considering, finally, the degree of task and role specialisation, firms are more likely to adopt a narrow and highly specialised division of labour when the training system does not produce broadly skilled workers who are able to develop new expertise fairly easily, thus requiring employers to undertake on the job training which is limited to the specific task being performed. In the case of many large Japanese firms, this is counteracted by the high level of employer-employee commitment which places a premium on flexibility of skills and roles to facilitate long term employment policies. Both employers and employees here have a vested interest in not establishing a narrow division of labour so that firms can deal with change without destroying this mutual commitment.

Specialisation is also encouraged by strong skill based trade unions and professional associations which control, standardise and certify relatively narrow skills without significant employer involvement. Because expertise in these economies is largely controlled by external agencies, firms adapt their job specifications and expectations to the available competences and find it difficult to develop broader, more interdependent and flexible roles. Where loyalties are primarily based on these certified skills, it is difficult to foster employer-employee commitment which would transcend their boundaries and so coordination costs can be considerable, as Child et al (1983) have argued is the case in Britain.

Contractual forms of authority also facilitate specialisation by institutionalising relatively formal and narrow delimitations of responsibilities and requirements so that roles can be formally specified and defined. Contrarily, more paternalistic sorts of authority place fewer restrictions on superordinate discretion and permit greater flexibility in allocating tasks and responsibilities. Formal delimitation of tasks and roles is therefore less strong and developed in these cultures than where authority relations are more specified and bounded by formal procedures.

These interconnections are summarised in Table 7.3, which highlights the links between particular combinations of institutional features and distinctive patterns of firm type and employment policies. In particular, the dominant characteristics of firms and their labour management practices in Anglo-Saxon and postwar Japanese economies can be clearly understood in terms of their quite different institutional environments. The combination of relatively weak states which distance themselves from direct involvement in firms' affairs, and do not wish to regulate markets formally with capital market based financial systems that facilitate a strong market for corporate control and high liquidity of share ownership in Anglo-Saxon societies has led to individual companies being relatively isolated and autonomous managers of risks. This, in turn, has encouraged diversification across products, markets and skills and portfolio approaches to managing a range of businesses which are often bought and sold as distinct, tradeable entities. Growth goals in this situation are subject to quite strong profit constraints due to capital market pressures. In combination with predominantly adversarial relations with the labour movement and decentralised bargaining systems, these institutional features discourage the development of long-term commitments to employees and instead have led to a reliance on the external labour market for acquiring new skills. Coupled with strong occupational associations and a traditional union structure based on relatively narrowly defined skills, this has resulted in quite segmented employment policies and specialised roles within firms. These connections are diagrammed in Figure 7.1.

In contrast, the postwar Japanese state has been quite "strong", especially in the 1950s and early 1960s, and has taken direct responsibility for managing economic development, particularly on a sectoral basis (Johnson, 1982). While not as focused on individual firms and as overweening as the post-1961 South Korean State (Amsden, 1989), it has coordinated investment policies and major strategic choices of leading enterprises and groups through the credit system and extensive regulatory discretion. Together with the credit based financial system which has generated close ties between large firms and banks, this has encouraged high growth policies with only weak profit constraints. The insignificant market for corporate control and major role of intermediary organisations, combined with strong conventions governing trust relations and reciprocity in Japanese society, has enabled Japanese large firms to remain

*Table 7.3   Interdependences between Institutional Features, Firms' Strategies and Employment Practices*

| Institutional Features | Firms' Strategies and Employment Practices | | | | | |
|---|---|---|---|---|---|---|
| | Highly Diversified | Radical Discontinuous Changes | High Growth Goals | High Employer-Employee Commitment | High Employee Segmentation | High Role Specialisation |
| Weak trust institutions | | + | | − | + | |
| Low collective loyalties | | | | − | | |
| Remote paternalistic authority | | | | − | | − |
| Reciprocal paternalist authority | | | | + | | − |
| Contractual authority | | | | | + | |
| Communal authority | | | | + | − | |
| Dominant state | | | + | | | |
| Low state risk sharing | + | + | − | − | | |
| Support for intermediaries | − | − | | | | |
| High regulation of markets | − | − | | + | | |
| Credit based financial system | − | − | + | | | |
| Capital market financial system | | | | − | | |
| Strong joint training system | − | − | | + | − | |
| Strong skill based unions | | | | | − | + |
| Centralised bargaining | − | − | | + | | |
| Strong labour movement | | − | + | + | − | |

relatively focused on particular sectors and manage risks through interdependent ties to suppliers, customers and employees which inhibit radical discontinuities in their activities and capabilities. The strength of the labour movement in the late 1940s and 1950s, together with the strong collective loyalties capable of being developed in Japan - as distinct from Korea and China - also encouraged such long term commitments between large firms and the male workforce. These were further facilitated by the absence of strong skill based occupational associations and unions which could generate horizontal loyalties and "efficient" external labour markets in specialised skills. Relatedly, the lack of a strong public training system in technical skills has allowed firms to develop firm specific skills which are flexible and allow considerable mobility within large organisations. Figure 7.2 summarises these relationships.

Similar connections between combinations of institutions and firm characteristics and policies help to account for the distinctive patterns found in the Chinese family business (cf. Redding, 1990; Silin, 1976), the Korean chaebol (see Janelli, 1993; Kim, 1992) and different Continental European economies (e.g. Lane, 1992; Lilja et al, 1992). For example, the relatively low level of trust in formal institutions and of collective loyalties beyond the family in South Korea, Taiwan and the Chinese diaspora in Asia has inhibited the development of strong employer-employee interdependence beyond the owning family and a few colleagues with whom strong, family-like personal loyalties have been developed in Chinese and Korean businesses. Similarly, the strong peak associations and trade unions in Germany and many Scandinavian countries have encouraged employers to cooperate with employees, limit segmentation of groups of employees and pursue growth goals incrementally within particular industries rather than discontinuously. Authority in these societies is also less focused on narrow forms of contractualism than in Anglo-Saxon ones, and so the establishment of a commitment to common objectives and acceptance of superiors' expertise is easier to achieve, especially when reinforced by legal requirements such as the Co-Determination Acts in Germany.

These examples indicate the complex interdependences that exist in any market economy between sets of institutional features and firm types so that the particular kind of labour management strategies and employment policies that develop, and change, among particular leading firms reflect a number of tendencies and pressures that not infrequently conflict. The postwar French state, for example, has been dominant and risk sharing through its control over the flow of credit (Green, 1986; Zysman, 1983), yet it has not encouraged the establishment of strong intermediaries or a strong collaborative training system. Unions are weak and fragmented in France, especially in the private sector, and typically rely on political actions to obtain their goals. Firms, therefore, can pursue growth goals with only weak profit constraints but have not been encouraged to develop

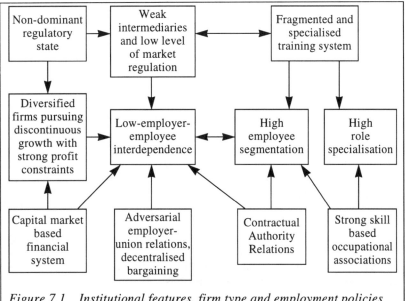

*Figure 7.1     Institutional features, firm type and employment policies
in Anglo-Saxon capitalism*

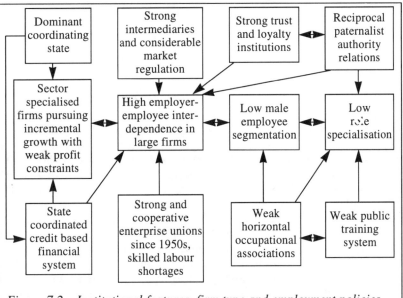

*Figure 7.2     Institutional features, firm type and employment policies
in postwar Japanese capitalism*

long term commitment to employees or common employment conditions. Indeed, the strongly hierarchical formal education system, and its influence on the allocation of social prestige and state positions, have entrenched highly differentiated strata in many large French firms. Despite, then, some similarities with Japanese institutions, other differences, not least the overall pattern of industrialisation, have led to quite contrasting employment patterns in France.

Such interdependences, and the remarkable longevity of many characteristics of firms and their preferred ways of managing employees, clearly structure responses to state employment initiatives, and long term patterns of employment growth and decline. The sorts of jobs that firms offer, how they recruit staff, reward, train and promote or dismiss them, are highly constrained and guided by the nature of dominant economic actors in any one market economy and, both directly and indirectly, by the nature of dominant institutions in each economy. Consequently, employment patterns, and the impact of efforts to change them, are highly dependent on the particular interdependences between business system characteristics and institutional features which have become established during and after industrialisation. These patterns can be changed, but only by also changing key institutions and taking into account the systemic connections between them.

## 7.4.   CONCLUSIONS

This discussion of employment policies and firms' strategies in different contexts has highlighted a number of conclusions. First, employment practices and labour management strategies are closely interlinked with the kinds of firms that dominate an economy. Thus, second, policies designed to modify firms' labour strategies need to consider their general pattern of growth and risk management if they are to be effective. Third, such general patterns are themselves dependent on the overall institutional context in which firms operate, especially the political and financial systems, and so changing labour market institutions without also modifying key features of these systems may be ineffective or even counter-productive. Fourth, since the state is itself both a key actor within each market economy, and an interdependent part of the overall system, the ways in which employment policies are developed and implemented are themselves structured by dominant logics and constraints. Standard recipes are, thus, inevitably transmuted into more idiosyncratic and context dependent actions. Finally, the institutional interdependence of firms' activities and development patterns means that any significant shift in their employment policies and practices - through, for instance, investing heavily in a public skill training system - will take a considerable time to develop and may well have unforeseen consequences.

# REFERENCES

Abegglen, James C. and George Stalk (1985) *Kaisha: The Japanese Corporation*, New York: Basic Books.

Amsden, A.H. (1989) *Asia's next Giant*, Oxford: Oxford University Press.

Aoki, M. (1988) *Information, Incentives, and Bargaining in the Japanese Economy*, Cambridge: Cambridge University Press.

Campbell, J., R. Hollingsworth and L. Lindberg (eds) (1991) *The Governance of the American Economy*, Cambridge: Cambridge University Press.

Chandler, A.D. (1990) *Scale and Scope,* Cambridge, Mass.: Harvard University Press.

Child, J., M. Fores, L. Glover and P. Lawrence (1983) "A Price to Pay? Professionalism in Work Organisation in Britain and West Germany", *Sociology* 17: 63-78.

Clark, R. (1979) *The Japanese Company*, Yale University Press.

Cox, A. (1986) "State, Finance and Industry in Comparative Perspective", in A. Cox (ed), *State, Finance and Industry*, Brighton: Wheatsheaf.

Cusumano, M.A. (1985) *The Japanese Automobile Industry: Technology and Management at Nissan and Toyota*, Harvard University Press.

Deyo, F.C. (1989) *Beneath the Miracle: Labour Subordination in the New Asian Industrialism*, Berkeley, Calif.: University of California Press.

Dore, R.P. (1973) *British Factory - Japanese Factory*, London: Allen and Unwin.

Eckstein, H. and T.R. Gurr, (1975) *Patterns of Authority a structural basis for political inquiry*, New York: John Wiley.

Fligstein, N. (1990) *The Transformation of Corporate Control*, Cambridge, Mass: Harvard University Press.

Friedman, A. (1977) *Industry and Labour*, London: Macmillan.

Fruin, M. (1992) *The Japanese Enterprise System*, Oxford: Oxford University Press.

Gerlach, M. (1992) *Alliance Capitalism*, Berkeley, Calif.: University of California Press.

Gold, T.B. (1986) *State and Society in the Taiwan Miracle*, Armonk, N.Y.: M.E. Sharpe.

Gospel, H.F. (1992) *Markets, Firms and the Management of Labour in Modern Britain*, Cambridge: Cambridge University Press.

Granovetter, M. (1985) "Economic Action, Social Structure and Embeddedness", *American Journal of Sociology,* 91:481-510.

Green, Diana (1986) "The State, Finance and Industry in France", in A. Cox (ed) *The State, Finance and Industry*, Brighton: Wheatsheaf.

Greenhalgh, S. (1984) "Networks and their Nodes: Urban Society on Taiwan", *The China Quarterly*, 99:529-552.

Greenhalgh, S. (1988) "Supranational Processes of Income Distribution", in E.A. Winckler and S. Greenhalgh (eds), *Contending Approaches to the Political Economy of Taiwan*, Armonk, N.Y.: M.E. Sharpe.

Hamilton, G. and C.S. Kao (1990) "The Institutional Foundation of Chinese Business:the family firm in Taiwan", *Comparative Social Research*, 12:95-112.

Hamilton, G., W. Zeile and W.J. Kim (1990) "The Network Structures of East Asian Economies", in S. Clegg and G. Redding (eds) *Capitalism in Contrasting Cultures*, Berlin: de Gruyter.

Hirst, P. and J. Zeitlin (1991) "Flexible Specialisation vs. Post-Fordism: Theory, Evidence and Policy Implications", *Economy and Society*, 20:1-56.

Hollingsworth, J.R. and W. Streeck (1993) "Countries and Sectors: concluding remarks on performance, convergence and competitiveness", in R. Hollingsworth, P. Schmitter and W. Streeck (eds), *Governing Capitalist Economies: Performance and Control of Economic Sectors*, Oxford: Oxford University Press.

Ingham, G. (1984) *Capitalism Divided? The City and Industry in British Social Development*, London: Macmillan.

d'Iribarne, P. (1989) *La Logique de l'Honneur*, Paris: Seuil.

Janelli, R.L (1993) *Making Capitalism: the Social and Cultural Construction of a South Korean Conglomerate*, Stanford: Stanford University Press.

Johnson, C. (1982) *MITI and the Japanese Miracle*, Stanford University Press.

Kagono, T., I. Alonaka, K. Sakakibara and A. Okumara (1985) *Strategic versus Evolutionary Management*, Amsterdam: North Holland.

Kenney, M., and R. Florida (1993) *Beyond Mass Production: The Japanese System and its Transfer to the US*, Oxford: Oxford University Press.

Kim, Choong Soon (1992) *The Culture of Korean Industry*, Tucson, Arizona: University of Arizona Press.

Koike, K. (1987) "Human Resource Development and Labour-Management Relations", in K. Yamamura and Y. Yasuba (eds) *The Political Economy of Japan* I, Stanford University Press.

Kristensen, P.H. (1992) "Strategies against Structure: Institutions and economic organisation in Denmark", in R.D. Whitley (ed) *European Business Systems*, London: Sage Publications.

Lane, C. (1989) *Management and Labour in Europe*, Aldershot: Edward Elgar.

Lane, C. (1992) "European Business Systems: Britain and Germany Compared", in R. Whitley (ed) *European Business Systems: Firms and Markets in their National Contexts*, London: Sage.

Lawrisky, M.L. (1984) *Corporate Structure and Performance*, London: Croom Helm.

Lazonick, W. (1991) *Business Organisation and the Myth of the Market Economy*, Cambridge: Cambridge University Press.

Lilja, K., K. Rasanen and R. Tainio (1992) "The Forest Sector Business Recipe in Finland and its Domination of the National Business System", in R.D. Whitley (ed) *European Business Systems*, London: Sage Publications.

Lodge, G.C. and E.F. Vogel (eds) (1987) *Ideology and National Competitiveness*, Boston, Mass.: Harvard Business School.

Macfarlane, A. (1978) *The Origins of English Individualism*, Oxford: Blackwell.

Marris, R (1964) *The Economic Theory of "Managerial" Capitalism*, London: Macmillan.

Maurice, M., F. Sellier and J.J. Silvestre (1986) *The Social Bases of Industrial Power*, MIT Press.

Nishida, J. (1991) "The Japanese Influence on the Shanghaiese Textile Industry and

Implications for Hong Kong", M.Phil Thesis, University of Hong Kong.

Numazaki, I. (1992) "Networks and Partnerships: the Social Organisation of the Chinese Business Elite in Taiwan", unpublished Ph.D. thesis, Michigan State University.

Penrose, E. (1959) *The Theory of the Growth of the Firm*, Oxford: Blackwell.

Piore, M.J. and C.F. Sabel (1984), *The Second Industrial Divide*, New York: Basic Books.

Pye, L.W., (1985) *Asian Power and Politics: The cultural dimensions of authority.* Harvard University Press.

Redding, G.R. (1990) *The Spirit of Chinese Capitalism*, Berlin: de Gruyter.

Richardson, G. (1972) "The Organisation of Industry", *Economic Journal*, 82:883-896.

Rohlen, T.P. (1974) *For Harmony and Strength - Japanese White-Collar Organisation in Anthropological Perspective*, University of California Press.

Sako, Mari (1992) *Prices, Quality and Trust,* Cambridge: Cambridge University Press.

Silin, R.H. (1976) *Leadership and Values. The Organisation of Large Scale Taiwanese Enterprises*, Harvard University Press.

Steers, R.M., Y.K. Shin and G.R. Ungson (1989) *The Chaebol*, New York: Harper and Row.

van Iterson, A. and R. Olie (1992) "European Business Systems: the Dutch Case", in R. Whitley (ed) *European Business Systems*, London: Sage.

van Wolferen, K. (1989) *The Enigma of Japanese Power*, London: Macmillan.

Wade, R. (1990) *Governing the Market*, Princeton University Press.

Whitley, R D. (ed) (1992a) *European Business Systems: Firms and Markets in their National Contexts*. London: Sage.

Whitley, R (1992b) "Societies, Firms and Markets: the Social Structuring of Business Systems", in R. Whitley (ed) *European Business Systems: Firms and Markets in their National Contexts*, London: Sage.

Whittaker, D.H. (1990) *Managing Innovation*, Cambridge: Cambridge University Press.

Wong, S-L. (1988) "The Applicability of Asian Family Values to other Sociocultural Settings", in P.L. Berger and H-H.M. Hsiao (eds) *In Search of an East Asian Development Model*, New Brunswick, New Jersey: Transaction Books.

Woo, Yung-En (1991) *The Race to the Swift*, Columbia University Press.

Zeile, W. (1991) "Industrial Policy and Organisational Efficiency: the Korean Chaebol Examined", in G. Hamilton (ed) *Business Networks and Economic Development in East and South-East Asia*, Hong Kong: University of Hong Kong (Centre of Asian Studies).

Zucker, L. (1986) "Production of Trust: Institutional Sources of Economic Structure, 1840 - 1920", *Research in Organisational Behaviour*, 8:53-111.

Zysman, John (1983) *Governments, markets and growth: Financial systems and the politics of industrial change*, Ithaca: Cornell University Press.

# 8. Knowledge and Ideas for Job Creation

José Luis Alvarez[*]

## 8.1. THE ROLE OF KNOWLEDGE AND IDEAS IN ECONOMIC AND BUSINESS ACTIVITIES

Discussion of the structural and cyclical causes of unemployment and of job-creation policies deals mainly with economic arguments. Apart from the prestige of Economics among the social sciences, there is an important practical reason for this: economic variables such as the cost of money, interest rates and even the public deficit, are more easily controlled by governments than are other social realities and institutions such as attitudes toward private property, the traditional role of the public versus the private sector in employment creation, the stigma of failure in entrepreneurial activities, the labour market, the structure of the family, the distribution of wealth, the role of trust and social networks, and so on.

Despite their limited malleability, these latter variables are of paramount importance for understanding the phenomenon of unemployment. And they are perhaps even more important for grasping the dynamics of entrepreneurship, here understood as the launching of new firms - one of the activities most directly related to employment creation. Among the social realities not strictly economic in nature that are critical for employment creation are knowledge and ideas about economic and business activities.

This paper focuses on the knowledge and ideas about entrepreneurial activities that triumphed and spread all over the world in the 1980s - what I here call the Entrepreneurship Movement. This paper assumes that entrepreneurial activities are crucially important for the creation of jobs. It studies the role played by management education and by other social institutions such as governments and business associations in the success and diffusion of entrepreneurial knowledge and ideas. It addresses the question of the extent to which entrepreneurial ideas differ in the various societies where they have succeeded, as well as how well-adapted they were to local contexts when an international transfer of entrepreneurship ideas took place. In short, this essay aims to provide some of the elements needed to address an important issue: the role of education in entrepreneurial endeavours and, therefore, in employment creation; and the feasibility of an international circulation of knowledge to support it.

However relevant a topic it may be, empirical studies of the diffusion and institutionalisation of economic ideas in general, and of business knowledge in particular, were very scarce until the 1990s, when interest in the subject grew rapidly.

The main reason for this scarcity of studies lies in the difficulty of the topic. Research is made difficult by the extreme complexity of business tasks - these are highly interdependent, contextual and systemic, relatively understandised, changeable and developing, involving both the maintenance and the modification of structures, rarely generating visible and separable inputs (Whitley, 1989a). This complexity requires the use of several types of knowledge by practitioners: from technical knowledge to decision-making habits, organisational savvy, or assumptions about the social features of human nature. These kinds of knowledge do not fit together in ordered patterns, but rather in the style of a bricolage or ideology (Bourricaud, 1980). Like any ideology, knowledge for business action consists of ideas whose purpose is to make sense of the countless data out there in the business world and to act upon that world. And like an ideology, business knowledge is in practice extremely difficult to fathom.

A further difficulty arises from the fact that there are no final and purely academic criteria for evaluating the utility of business notions. Consequently, administrative knowledge needs to be socially legitimated by, for instance, top business schools, business media, management "gurus" or other mediating institutions before it can be adopted by practitioners and make its impact on practices (Cohen and March, 1986; Abrahamson, 1991). This means that research should deal with both epistemological issues and institutional processes.

Moreover, given the innumerable variables and redundancies at play in organisational action, there is still considerable uncertainty about the real influence of management concepts on organisational practises (Hackman, 1985). For instance, there is debate about the relationship between the spread of pro-entrepreneurship ideas and the actual creation of new firms or intrapreneurial activities and, in turn, of employment. Several authors have suggested that economic conditions have been much more important in the revival of entrepreneurial activities than has the success of new ideological trends and the spread of entrepreneurial knowledge (Curran and Burrows, 1986; Whitley, 1989b; Harrison, 1994). Whitley puts forward five structural or non-ideological reasons for the revival of small business in Europe: "the decline of manufacturing employment and the growth of the service sector; second, the rise in unemployment since the early 1970s; third, income growth in the 1960s and 1970s leading to changing market structures for consumer goods; fourth, technological changes reducing the minimum efficient size of plants; and, fifth, a move by many large firms to disintegrate their activities and rely on sub-contractors to a greater extent". He concludes that "the increasing significance of small businesses in many European countries since the mid-1970s is as much a result of changes in large firms' policies and practices as of an upsurge of 'entrepreneurship' in Europe."

The success of ideas and knowledge (from scientific to denotative and to performative) about entrepreneurship may have been more important for legitimation than for practical results. The fact remains, though, that ideas and knowledge are crucial to an understanding of business action. Moreover, the neo-institutional school of organisational theory, in accordance with the hypothesis traditionally held by the sociology of knowledge, has shown the importance of knowledge, values and beliefs held by organisational actors and their normative ideas for explaining practices. Hence the importance of understanding the origin, legitimation, reception and consumption of business knowledge and ideas. Without this understanding, the contribution of business education to business action, and therefore also such education's contribution to the creation of employment, will remain largely unrecognised.

This is particularly important in a situation where policies for job creation are being recommended by international agencies, or where an approach that has proved successful in some countries is being imitated by others. The feasibility of those recommendations and the conditions for their success cannot be assessed without understanding the processes whereby knowledge for entrepreneurial action is diffused.

## 8.2.   A FRAMEWORK FOR STUDYING IDEAS FOR BUSINESS ACTION

In the 1980s, entrepreneurship was a huge success in management education. A new branch of scholarly literature emerged, new academic associations were formed, courses made obligatory, chairs endowed, research centres created, etc. Entrepreneurship was also a great success as a political idea in the context of wider trends, such as the reinstatement of enterprise as the most important institution of economic life, and the diminishing role of the state (Bourricaud, 1986). In the social and cultural domains, entrepreneurship had obvious links with the rising demand for high psychological and professional rewards, the reevaluation of personal merit and the parallel devaluation of egalitarian tendencies (Stevenson and Sahlman, 1986). Moreover, entrepreneurial fervour in the 1980s became a worldwide movement, spreading across countries, regardless of their level of development or even of their basic mentality or value orientation toward business activities. The argument that entrepreneurship was the single most important device for creating employment (an argument popularised by MIT's Birch, 1979) became a widely held belief. As this paper shows, it was the main reason for the success of the entrepreneurship idea.

This paper focuses on three processes:

1) how entrepreneurship came to be a part of management education, both formal (academic) and informal (popular business media);

2) how the promotion of entrepreneurship came to be accepted by governments of all political persuasions as an essential task; and

3) how praise of entrepreneurship came to be the core of pro-business arguments during the 1980s.

The three countries in the study - Britain, Mexico and Spain - do not constitute a representative sample of countries around the world, although preliminary data had suggested that they could be illustrative enough for the purposes of this study. There is an "early industrialised" country, Britain, as well as a "late industrialised" society: Spain. These two have similar political and economic systems, although in the 1980s they had governments of very different political orientation. Mexico, a developing country with a highly interventionist state, is quite an attractive case on account of its recent brisk transition toward a more open market economy. The three-country comparison offers an opportunity to develop hypotheses about the relationship between social groups and external events, on the one hand, and the popularisation of entrepreneurial knowledge on the other (see Figure 8.1).

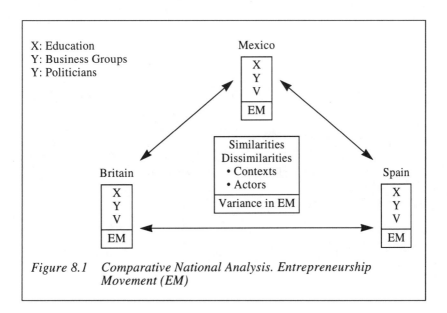

*Figure 8.1 Comparative National Analysis. Entrepreneurship Movement (EM)*

The literature generally agrees about which three groups are most important in the process of diffusion and institutionalisation of knowledge analogous to business knowledge and ideas. First, there are the educators. These may be divided into two groups. On the one hand, we have professors and researchers in institutions of management education. On the other are the agents of so-called "informal education", such as groups of intellectuals, management gurus, and organisations that diffuse non-academic business knowledge through magazines, popular books and other mass media. The second group is made up of governments and the politicians and administrators who work for them. The third group, specifically for this case, consists of businessmen and women and their professional associations. Two resources - cultural (the availability of ideas and knowledge for articulating a public discourse) and organisational (institutional support for social action) - are viewed as necessary in order for these groups to be able to receive, legitimate and disseminate knowledge.

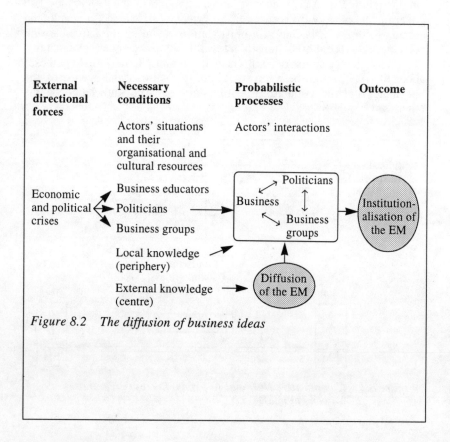

Figure 8.2    *The diffusion of business ideas*

Many authors (from classics like Weber and Mannheim to contemporary sociologists of knowledge such as Berger et al., 1974; Boudon, 1986; and Wuthnow, 1989) coincide on the basic sequences leading to the popularisation of social ideas. These authors suggest that, first, the right environmental conditions must exist in the economic, social and political realms to act as prompting events or external directional forces by delegitimating old ideas and creating a need for new ones. A second condition for a process of popularisation of business ideas is the presence of certain necessary conditions or institutional contexts: carriers or social agents - producers, transmitters and consumers of business knowledge with their cultural and organisational resources - who are affected by those external directional forces. The third requirement is probabilistic processes or action sequences: these social actors' actions and reactions of selection, dissemination, consumption and reproduction of ideas, based on their institutional location or "position" and their willingness to act socially: their "dispositions" (Boudon, 1986). And fourth, there is the outcome: the diffusion and institutionalisation of ideas. Since prompting events and the social actors and their resources depend in part on the economic, social and political dynamics of individual countries, the popularisation of ideas should present specific national contents and strengths. However, since those same factors, as well as the educational system (especially the business education sector) also have very powerful international dynamics, these should also be incorporated into the model. Figure 8.2 presents a graphic summary of this framework as applied to the process of the Entrepreneurship Movement.

## 8.3. THE ENTREPRENEURSHIP PHENOMENON IN THE 1980s

The first variable in this framework is the *External Directional Forces*: economic, social, political or ideological crises that delegitimate the dominant ideas and knowledge and clear the way for new concepts and points of view. In each of the three countries under study it was possible to find these "prompting events" at work.

In the 1970s and 1980s Britain experienced nothing like the extremely acute political and economic crises of Mexico and Spain. First of all, it had no need for a sweeping change of its political regime. Secondly, Britain's economic problems were not as serious as those of Mexico and Spain. Unemployment in Britain in the 1970s and 1980s was never as high as in Spain, and there were fewer years with over 10% inflation. See Table 8.1.

However, in the later 1970s Britain suffered from an acute sense of crisis, the so-called "British disease". This perception of national decline was not so much the result of a sharply declining economy as of comparisons with other countries (although Britain grew more rapidly

Table 8.1    UK Basic Economic Data (per cent)

| Year | 1974 | 1975 | 1976 | 1977 | 1978 | 1979 | 1980 |
|---|---|---|---|---|---|---|---|
| Inflation | 8.6 | 24.2 | 16.5 | 15.8 | 8.3 | 13.4 | 18.0 |
| Unemployment | 3.1 | 4.6 | 6.0 | 6.4 | 6.3 | 5.6 | 6.8 |
| GDP Growth | −1.7 | −0.7 | 2.7 | 2.3 | 3.4 | 2.7 | −2.1 |

| Year | 1981 | 1982 | 1983 | 1984 | 1985 | 1986 | 1987 |
|---|---|---|---|---|---|---|---|
| Inflation | 12.0 | 8.6 | 4.6 | 5.0 | 6.1 | 3.4 | 4.1 |
| Unemployment | 9.9 | 11.5 | 12.3 | 11.8 | 11.2 | 11.2 | 10.7 |
| GDP Growth | −1.2 | 1.7 | 3.6 | 2.3 | 3.7 | 4.2 | 4.8 |

| Year | 1988 | 1989 | 1990 | 1991 | 1992 |
|---|---|---|---|---|---|
| Inflation | 4.9 | 7.8 | 9.5 | 5.9 | 3.7 |
| Unemployment | 8.8 | 7.2 | 6.8 | 8.3 | 9.6 |
| GDP Growth | 5.0 | 4.9 | 3.9 | −2.2 | −0.6 |

Sources:   OECD Economic Outlook, December 1994; Year Book of Labour Statistics, 1994, ILO, Geneva; International Financial Statistics Year Book, 1994.

than ever before, it grew less than Germany, Japan and Italy) along with the realisation that Britain had lost its world economic and geo-strategical hegemony. The nation with Europe's highest per capita national product in 1945 ended up on the lower end of the scale in 1985. This "malaise", combined with increasingly powerful trade unions and the perception of a weak political leadership, paved the way, after the famous "winter of discontent", for Thatcher's rise to power and a thorough reversal of British postwar political and social traditions.

For the four decades between the 1940s and the 1980s, Mexico's rate of economic growth was positive and usually above 4%. And it was only in the 1970s that inflation stayed above 10%. Moreover, in sharp contrast to other Latin American countries, the political system born of the Mexican Revolution proved extremely stable. However, in the late 1960s the gradual disaffection of the social groups that had supported the regime for decades led to an economic-cum-political crisis. First, after the 1968 student uprising and its police repression, the PRI regime lost most of its "progressive" support. A few years later, in 1973, the assassination of Eugenio Garza Sada, one of Mexico's most prominent industrialists and founder of the Instituto Tecnológico y de Estudios Superiores de Monterrey (ITESM), alienated businessmen, the other pillar of PRI support. Until then they had supported the economic policies of the regime: subsidised prices, low taxes, a high public deficit and protectionism. With this support declining, the PRI regime became highly dependent upon a final source of legitimacy: the continuation of economic development, for which the state was mainly responsible.

This political isolation was exacerbated by serious tensions in the economic and social domain. One of the causes was population growth: from 25.7 million people in 1950 to 82.7 in 1988. Unemployment was rampant. Table 8.2 reflects only the "open" or registered unemployment, widely considered to be well below the real level.

There was also widespread underemployment. Illiteracy, malnutrition, high mortality and disease, lack of housing: all these became overwhelming problems accentuated by the concentration of population in the cities. With all the caution that figures on the informal economy deserve, it can be said that, from an insignificant percentage in the 1960s, the informal economy rose to a percentage of more than a third of GDP in the 1980s, as the spontaneous alternative to the inability of the state and the official private sector to generate jobs (García, 1989; Roberts, 1989).

The PRI regime responded with a sharp increase in public investment, fuelled by the profits derived from the rise in oil prices, which set up the external debt trap. Figure 8.3 shows, in billions of US dollars, the level of external debt over the last two decades, and the depth of the crisis at the beginning of the 1980s.

But the external debt crisis was only one of the many problems that Mexico faced in the 1980s. At the beginning of that decade (the end of López Portillo's presidency) the banking system was nationalised. This furthered the confrontation between certain very important business groups and the PRI Government, in spite of measures taken by the new president, De la Madrid (1982-1989). De la Madrid reformed the constitution, adding new articles in which the preeminence of the market over state economic activities was recognised.

During the presidencies of López Portillo and De la Madrid, Mexico was a country on the road to instability: economic instability, because the payment of the external debt made it almost impossible to improve standards of living for the population; and political instability, because demands for a better life were increasingly channelled through the ballot box, making it difficult to gain electoral support for tough economic policies. This, in turn, rendered the whole process of political and economic transition increasingly uncontrollable. There was ideological

Table 8.2   Mexico Basic Economic Data (per cent)

| Year | 1980 | 1981 | 1982 | 1983 | 1984 | 1985 | 1986 |
|------|------|------|------|------|------|------|------|
| Inflation | 26.3 | 27.9 | 58.8 | 101.8 | 65.4 | 57.7 | 86.2 |
| Unemployment | 6.8 | 4.0 | 8.0 | 9.2 | 6.0 | 4.4 | 4.3 |
| GDP Growth | 8.3 | 6.4 | 0.7 | –4.1 | 3.6 | 2.5 | –3.7 |

| Year | 1987 | 1988 | 1989 | 1990 | 1991 | 1992 | |
|------|------|------|------|------|------|------|---|
| Inflation | 131.8 | 114.1 | 19.7 | 20.0 | 17.0 | 12.0 | |
| Unemployment | 3.9 | 3.6 | 3.0 | 2.8 | 2.6 | 2.8 | |
| GDP Growth | 1.8 | 1.2 | 3.3 | 4.3 | 3.6 | 2.8 | |

*Sources*:   *Year Book of Labour Statistics,* 1994, ILO, Geneva; *International Financial Statistics Year Book*, 1994; Banco de México, *Informe Anual*, 1993.

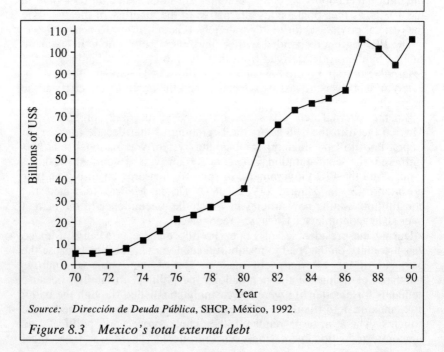

*Source:   Dirección de Deuda Pública*, SHCP, México, 1992.

Figure 8.3   Mexico's total external debt

instability besides, because the populism and nationalism upon which the legitimacy of the PRI regime was based had grown politically and economically counterproductive. The Entrepreneurship Movement was one of the reactions to the economic and political crisis that began in 1982.

Spain also underwent acute economic and political problems. In the 1960s, after two decades of economic and political isolation and very low growth, the Spanish economy started to grow at rates comparable to those of the Southeast Asian countries in the 1980s. (Between 1961 and 1974, average GNP growth was 6.8%.) This was due to a combination of factors, including a less regulated economy, trade liberalisation with Europe, and the influx of foreign exchange from tourism and emigrants. Spain became the tenth largest industrial economy in the world. In the 1970s, however, political and economic crises converged. The political difficulties of the transition to democracy were compounded by a complicated economic situation deriving from the country's energy dependence, the external deficit, and the relative importance for the Spanish economy of the sectors most affected by the international crisis, such as the iron and steel industries, shipbuilding, and so on.

These economic problems were extremely serious, as the main economic indicators show. Inflation reached 24% in 1977. In 1979 and 1981 the growth of GNP was negative and unemployment figures were among the worst in Europe. See Table 8.3 for a summary of the main economic variables, and Figure 8.4 for the evolution of the number of officially registered new firms.

It was under these circumstances that the Socialist Party came to power in 1982 - as in the case of the Conservatives in Britain, this occurred amid a general atmosphere of crisis and with a clear mandate for change.

These were the "external directional forces" of the Entrepreneurship Movement. According to the "displacement thesis" of the diffusion of ideas, these prompting events are shocks that change the content and function of predominant ideas (Gamble et al., 1989). By breaking the inertia that prevents social actors such as scholars, intellectuals, public officials and businesspeople from operating and interacting among themselves, or by providing them with the incentives and motives to do so, the "environmental conditions" set off the "probabilistic processes" (Mohr, 1982), or "action sequences" (Wuthnow, 1989), that lead to the diffusion and institutionalisation of new business values and organisational and economic knowledge.

The economic and political circumstances of Britain, Mexico and Spain - which triggered the diffusion and institutionalisation of the Entrepreneurship Movement - present two basic constants: deep economic crises and profound political changes. The economic crises were not simply part of the recurrent short cycles of growth and recession in post-World War II Western economies. In each country it was the worst crisis in many years: in Britain, the worst since Labour defeated Churchill in

*Table 8.3    Spain Basic Economic Data (per cent)*

| Year | 1977 | 1978 | 1979 | 1980 | 1981 | 1982 | 1983 | 1984 |
|---|---|---|---|---|---|---|---|---|
| Inflation | 24.5 | 19.8 | 15.7 | 15.6 | 14.5 | 14.4 | 12.2 | 11.3 |
| Unemployment | 5.7 | 7.5 | 9.2 | 11.8 | 14.4 | 16.3 | 17.8 | 20.3 |
| Growth GDP | 2.8 | 1.4 | 0.0 | 1.2 | –0.7 | 1.5 | 2.2 | 1.4 |

| Year | 1985 | 1986 | 1987 | 1988 | 1989 | 1990 | 1991 | 1992 |
|---|---|---|---|---|---|---|---|---|
| Inflation | 8.8 | 8.8 | 5.2 | 4.8 | 6.8 | 6.7 | 5.9 | 5.9 |
| Unemployment | 21.6 | 21.2 | 20.5 | 19.5 | 17.3 | 16.3 | 16.4 | 18.4 |
| Growth GDP | 2.6 | 3.2 | 5.6 | 5.1 | 4.9 | 3.6 | 2.2 | 0.7 |

*Sources*:   OECD *Economic Outlook*, December 1994; *Year Book of Labour Statistics,* 1994, ILO, Geneva; *International Financial Statistics Year Book*, 1994.

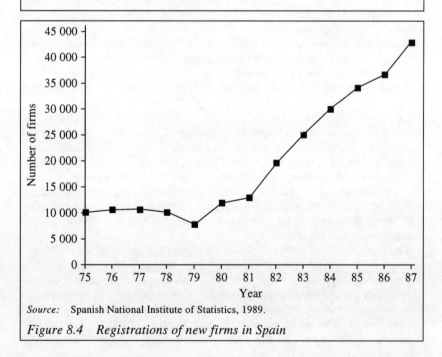

*Source:*   Spanish National Institute of Statistics, 1989.

*Figure 8.4    Registrations of new firms in Spain*

1945; in Spain, since the Modernisation Plan of the late 1950s; and in Mexico, since the establishment of the PRI regime in the 1930s.

The importance of these economic shocks was matched by that of the changes in the political domain. Margaret Thatcher's victory in 1979 meant more than a change in the political affiliation of Ten Downing Street's resident. It heralded a radical attempt to change the way post-World War II British politics was played. In Mexico the 1980s was the first time the hegemony of the PRI was seriously contested. And in Spain there was not only a change in the political system - from dictatorship to constitutional monarchy - but also, in 1982, in the middle of the economic crisis, with almost no economic growth, unemployment above 15% and inflation at 14.4%, the Left gained political hegemony for the first time in half a century.

The "times", or environmental conditions, that accompanied the growth of the Entrepreneurship Movement throughout the 1980s were hard. But apart from that they had another interesting feature that could explain some of that movement's paradoxes. The Entrepreneurship Movement became ideologically linked with economic policies based, in simple terms, on the neo-classical economic hypothesis. These policies were generally successful in fighting inflation and promoting growth, but unemployment remained an unresolved problem. However, it was not until almost the mid-1990s that the persistence of unemployment was linked to the implementation of those neo-classical policies, and that entrepreneurship and related practices, such as the promotion of small businesses, were being considered as anything other than definite contributors to the unemployment problem's solution (Harrison, 1994).

In sum, the simultaneous success of neo-classical policies (regarding inflation and growth in the 1980s) and the widespread failure to bring down unemployment figures (a failure decoupled from those policies in the same decade) gave the Entrepreneurship Movement both legitimation, via its ideological affinities with economic liberalism, and an enduring justification until the mid-1990s: namely, the need to solve the apparently intractable problem of high unemployment.

The reactions to these crucial events of the three social actors most involved in the popularisation of business and entrepreneurial ideas are described in the following pages.

## 8.4.   MANAGEMENT EDUCATION

In Britain, education in entrepreneurship stands in sharp contrast to that of Mexico and Spain. It was initiated much sooner, in the early 1970s, after the publication in 1971 of the Bolton report, an inquiry into British economic decline, commissioned by the government and leading industrialists. This report recommended fostering small businesses as a way of revitalising the decaying industrial fabric. The report prompted a wave of research into small firms, as well as a series of entrepreneurship courses, in many cases supported by public agencies. In the long run, this made British management education less dependent on foreign sources of entrepreneurial knowledge and pedagogical materials. Management education institutions produced their own entrepreneurship knowledge, mostly related to small businesses. They also distributed it, through special programmes, to those who planned to start up new businesses or already owned small firms and, through MBA programmes and university courses, to business students. Business educators provided the mediators of administrative knowledge - business journalists, for instance - with a good deal of the "raw material" on which to base their articles in newspapers and in the numerous magazines and publications on start-ups, small businesses and joint ventures that began to appear in the 1980s.

The main characteristic of entrepreneurship education in Mexico, both formal and informal, is its strong thematic cohesiveness and clear-cut content. Entrepreneurship in Mexican management schools, at both undergraduate and graduate levels, means, almost always, micro-firms and self-employment. This orientation was not the result of deliberate decisions but of the lack of research and teaching capabilities of Mexican business schools and universities.

In Mexico, the formal education front of the Entrepreneurship Movement developed in two phases. The first phase was dominated by the Instituto Tecnológico y de Estudios Superiores de Monterrey (ITESM), the most prestigious private university in Mexico, which pioneered entrepreneurship education. It did so for predominantly socio-political reasons. In 1983, in order to help change the economic culture of Mexico, the business groups of Monterrey - the most influential in the country, the most US-oriented and the founders and financial backers of ITESM - modified the institute's goals. Entrepreneurship education became obligatory in all programmes and schools. This change was quite deliberate. In 1982, the Mexican government nationalised the banking system, and business groups, fearing for the fate of the private sector, started to actively defend the legitimacy of private enterprise. The idea of entrepreneurship became one of the most important vehicles for that effort.

However, the lack of local capabilities for developing entrepreneurship knowledge and education forced ITESM to import foreign teaching materials, from course outlines to slides for use in class. Most of these materials were imported from "US Junior Achievement", an organisation which, through courses on how to start micro-firms, promotes free enterprise in US high schools. US Junior Achievement had a delegation in Mexico, and instructors from Mexican Junior Achievement were recruited by ITESM. The materials drawn from Mexican Junior Achievement, which were copied almost literally from US Junior Achievement, were at a very basic level. This meant that they were readily adopted by ITESM's faculty, readily applied across all types of programmes and readily accepted by students.

In the second phase, most of the other Mexican universities and schools started to teach entrepreneurship courses. Their motivation was what the neo-institutional school of organisational theory would recognise as more typically mimetic: they were following the successful example of ITESM, from which they copied most of their materials. In this way, the very basic and motivational entrepreneurship knowledge produced and used by US Junior Achievement, at first in literal translation, has been imported and spread through most Mexican educational institutions, at least until the end of the 1980s, when adaptation to the local context became significant. Table 8.4 below shows the years in which courses on entrepreneurship were first offered at the country's main management schools. A few years after the nationalisation of the banking system - and business groups' response to it - entrepreneurship education was already a widespread phenomenon in management education in Mexico.

As far as informal business education in Mexico is concerned, it is remarkable how much importance was acquired by a handful of "intellectuals of entrepreneurship". Through frequent articles in the most important newspapers and through other media such as books, seminars and the like, these intellectuals reached an adult audience of self-employed businessmen and owners of small firms or family businesses. The message of these "entrepreneurship gurus" was very motivational. They addressed the occupational concerns of their audiences and voiced the interests of a group that had never - until the second half of the 1980s - been appreciated by the dominant PRI ideology. In Mexico, then, there is one basic message - firms and self-employment - conveyed to two different audiences or social groups through two main channels: first, through universities to young students and, second, through popular business media to adult entrepreneurs.

Although most of the manifestations of the popularisation of entrepreneurial ideas that exist in Britain and Mexico are also present in Spain, they lack thematic unity and intensity there. There were entrepreneurship courses at the main business schools in the latter half of the 1980s, but entrepreneurship education was not as generalised in Spain as in Mexico, nor was it as research-oriented or institutionalised as in Britain. It was not until after the economic crisis that, with few exceptions, entrepreneurship became an established part of the curriculum in graduate business education in Spain. Table 8.5 reflects the international academic sources and the year of the first entrepreneurial sources in each of the three major Spanish business schools.

The diffusion and institutionalisation of entrepreneurship education in Spanish business schools has followed an international mimetic pattern: institutions on the periphery (or, like Spain, on the semi-periphery)

*Table 8.4   Entrepreneurrship Education in Mexico*

| School | Origins | First entrepreneurship courses | | |
|--------|---------|---------|-----|-------|
| | | College | MBA | Other |
| 1. ITESM | US/Mexican Junior Achievement | 1986 | 1989 | 1989 |
| 2. UNAM | US/Mexican Junior Achievement | 1989 | 1989 | |
| 3. ITAM | US/Mexican Junior Achievement | 1987 | 1989 | |
| 4. IPADE | IESE (Spain)/Harvard (US) | | 1976 | |
| 5. LA SALLE | US/Mexican Junior Achievement | 1990 | | |
| 6. ANAHUAC | Local | | | 1986 |

*Source*:   Research by the author.

*Table 8.5   Entrepreneurship Education in Spain*

| School | Origins | First entrepreneurship courses | | |
|--------|---------|---------|-----|-------|
| | | College | MBA | Other |
| 1. ESADE | Stanford | 1983 | 1983 | |
| 2. IESE | Harvard | | 1975 | |
| 3. IE | Several sources | | 1983 | |

*Source*:   Research by the author.

followed the model of US institutions in the "centre". They sought to legitimate themselves through their similarity to US business schools. However, an important observation has to be made regarding these isomorphic dynamics. They were not the result of organisational mimesis, of built-in academic pressure to incorporate new academic fields, of decisions taken by the boards of Spanish business schools, or even of pressure from the businessmen who gave donations to these schools. Instead, the new courses were the result of individual initiatives of professors with academic education and contacts in the US. These professors were the carriers (sociologically and literally) of case studies, course outlines, books, and so on - the elements of entrepreneurship courses - to Spanish business schools. That is, the mimesis was professional and personal, rather than strictly organisational. The importance that entrepreneurship education has acquired in Spanish business schools is due to the skills of the professors who at their own risk, in an academic "intrapreneurial" way, pushed for an acknowledgement of the field's importance in their own organisations.

At the same time, the role of informal entrepreneurship education in Spain is very minor. There are no relevant media, such as magazines dedicated to the subject, or acknowledged social champions of entrepreneurship. In sum, the absence of a dominant theme equivalent to that of micro-firms in Mexico or small firms in Britain, coupled with the lack of social visibility, give Spain's entrepreneurship education a very amorphous character in comparison with that of the other two countries.

## 8.5.　GOVERNMENTS

The idea of entrepreneurship has spread well beyond the academic domain. It has been adopted by governments of all creeds, which jumped onto the bandwagon of entrepreneurship in the 1980s with an ardour laden with what even the Financial Times described as "banal attitudes and exaggerated claims" (quoted by Rainnie, 1985). This enthusiasm also surprised researchers, who had frequently cautioned that their research did not merit uncritical acceptance (statistics on entrepreneurship and its actual impact on job creation are highly disputable). (For some British examples of such caveats, see Curran and Stanworth, 1986; Hall, 1986; Gallagher and Doyle, 1986; Bannock and Peacock, 1989; Whitley, 1989b).

The Entrepreneurship Movement's emergence into the realms of public administration and education was more or less simultaneous. In Britain, early in the 1970s, the Bolton report was the starting point for a series of legal measures aimed at promoting small firms. And it was Mrs. Thatcher's rise to power, with small firms as the epitome of her enterprise culture, that gave entrepreneurship ideas a second push in the 1980s.

In Mexico, the movement's two fronts - academic and governmental - do not share a single source parallel to the Bolton Report in Britain. They do, however, share its "timing". It was two to three years after the external debt crisis of 1982 that the PRI government began to promote entrepreneurship, especially micro-firms and self-employment. As in the case of education, this reaction would not have been possible in Mexico without the influx of knowledge from other countries. Foreign experience in the promotion of new firms and micro-firms was channelled to the Mexican government after 1983 through the United Nations Organisation for Industrial Development. The impact of this foreign influence was similar to the impact on business education. Just as the teaching materials imported from the US were literally reproduced in Mexican classrooms, some of the recommendations of the UN agency were also reproduced verbatim in programmes and in laws on self-employment and micro-firms enacted after 1985 by the Mexican government (no specific laws were promulgated then on small and medium firms).

In Spain, central and local government activity started, as did most entrepreneurship education, after the economic crisis, which peaked in 1979. For instance, the IMPI (Institute for Small and Medium Industries), an agency of the Ministry of Industry, was created in 1978. As in Mexico, foreign influence was decisive with regard to the activities of local, regional and central governments. Most public support for new and small companies, from financial aid to databases, came from European programmes, like the EC's Local Employment Development Action, the European Business Centres Network, the European Federation of Development Agencies, the EC's Sprint programme on technological transfer, the IRIS (Initiatives for Women's Employment) and many others.

There is a common impetus behind the enthusiasm of governments for the celebration and promotion of entrepreneurship: the fight against unemployment, the most recalcitrant problem for the neo-classical economic policies that spread after the energy crises of the 1970s. But there was more to the Entrepreneurship Movement's political front than a search for new employment. The idea of entrepreneurship - which maintains that the creation of enterprises, and consequently of employment, takes place within the private economic domain - was also one of the main justifications for politicians of all ideologies to drop from their political discourse the idea of government's responsibility for employment, which had been a constant in Keynesian economics and corporatist politics. Entrepreneurship has signalled a retreat in the economic and employment expectations that the public domain had set up for itself in the post-World War II era.

## 8.6. BUSINESS GROUPS

The actions of businesspeople - the social group with the highest stake in the spread and acceptance of entrepreneurship, since entrepreneurship lends it part of its identity and legitimacy - further reinforced some of the motives for the popularisation of entrepreneurial ideas.

It may be said that business groups shared a basically similar context in the 1980s: the exhaustion - signalled by the deep crises of the late 1970s - of the corporatism in place since the Cárdenas presidency in Mexico, the end of World War II in Britain, and dominant through most of Franco's regime in Spain, a corporatism with which, in general, business groups in these three countries collaborated. But business participation in this corporatism was not backed by a self-legitimating discourse, so that business, by default, found its justification merely in its ability to bring about general economic well-being. When the crises occurred, business faced both an economic crisis and a legitimation crisis (Useem, 1984). Despite this basic common denominator, important differences between businessmen's "positions" and "dispositions" (Boudon, 1986) still existed. The reactions to these dissimilar circumstances gave plurality to the diffusion of entrepreneurial ideas.

The literature suggests that, in general, there are two main variables for explaining business groups' activism (Useem, 1984). First, there are the incentives these groups may have for participating in political activities. These incentives must be quite strong, given business's traditional reluctance to become involved in politics. The urgency of the incentives in this case varied greatly from country to country. In Britain, decreasing profits and the increasing role of the state under a Labour government were the trigger for political activism. In Mexico, the incentives were much more powerful. The very legitimacy of private business was considered by business groups to be at stake. Consequently, they grew hyperactive in changing a political regime not fully committed to private enterprise (as the 1982 nationalisation of the banking system showed). And the great opening for a pro-business offensive was the external debt crisis of 1982, which questioned the most important basis of the PRI regime's legitimacy: economic development. Whereas the strongest motives for a high-profile social offensive were present in Mexico and Britain, in Spain the possible incentives were quickly diminished by a constitutional agreement that recognised the hegemony of the market economy and by the economic recovery in the latter half of the 1980s.

The second variable for explaining processes of institutionalisation is the resources that business groups have at their disposal for social action, from self-organisation and financing to political skills and slogans. Only Mexican businesspeople, thanks to their control over important universities, were able to launch massive campaigns of entrepreneurial education in order to increase their social legitimation. In Britain, the most liberal wing of the Conservative Party was even ahead of businesspeople in promoting the enterprise culture. However, in Spain, businesspeople had neither the backing nor the "pull" of an openly pro-business party for launching anything like Mrs. Thatcher's enterprise culture campaign, nor did they own prestigious educational institutions. In short, the generalised social activism of business groups in the late 1970s and 1980s was based on an active self-legitimating discourse defending the autonomy and preeminence of the market economies and businessmen's irreplaceable role in them. Entrepreneurship - an element of civil society, independent of the state, even considered to help defeat unemployment - became for businesspeople an ideal concept upon which to base their increased social presence as well as their retreat from corporatism. The position, incentives and resources of business groups in each country have caused the importance and content of entrepreneurial ideas to vary. Whereas in Mexico entrepreneurship in the form of self-employment was the main self-legitimating idea for businesspeople of all categories, and in Britain the management of small firms - rather than start-ups - has been the representation of the social virtues of the enterprise culture, in Spain the situation is different. Entrepreneurship did not serve as an active legitimation of market values in the 1980s, although it could have been a critical element of such a process.

## 8.7.　SUMMARY

The popularisation of entrepreneurial ideas displays a fundamental contrast. It has taken place more or less simultaneously in Britain, Mexico and Spain, as well as in most other countries. Owing to the international circulation of business knowledge, some of its manifestations are fairly isomorphic across societies. And yet the movement presents very different profiles in the three countries where it has been studied, as Table 8.6 shows in summary form.

In Britain, the Entrepreneurship Movement began to develop about a decade earlier than in Mexico and Spain as one of the first reactions to the decline of Britain as an industrial power. In the early 1970s, the Bolton Report started a tradition of research on small firms, probably the strongest in Europe. It also prompted a series of government actions in support of small businesses and gave the Entrepreneurship Movement in Britain its dominant theme: small firms.

The arrival of Margaret Thatcher gave this tradition a high political profile. Entrepreneurship, represented by small firms, became one of the most important ideas of the "enterprise culture" promoted by the liberal and populist wing of the Conservative Party, drawing the most active groups of businesspeople after it. This "enterprise culture" was to be one

*Table 8.6 The Entrepreneurship Movement in Britain, Mexico and Spain*

| | *Triggering events* | *Social champions* | *Diffusing institutions* | *Dominant theme* | *Origin of knowledge* |
|---|---|---|---|---|---|
| *Britain* | British decline and energy crisis 1970s | Conservative politicians | Enterprise culture and education | Small firms | Local |
| *Mexico* | External debt crisis early 1980s | Business groups | Entrepreneur-ship education | Micro-firms | USA |
| *Spain* | Energy crisis late 1970s | No leaders | No salient institutions | No dominant theme | USA |

of the key elements in the economic revitalisation of Britain and the end of the Keynesian consensus that had been in place since the end of World War II. During the years of Conservative government in the 1980s, private and public schemes for promoting and supporting the creation of new firms and the management of small companies multiplied nationally and locally, as did pro-enterprise education.

In Mexico, the movement was launched in the wake of the external debt crisis of 1982 and the nationalisation of the banking system in the same year by the groups of businessmen most inimical to the PRI regime. It was initiated with a massive campaign of entrepreneurship education that started in the educational institutions these businessmen influenced, such as the prestigious Instituto Tecnológico de Monterrey (ITESM), which they founded and supported financially. Other schools and universities soon followed suit. At the same time, some public champions of the movement began to diffuse the idea of entrepreneurship in the popular media. Finally, the government, in a marked switch of policy, also started to promote entrepreneurship through several public bodies which relied on foreign knowledge channelled through a United Nations agency.

The theme of the Entrepreneurship Movement in Mexico is self-employment or micro-firms. The dominance of this theme is due to a combination of factors: the lack of academic resources capable of disseminating a more sophisticated version of entrepreneurship, the urgent need for new sources of employment, and ideological considerations. Entrepreneurship in the form of "micro-firms" is a perfect popular "idea-force" for legitimating a more active role for civil society, as opposed to the traditional statism of the PRI regime.

In Spain, after the serious economic crises resulting from energy-price increases, most of the educational, social and political manifestations of the Entrepreneurship Movement found in Mexico and Britain were also in evidence. However, although free enterprise and the world of business came to be evaluated more positively in the 1980s as a result of the booming economy, the movement had no single dominant theme and its social visibility was not as great as in the other two countries. This may have been due to the absence of a social group with the necessary organisational and cultural resources and deep commitment to the diffusion and institutionalisation of the idea of entrepreneurship.

## 8.8. CONCLUSIONS

What lessons can we draw from the popularisation of entrepreneurial ideas in the 1980s that could be applied to the spread of knowledge for the promotion of business activities and job creation?

The first point is that values and ideas regarding economic activities matter, and that knowledge plays a critical role in business action, and therefore in job creation. The case of entrepreneurship in the 1980s demonstrated this. Whether these knowledge variables have practical consequences or play more of a socially legitimating role, or both, and in which order of importance, will depend on specific cases and situations. For instance, whereas the economic recovery that took place in Mexico and the UK in the latter half of the 1980s cannot be explained without taking into account the renewed social legitimation of business - to which the immense success of entrepreneurship greatly contributed - in Spain, that relationship has been much more tenuous.

What the entrepreneurship phenomenon shows, then, is that if job creation is to become a permanent central task of businesses as well as of society as a whole, it has to be normatively accepted, to become a shared belief, and this cannot be accomplished without the promotion of knowledge and ideas for employment creation.

A second point is that, as the neo-institutional school of organisational theory has also stated, we cannot consider ideas or knowledge (or, for that matter, culture, beliefs or mentalities) in isolation from the social actors and institutions which directly or indirectly spread them (educational institutions or the media) or support their transmission and consumption (for instance, governments or business groups). For a social idea to gain the extraordinary importance and visibility that entrepreneurship gained in Mexico and Britain, the decisive action of social groups motivated by exceptional circumstances and opportunities was needed. Spain is a good example of how the lack of activism by those social groups led to a lesser degree of acceptance of entrepreneurship.

For job creation to become a social value, or for management knowledge regarding business action and employment creation to be widely disseminated, it is not enough to have a social structure of educational institutions. Social groups with resources at their disposal also need to be active promoters of such values and knowledge. Ideas and values do not spread of their own accord. They do not succeed without socially active defenders, no matter how necessary the ideas or values may be. Promoting pro-job creation values requires decisions and actions that are not only of an economic, or even of a cultural or academic nature; they should also be social and institutional.

A third point has to do with the international transit of business knowledge. One lesson from the case of entrepreneurship in the 1980s - to echo the conclusions of several other pieces in this volume - is the need for caution when exporting business knowledge or economic policies from one society to another one with a different institutional or social framework. Despite the need for local adaptation, the international circulation of business ideas and recipes is a fact and, properly channelled, could be very positive. It is impossible to explain the spectacular success of entrepreneurship ideas in the 1980s in countries at different levels of development without reference to the reception of academic and other knowledge materials diffused from other societies that are traditional exporters of management knowledge, especially the US.

But, very importantly, the initiative for this diffusion has come from the "receiving end" of the transmission. It has not been the centre of the US business education establishment or even the promoters of free market values, such as think tanks in the United States which have systematically promoted the Entrepreneurship Movement across national borders. Local actors on the periphery have imported entrepreneurship courses, publications and social ideas. This is also true of the actions carried out by governments. In the cases of Mexico and Spain a good number of these actions enjoyed the support of international agencies. And although there is no doubt that international institutions contributed a great deal to the Movement - ranging from knowledge to political backing - most of the first steps and connections were established on the initiative of the receptor countries.

In conclusion, then, job creation is not just an economic problem to be solved with purely economic solutions. It is a problem that cuts across social and institutional structures, which in turn are tightly intertwined with the types of knowledge and ideas available for organisational action, as I have tried to demonstrate in this essay for the case of entrepreneurship.

Although these non-economic variables are more systemic and less modifiable, and so do not justify facile optimism, acknowledging their importance has an indisputable advantage: long-term solutions can only be built on the realism demanded by the complexity of social systems and their dynamics of change.

## NOTES

* The author thanks his Research Assistant, Blanca Franco, for her help in the final stages of this paper.

## REFERENCES

Abrahamson, E. (1991). "Managerial Fads and Fashions." *Academy of Management*, Vol. 16, No. 3.

Bannock, G. and A. Peacock (1989). *Governments and Small Business*. London, U.K.: Paul Chapman.

Berger, P. et al. (1974). *The Homeless Mind: Modernization and Consciousness*. New York: Vintage Books.

Birch, D. (1979). *The Job Generation Process*. Cambridge, Mass.: MIT Press.

Boudon, R. (1986). *L'Idéologie ou l'Origine des Idées Reçues*. France: Fayard.

Bourricaud, F. (1980). *Le Bricolage Idéologique: Essai sur les Intellectuels et les Passions Démocratiques*. Paris: Presses Universitaires de France.

Bourricaud, F. (1986). *Le Retour de la Droite*. France: Calmann-Lévy.

Castels, M. and A. Portes (1989). "World Underneath: The Origins, Dynamics, and Effects of the Informal Economy." In A. Portes, M. Castells and L.A. Benton. *The Informal Economy. Studies in Advanced and Less Developed Countries*. Baltimore: Johns Hopkins University Press.

Cohen, M. and J. March (1986). *Leadership and Ambiguity*. Boston, Mass.: Harvard Business School Press.

Curran, J. and J. Stanworth (1982). "The Small Firm in Britain - Past, Present and Future." *European Small Business Journal*, Vol. 1, No. 1.

Curran, J. and R. Burrows (1986). "The Sociology of Petit Capitalism." *Sociology*, Vol. 20, No. 2.

DiMaggio, P. (1988). "Interest and Agency in Institutional Theory." In L. Zucker (ed.). *Institutional Patterns and Organizations: Culture and Environments*. Cambridge, Mass.: Ballinger.

Eccles, R. and N. Nohria (1992). *Beyond the Hype: Rediscovering the Essence of Management*. Boston, Mass.: Harvard Business School Press.

Gallagher, C. and J. Doyle (1986). "Job Generation Research: A Reply to Storey and Johnson." *International Small Business Journal*, Vol. 4, No. 4.

Gamble, A, et al. (1989). *Ideas, Interests and Consequences*. London, U.K.: Institute of Economic Affairs.

García, J. "Recuperar el rumbo. Enterrar el pasado." *Excelsior,* 25 October 1989.

Geertz, C. (1973). *The Interpretation of Cultures*. New York: Basic Books.

Hackman, R. (1985). "Doing Research that Makes a Difference." in E.E. Lawler et al. (eds.). *Doing Research that is Useful for Theory and Practice*. San Francisco, Calif.: Jossey-Bass.

Hall, P. (1986). *Governing the Economy: The Politics of State Intervention in Britain and France*. New York: Oxford University Press.

Harrison, B. (1994). "The Small Firms Myth." *California Management Review*, Spring.

McCloskey, D. (1994). *Knowledge and Persuasion in Economics*. Cambridge, U.K.: Cambridge University Press.

Mohr, L. (1982). *Explaining Organizational Behavior: The Limits and Possibilities of Theory and Research*. San Francisco, Calif.: Jossey-Bass.

Rainnie, A. (1985). "Small firms, big problems: the political economy of small business." *Capital and Class,* Vol. 35.

Roberts, B.R. (1989). "Employment Structure, Life Cycle, and Life Chances: Formal and Informal Sectors in Guadalajara. The Informal Economy". In A. Portes, M. Castells and L.A. Benton. *Studies of Advanced and Less Developed Countries*.

Stevenson, H. and W. Sahlman (1986). "Importance of Entrepreneurship in Economic Development". In R. Hisrich (ed.). *Entrepreneurship, Intrapreneurship, and Venture Capital: The Foundation of Economic Renaissance*. Lexington, Mass.: Lexington Books.

Useem, M. (1984). *The Inner Circle: Large Corporations and the Rise of Business Political Activity in the US and UK*. Oxford, U.K.: Oxford University Press.

Whitley, R. (1989a). "On the Nature of Managerial Tasks and Skills: Their Distinguishing Characteristics and Organisation." *Journal of Management Studies*, Vol. 26, No. 3.

Whitley, R. (1989b). "The Revival of Small Business in Europe". Working Paper, Manchester Business School.

Wuthnow, R. (1987). *Meaning and Moral Order: Explorations in Cultural Analysis*. Berkeley, Calif.: University of California Press.

Wuthnow, R. (1989). *Communities of Discourse*. Cambridge, Mass.: Harvard University Press.

# Index

Abegglen, J.C. 163
Abrahamson, E. 191
Active Population Survey 119, 143
AFDC 63
aggregate demand 7–8, 31–5
agriculture 111
Alogouskoufis, G. 8, 21
Alvarez, J.L. 11, 13, 190–212
Amsden, A.H. 161, 163, 172, 176, 178, 182
Antolín, P. 111
Aoki, M. 180
Asia 184
   see also East; Southeast
Austria 74, 82, 172
Autonomy Law 114

Bank of Spain 114
Bannock, G. 205
Bean, C. 7
Belgium 31, 35, 37, 41, 55
Bentolila, S. 107, 134, 135
Berger, P. 195
Berman, E. 6
Birch, D. 193
Blanchard, O. 8, 11
Bolton report 201, 205, 206, 208
Boudon, R. 195, 207
Bourricaud, F. 191, 192
Bover, O. 111
Budget Act 1995 147, 148
budget cost 75–6
Burrows, R. 191
business action 192–5
business groups 207–8
business ideas diffusion 194

Calmfors, L. 109
Campbell, J.R. 179
Canada
   labour practices 72, 73, 74, 75–6, 78, 79–80
   long-term unemployment prevention 55, 56
capacity utilisation 34
Cárdenas, L. 207
Central de Balances 132
Chandler, A.D. 157
Child, J.M. 174, 181
China 168, 171, 176, 180, 184
Churchill, W. 199
Clark, R. 158, 160, 163, 164, 165, 167, 175, 180
Clinton, B. 71
Co-Determination Acts 184
Cohen, M. 191
collective bargaining 108–10, 139–41
collective representation 73, 79–81
Common Agricultural Policy 111
Community Programme 57
Comparative National Analysis Entre-preneurship Movement 193
compensation per employee 104
competition, lack of in labour market 106–8
Conservative Party 199, 208, 209
consumer price index 128, 129, 138
Convergence Programme 114
convertibles 51
Cox, A. 172
Curran, J. 191, 205
Cusumano, M.A. 161
cyclical movements 96

De la Madrid 197
De Lamo, A. 110
Denmark 181
Deyo, F.C. 180
Directorate for Economic and Financial
    Affairs (DGII) 40
d'Iribarne, P. 170, 171
displacement 57–8, 59–63
Dolado, J.J. 107, 110, 129, 135
Dore, R.P. 158, 165, 168
Doyle, J. 205
Drèze, J.H. 6, 7, 9, 29–54
Drifill, J. 109
Drugman, P. 17
Dunlop, J.T. 82

Earned Income Tax Credit 79
East Asia 147
Eckstein, H. 170
economic and monetary union 113, 114
economic policies 114–16
education 73–4
    management 201–5
    *see also* training
employability 60–2
employee representation 73, 75
employment 36, 41–3, 94, 95
    by sector 94, 95, 101
    change in 125, 136
    gross domestic product ratio 121
    1960–91 36
    patterns 176–86
    policies 159–68, 175, 183, 185
    United States 100
    *see also* Spain
Employment Service 58, 59
enterprises, participation in 75
entrepreneurship education 204
Entrepreneurship Movement 190, 195–
    201, 205, 206, 208, 209, 210, 211
environment 47, 49–50
EPA *see* Active Population Survey
European Business Centres Network 206
European Commission 3, 38, 39, 40, 49,
    50
European Council 3, 49, 51
European Currency Unit 43
European Federation of Development
    Agencies 206

European Free Trade Area 51
European Investment Bank 50, 51
European Investment Fund 50, 51
European Monetary Union 38, 42–3
European Parliament 49, 51
experience, relevant 63–7

firm type 185
firms' strategies, institutional structuring
    of 157–86
    employment policies 159–68, 175,
        183
    interdependencies between institu-
        tions and employment patterns
        176–86
    major institutional features 168–76
Fligstein, N. 158
Florida, R. 157
Ford, H./Fordism 157, 161
foreign direct investment 14
foreign practices 81–2
France 122
    employment 43
    firms' strategies 163, 166, 172, 173,
        177, 184, 186
    labour costs and tax wedge 106
    labour market structure and employ-
        ment 14
    labour practices 72, 74, 79, 86
    technological change and employ-
        ment 6
    user cost of labour 135
    wage moderation 37
Franco, F. 122, 207
Freeman, R.B. 9, 11–12, 13, 70–88
Friedman, A. 180
Fruin, M. 158, 161, 163

Gallagher, C. 205
Gamble, A. 199
García, J. 197
García Perea, P. 106
Gerlach, M. 157, 160, 163
Germany 122
    aggregate demand 35
    employment 43
    Entrepreneurship Movement 196
    firms' strategies 161, 163, 166, 168,
        172–7*passim*, 184

labour costs and tax wedge 106
labour market structure and employment 11–12
labour practices 70, 72, 73, 74, 75, 78, 80, 86
user cost of labour 135
Gold, T.B. 164
Gómez, R. 106
Gospel, H.F. 180
Gould, W. 70, 80, 81
governments 205–6
Granovetter, M. 157
Green, D. 184
Greenhalgh, S. 164
gross domestic product 35, 36, 39, 40, 76, 102, 135, 197
change in 125, 136
real growth rates 32
United States 100
*see also* Spain
gross national product 29, 58, 199
growth policies 38–41
investment 40
recommendations 38–40
wages 40–1
Gual, J. 3–24
Gueron, J.M. 63
Gulf War 31
Gurr, T.R. 170

Hackman, R. 191
Hall, P. 205
Hamilton, G. 170
Harrison, B. 191, 201
Heckscher-Olin model 16
Helpman, E. 17
Hirst, P. 157
Hollingsworth, J.R. 175
Hong Kong 161, 162

IESE *see* International Graduate School of Management
IMAC 145
income tax 46
industrial prices 128
INE *see* National Institute for Statistics
INEM *see* National Institute of Employment
inequality 72

inflation constraint 65
Ingham, G. 158
Initiatives for Women's Employment (IRIS) 206
Institute for Small and Medium Industries 206
institutional factors 74, 185
institutional support 74–5
institutions, malleable and catalytic 85–7
International Graduate School of Management 3–4
investment 40
in competitiveness of Europe 49–51
growth rates 32
*see also* foreign direct investment
Ireland 55, 80
IRIS *see* Initiatives for Women's Employment
Italy
employment 43
Entrepreneurship Movement 196
firms' strategies 157, 163
labour costs and tax wedge 106
labour practices 72
user cost of labour 135
ITESM 202, 203, 209

Jackman, R. 65, 129
Janelli, R.L. 163, 184
Japan
Entrepreneurship Movement 196
firms' strategies
and employment policies 157, 160–5*passim*, 167, 168, 185
interdependencies between institutions and employment patterns 179, 180, 181, 182, 184, 186
major institutional features 171, 172, 173, 175, 185
labour practices 70, 72, 74, 75, 77, 78
long-term unemployment prevention 55, 56, 63
unemployment rate 120
job fund, lack of 60
Johnson, C. 172, 182

Kagono, T. 162, 179

Kao, C.S. 170
Kauffman, S. 83
Kenney, M. 157
Keynes, J.M. 31, 32, 148, 149, 206, 209
Kim, C.S. 184
knowledge and ideas for job creation
    190–212
  business action 192–5
  business groups 207–8
  Entrepreneurship Movement 195–201
  governments 205–6
  management education 201–5
  role 190–2
Koike, K. 180
Korea 157, 161, 168, 171, 176, 184
  *see also* South Korea
Kristensen, P.H. 181

labour
  contracts 137–8
  costs 106, 132–7
  force 67, 93, 94, 120, 121
  institutions, new 79–81
  laws and regulations 75, 79–81
  markets 8–14, 106–8, 124
  participation 111
  reform 1994 144–8
  unskilled 30–1
  user cost of *see* Spain
  *see also* labour practices
Labour Ordinances (National Labour
    Regulations) 136–7, 142, 146–7
Labour Party 199, 207
labour practices, differing 70–88
  analysis, framework for 82–7
    malleable and catalytic institutions
      85–7
    Working Under Different Rules
      project 71–7
Lane, C. 175, 176, 177, 179, 180, 184
Latin America 196
Lawrence, R.Z. 16–17
Lawrisky, M.L. 158
Layard, R.G. 5, 55–68, 129
Lazonick, W. 157
Lilja, K. 184
Lindbeck, A. 36
Local Employment Development Action
    206

local services 47
Lodge, G.C. 170, 171
long-term unemployment prevention
    55–68
  benefits and costs 58–9
  carrot and stick 59
  causes 56
  effects 55
  experience, relevant 63–7
  substitution and displacement 57–63
    employability 60–2
    no job fund 60
    people causing jobs 63
    proposed scheme 62

Maastricht Treaty 31, 38, 49, 114
Macfarlane, A. 177
macroeconomic employment policy
    114–15, 148–9
Malinvaud, E. 39, 48
Malo de Molina, J.L. 129
management education 201–5
mandatory severance pay 105
Mannheim, K. 195
manufacturing wages 128
March, J. 191
market regulations and imperfections
    *see* Spain
Marris, R. 163
Mateos, B. 134
Maurice, M. 166, 173, 176
Mexico 209, 210, 211
  basic economic data 198
  business action 193
  business groups 207, 208
  entrepreneurship education 204
  Entrepreneurship Movement 195,
    196, 197–8, 199, 201, 209
  governments 206
  ITESM 202, 203
  Junior Achievement 202
  management in education 202, 203,
    205
  total external debt 198
  trade and employment 15
Milgrom, P. 83–4
minimum wages 45
Ministry of Industry 206
Ministry of Labour 74

Modernisation Plan 201
Mohr, L. 199
Morris, B. 70

NAIRU *see* non-accelerating inflation
    rate of unemployment
Nash equilibrium 33
National Accounts 132
National Bureau of Economic Research
    charter 72, 80
National Institute of Employment 108,
    131, 146
National Institute for Statistics 131
national labour relations 81–2
Netherlands 72, 73
Neven, D. 17, 18
new facilities 51
new jobs, sources of 47
New Zealand 84
Nickell, S. 65, 129
Nishida, J. 161
non-accelerating inflation rate of unem-
    ployment 10, 103, 109, 110, 148
non-wage costs 132
North Africa 49, 51
North America 102, 135
    *see also* Canada; United States
notice 105
Numazaki, J. 170

oil shock 1974–81 125
Olie, R. 173
Oliveira Martins, J. 17
Organisation of Economic Cooperation
    and Development 17, 38, 40, 41,
    71, 76, 129, 135
Ortega, R. 14

Peacock, A. 205
Penrose, E. 161, 163
pensions system, financing of 138–9
Phillips curve 38, 41, 60, 99
Pigou, A.C. 33
Piore, M.J. 157
Portillo, L. 197
Portugal 111, 135
poverty rates 75–6, 78–9
PRI regime 197, 199, 201, 203, 206,
    207, 209, 210

price pressure 104–5
Program in Labor Studies 72
Public Administration 115
Pye, L.W. 171

quality of life, improvements in 47

Railway Labor Act 81
Rainnie, A. 205
Reagan, R. 31
real wages 36, 76–7
Redding, G.R. 162, 164, 168, 170, 176,
    180, 184
replacement rate 107
research and development 6
Revenga, A. 17, 18
Richardson, G. 59
Roberts, B.R. 197
Roberts, J. 83–4
Rogerson, R. 134
Rohlen, T.P. 171

Sabel, C.F. 157
Sachs, J. 16
Sada, E.G. 197
Sahlman, W. 192
Saint-Paul, G. 134
Sako, M. 161, 169
Say's Law 33
Scandinavia 74, 168, 171, 184
    *see also* Denmark; Sweden
Sebastián, C. 10–11, 12, 119–51
Servén, L. 138
Shatz, H.J. 16
short-term unemployment 62, 64
Silin, R.H. 171, 176, 180, 184
single market 111–13
skills 74
Slaughter, M. 16–17
Sneesens, H. 6
Snower, D. 59
Social Charter 70
social insurance contributions 46
social protection policies 75–6
Social Security 106, 132, 138–9, 143,
    147–8
social security contributions 132
Socialist Party 199
South Korea 163, 172, 178, 182, 184

Southeast Asia 199
Spain 21, 91–117, 119–51, 208, 210,
    211
  agriculture 111
  Autonomy Law 114
  Bank of Spain 114
  basic economic data 200
  Budget Act 1995 147, 148
  bureaucratised system (IMAC) 145
  business action 193
  business groups 207
  Central de Balances 132
  collective bargaining 108–10
  compensation per employee 104
  competition, lack of in labour market
    106–8
  conceptual framework 103
  consumer price index 138
  Convergence Programme 114
  economic and monetary union 113
  employment 43, 102
    growth 100
    inability to generate 119–22
    in public and private sector 101
  entrepreneurship education 204
  Entrepreneurship Movement 195,
    199, 201, 209
  EPA 143
  governments 206
  gross domestic product 95, 96–7, 100,
    119, 122, 148
  IMPI (Institute for Small and Medium
    Industries) 206
  International Graduate School of
    Management 4
  ITESM 209
  labour costs and tax wedge 106
  labour market structure and employ-
    ment 10–13, 120, 121
  Labour Ordinances (National Labour
    Regulations) 136–7, 142, 146–7
  labour participation 111
  labour practices 74, 76, 80
  labour reform 1994 144–8
  long term trends 92–6
  long-term unemployment prevention
    55
  macroeconomic policy 114–15, 148–9
  management in education 203, 205

  market regulations and imperfections
    137–44
    collective bargaining and wage-
      setting 139–41
    labour contracts 137–8
    pensions system, financing of 138–
      9
    unemployment protection 142–3
    work organisation 142
  Ministry of Industry 206
  Modernisation Plan 201
  National Accounts 132
  National Institute of Employment
    (INEM) 146
  non-accelerating inflation rate of
    unemployment 110
  price pressure 104–5
  private and public sector employment
    cumulative variation 94
  Public Administration 115
  registrations of new firms 200
  short term cyclical fluctuation 96–7
  single market 111–13
  Social Security 132, 138–9, 143, 147–
    8, 148
  structural policies 115–16
  unemployment 97–101, 120
  user cost of labour 122–37
    implicit 132–7
    non-wage 132
    wages 123–31
  value-added tax 138–9, 147
  wage pressure 105–6
  wages and employment growth 130
  Workers' Statute 134, 141
Sprint programme on technological
    transfer 206
Stalk, G. 163
standards of living 73, 78–9
Stanworth, J. 205
state employment agency 131
Steers, R.M. 161
Stevenson, H. 192
stocks and flows 66
Stolper-Samuelson theorem 17
Streeck, W. 175
structural policies 115–16
substitution 57–8, 59–63
Sweden

agriculture 111
labour practices 72, 76, 79, 84
long-term unemployment prevention
55, 56, 58, 59, 63

Taiwan 162, 164, 184
tax 79
cost 75–6
wedge 106
*see also* value-added
technological change and employment
4–6
telecommunications 49
TENS 51
Thatcher, M. 201, 205, 208
Third World 14
total factor productivity 17, 18
trade and employment 14–19
training 74–5, 78–9
trans-European networks, financing of
50
transport and energy 49

unemployment 29–30, 94
protection 142–3
rates 34, 109, 120
by level of educational attainment
44
1960–91 36
1964–94 93
1970–94 98
*see also* long-term; non-accelerating;
short-term; Spain
union bonds 51
unit labour cost in manufacturing 126
United Kingdom 209, 210, 211
basic economic data 196
business action 193
business groups 207, 208
Entrepreneurship Movement 195,
196, 199, 209
firms' strategies 165, 174, 176, 177,
180, 181
governments 206
labour practices 72, 80, 86
long-term unemployment prevention
57, 58, 59
management in education 201–2, 203,
205

technological change and employment 6
United Nations 209
Organisation for Industrial Development 206
United States 73, 97, 103, 122, 211
Commission on the Future of Worker-
Management Relations 87
differing labour practices 77–82
employment 36, 43, 102
growth 100
in public and private sector 101
firms' strategies 157, 160, 161, 162
governments 206
gross domestic product 100
growth rates 36
Junior Achievement 202, 203
labour market structure and employment 8–9, 11
labour practices 70, 71, 82, 84
long-term unemployment prevention
55, 56, 59, 63
management in education 202, 205
trade and employment 14–19
unemployment 98, 100
rate 36, 99, 120
unit labour cost in manufacturing 126
unskilled labour 30, 31
user cost of labour 123, 129, 135, 136
wage moderation 35, 37
wages and employment growth 130
*see also* Working Under Different
Rules project
unskilled labour 30–1
Useem, M. 207
user cost of labour *see* Spain

value-added tax 40, 138–9, 147
van Iterson, A. 173
van Wolferen, K. 171, 175
Viñals, J. 8, 10–11, 91–117
Vogel, E.F. 170, 171

Wade, R. 172
wages 40–1
agreements by company and industry
141
-determination 78–9
differentials 72

and employment growth 130
growth 128
inequality 73–4, 76–7
moderation 35–8
pressure 105–6
real 36, 76–7
-setting 139–41
Spain 123–31
Wagner Act 78, 81
Weber, M. 195
Whitley, R. 11, 13, 14, 157–86, 191–2, 205
Whittaker, D.H. 165, 168
Wong, S.-L. 161

Woo, Y.-E. 176
work organisation 142
Workers' Statute 134, 141
Working Under Different Rules project 71–7, 87
Wright, S. 83
Wuthnow, R. 195, 199
Wyplosz, C. 17, 18

Zabalza, A. 138
Zeile, W. 161
Zeitlin, J. 157
Zucker, L. 169
Zysman, J. 163, 167, 172, 179, 184